THE FORTUNES OF LIBERALISM

F. A. HAYEK

THE COLLECTED WORKS OF

F. A. Hayek

THE FORTUNES OF LIBERALISM

Essays on Austrian Economics and the
Ideal of Freedom

F. A. HAYEK

Edited by Peter G. Klein

Liberty Fund

This book is published by Liberty Fund, Inc., a foundation established to encourage study of the ideal of a society of free and responsible individuals.

The cuneiform inscription that serves as our logo and as the design motif for our endpapers is the earliest-known written appearance of the word "freedom" (*amagi*), or "liberty." It is taken from a clay document written about 2300 B.C. in the Sumerian city-state of Lagash.

The Fortunes of Liberalism is volume 4 of The Collected Works of F. A. Hayek, published by The University of Chicago Press.

This Liberty Fund paperback edition of *The Fortunes of Liberalism* is published by arrangement with The University of Chicago Press and Taylor & Francis Books, Ltd., a member of the Taylor & Francis Group.

Library of Congress Cataloging-in-Publication Data

Hayek, Friedrich A. von (Friedrich August), 1899–1992.
The fortunes of liberalism: essays on Austrian economics and the ideal of freedom/F. A. Hayek; edited by Peter G. Klein.—Liberty Fund paperback ed.
p.   cm.—(The collected works of F. A. Hayek; v. 4)
"The Fortunes of Liberalism is volume 4 of The Collected Works of F. A. Hayek, published by The University of Chicago Press."
Includes bibliographical references and index.
ISBN 978-0-86597-741-9 (pbk.: alk. paper)
1. Austrian school of economics.   2.   Free enterprise.
3. Liberalism.   4.   Economics.   5.   Social Sciences.
I. Klein, Peter G.   II. Title.
HB98.H395   2008
330.15'7—dc22   2008028379

Liberty Fund, Inc.
11301 North Meridian Street
Carmel, Indiana 46032
libertyfund.org

Cover design by Erin Kirk New, Watkinsville, Georgia
Printed and bound by Sheridan Books, Inc., Chelsea, Michigan

THE COLLECTED WORKS OF F. A. HAYEK

Founding Editor: W. W. Bartley III

General Editor: Stephen Kresge

Assistant Editor: Gene Opton

Published with the support of

The Hoover Institution on War, Revolution and Peace,
Stanford University
Anglo American and De Beers Chairman's Fund, Johannesburg
Cato Institute, Washington, D.C.
The Centre for Independent Studies, Sydney
Chung-Hua Institution for Economic Research, Taipei
Earhart Foundation, Ann Arbor
Engenharia Comércio e Indústria S/A, Rio de Janeiro
Escuela Superior de Economia y Administración de Empresas
(ESEADE), Buenos Aires
The Institute for Humane Studies, George Mason University
Instituto Liberal, Rio de Janeiro
Charles G. Koch Charitable Foundation, Wichita
The Vera and Walter Morris Foundation, Little Rock
Verband der Osterreichischen Banken und Bankiers, Vienna
The Wincott Foundation, London

CONTENTS

CONTENTS

EDITORIAL FOREWORD

I

The Collected Works of F. A. Hayek is the product not of the design but of the perception of W. W. Bartley III that the great importance of Hayek's thought would not be fully grasped without a complete, newly ordered, and annotated presentation of his writings. Thus the series is an unplanned outcome of Hayek's offer to place at Bartley's disposal all of his papers, should he undertake Hayek's biography, which Bartley did agree to do. In the course of their many talks—about Popper, about Wittgenstein, about Vienna—Hayek realised that Bartley had acquired a unique understanding of the Vienna of Hayek's birth and youth. Bartley, for his part, as he examined the depth and range of Hayek's writings, came to realise that the knowledge of Hayek's ideas held by contemporary thinkers was at best fragmentary and at worst woefully non-existent. Just as Ludwig Wittgenstein's English followers knew little of his Austrian life until Bartley wrote of it, Hayek's English and American readers knew little of Hayek's early work written in German. Even most economists had ceased to read Hayek's work on economic theory, and neglected entirely Hayek's ideas about theories of perception and the growth of knowledge. Yet none of Hayek's writing is entirely unconnected to the whole, and now, placed within its historical, theoretical, and critical context, which is the rewarding labour of the editors, Hayek's collected writing provides an invaluable education in a subject which is nothing less than the development of the modern world.

This new collection of essays, *The Fortunes of Liberalism: Essays on Austrian Economics and the Ideal of Freedom*, is the fourth volume of the Collected Works of F. A. Hayek and the third volume in order of appearance. Of particular interest is the essay "The Economics of the 1920s as Seen from Vienna", which is published here for the first time, and the essay "The Rediscovery of Freedom: Personal

Recollections", which is published for the first time in English. Also published for the first time is the Addendum to chapter 1, and for the first time in English chapters 3 and 7 and sections of chapters 4 and 6. With but two exceptions the remaining chapters have not been readily accessible and are here collected for the first time.

II

Much has changed in the world since the inception of this series. The fall of the Berlin wall is the dramatic and symbolic event that had long been prefigured in the criticisms of socialism made by Hayek, Mises, and their followers. Now irrefutable, Hayek's arguments may come to be read as a touchstone in a renewed examination of the evolution of the extended order of society. For the Hayek specialist who is encouraged to discover how Hayek's ideas have evolved in terms of his unfailing sense of what is the key problem to be solved, the essays in this volume about Hayek's teachers and colleagues will be of considerable interest. One may well be startled to see in chapter 3 a young Hayek in 1926 writing of "the most important economic problem, the laws of income distribution". Even then there were hints that these 'laws' would be merely foothills beyond which a high range of unexplored difficulty could be glimpsed. So Friedrich von Wieser, Hayek's teacher, writes of himself, "Henceforth it became my dream to write anonymous history. This too, however, came to nothing. The most obvious social relationship manifests itself in the economy—that had to be clarified first, before one could even consider fathoming more deeply concealed relations".

The question of the place of history in social evolution and the role historians play in our national identities connect all of the essays in this volume. Like an *ostinato* figure, the theme is sounded at the very start in Menger's epochal controversy with the German historical school, the *Methodenstreit*, over whether it is possible to discover laws of history that explain or predict or determine the destiny of nations. The great tragedy of the twentieth century was the twin monstrosities, the social calamities of Nazi Germany and Soviet Communism, which proved that if history is not "bunk", to use Henry Ford's famous monosyllable, *historicism* is not only wrong, but dangerously wrong. In the end it is clear the fortunes of liberalism rest on the objectivity of the historians—among whom Hayek enlists all students of social phenomena—"of the possibility of a history which is not written in the service of a particular interest".

How to reconcile the "supremacy of truth" that Hayek holds as the standard for all historians with the obscurity of events that economists must discern is the task that emerges from these pages. But then, as Hayek reminds us in the essay on Röpke, "an economist who is nothing but an economist cannot be a good economist".

III

This volume was assembled under painful circumstances. The founding editor of the Collected Works of F. A. Hayek, W. W. Bartley III died of cancer in February 1990. Nothing can prepare one for such a loss. But we were prepared to do the work that will remain as a testament to his foresight, perseverance, and intelligence. Of those who have kept the project together and moving forward during this difficult year, I am most grateful to Mr. Walter Morris of the Vera and Walter Morris Foundation. His has been, as Bartley wrote, the presiding genius behind the larger project, without whose advice and support it never could have been organised or launched and, I will now add, without whose unflagging counsel and sympathy the project would not have continued.

A similar debt of gratitude must also go to Mr. John Blundell of the Institute for Humane Studies. I should also like to express my thanks to Ms. Penelope Kaiserlian of the University of Chicago Press and to Mr. Peter Sowden of Routledge, not only for their renewed commitment to the series but for their patience and acceptance of the complexity of this undertaking; which complexity would not be resolved nor books produced without the knowledge and determination of the Assistant Editor, Ms. Gene Opton. We are also fortunate to have the translations of Dr. Grete Heinz. Thanks are due to Ms. Charlotte Cubitt, Ms. Leslie Graves, and Mr. Eric O'Keefe; and especially to Peter Klein for being curious and energetic enough to complete with great distinction the very painstaking work of editing this volume, and for being modest enough not to expect that virtue has any other reward.

Finally, the project could not have been carried through successfully without the generous financial assistance of the supporting organisations, whose names are listed prominently at the beginning of the volume and to which all associated with the volume are grateful. The support of these sponsors—institutions and foundations from six continents—not only acknowledges the international appreciation of Hayek's work, but also provides very tangible evidence of the extended order of human cooperation of which Hayek writes.

Stephen Kresge
Oakland, California
February 1991

INTRODUCTION

"Can capitalism survive?" asked Joseph Schumpeter in 1942. "No. I do not think it can".[1] But capitalism survived: Now half a century later we find socialism facing self-destruction, the ideal of central planning collapsing with the failed economies of East and Central Europe. If there is any lesson to be learned from the events of 1989, it is this: The rebirth of liberalism in that part of the world is largely, if not completely, a rebirth of capitalism—a recognition that only the market order can provide the level of well-being that modern civilisation requires. Though not yet fully understood, this is now widely recognised. Robert Heilbroner, certainly no friend of capitalism, writes that recent history "has forced us to rethink the meaning of socialism. As a semi-religious vision of a transformed humanity, it has been dealt devastating blows in the twentieth century. As a blueprint for a rationally planned society, it is in tatters".[2]

For F. A. Hayek this is but a mild surprise. As an 'Austrian' economist Hayek has always had an understanding of the market somewhat different from that of his contemporaries, not only those who oppose capitalism, but many of those who defend it as well. Throughout most of this century 'the economic problem' has been seen as the *allocation of resources*, the problem of finding a distribution of productive resources to supply a set of competing and potentially unlimited demands—for which a solution can in principle be computed by an outside observer (and, by implication, a central planner). For Hayek and the Austrians, by contrast, economics is about the *coordination of plans*, the means by which a 'highly complex

---

[1]Joseph A. Schumpeter, *Capitalism, Socialism, and Democracy* (New York: Harper & Brothers, 1942; third edition, 1950), p. 61.

[2]"Reflections After Communism", *The New Yorker*, September 10, 1990, pp. 91–100, esp. p. 98. An expanded version appears as "Analysis and Vision in Modern Economic Thought", in the *Journal of Economic Literature*, vol. 28, September 1990, pp. 1097–1114.

order' of human cooperation emerges from the plans and decisions of isolated individuals, operating in a world of tacit and dispersed knowledge. Explaining the regularity of phenomena like prices and production, money, interest, and business fluctuations, and even law and language, when these phenomena are part of no one's deliberate intention, is the task of economic science. Only by viewing the social order from this perspective can we hope to know why markets *work*, and why efforts to construct societies without markets are bound to fail.

Hayek belongs to the fourth generation of the Austrian school of economists, the generation of the diaspora that flowed out of Vienna to places like London and Chicago, Princeton, and Cambridge, Mass., so that the adjective 'Austrian' is now of purely historical significance. Throughout his migrations to England and the United States, though, Hayek has retained much of the perspective of the school founded by Carl Menger. Since its beginnings, the Austrian school has been known for its distinct and original understanding of the economic order, some parts of which have (to an extent) been incorporated into the mainstream of economic thought while others were tossed aside and forgotten. Among the former we may include the once-revolutionary theory of value and exchange offered in Menger's *Grundsätze der Volkswirtschaftslehre*, whose 1871 publication marked the beginnings of the school; among the latter is the attack on the feasibility of economic calculation under socialism developed by Hayek's senior colleague and mentor Ludwig von Mises in the 1920s, a theory which formed the basis for the modern Austrian understanding of the market as a *process* of learning and discovery, rather than an equilibrium state of affairs. Conventional neoclassical economics, believing Mises to have been refuted long ago by the Lange and Taylor models of 'market socialism', has had virtually nothing to say on the viability of central planning. Not so for the Austrians. Hayek's conception of what the market *is*, and how the market process works, has led him to the conclusion that socialism is a grave mistake—if you will, a 'fatal conceit'. And it is upon this understanding that he builds his defence of the liberal order.

This is the spirit in which the present volume is offered. In these essays Hayek writes on Austrian economics, the starting point for his own intellectual odyssey, and on the fortunes of liberalism, the social philosophy of the market order with which his work is so closely associated. The first part contains essays and lectures on the major figures of the Austrian school: Carl Menger, Hayek's teacher Friedrich von Wieser, Ludwig von Mises, and Joseph Schumpeter (Austrian by training and one of the dominant personalities in twentieth-century economic thought, though not a member of the Austrian school *per se*); the lesser-known economists Ewald Schams and Richard von Strigl; and two related figures on the Viennese intellectual scene, the philosophers Ernst Mach and Ludwig Wittgenstein, Hayek's second cousin. The second Part collects writings on the rediscovery of freedom in post-war Europe, with special reference to Germany and the international Mont Pèlerin Society, an influential organisation of liberals founded by Hayek in 1947. Both Parts touch on a theme that pervades all Hayek's work on the social order: the role of ideas—economic theory in particular—in the preservation of liberal society.

The remainder of this Introduction will sketch Hayek's career and try to place parts of his thought in historical and theoretical perspective. Before we continue, however, one terminological note is in order. Hayek uses the word 'liberalism' in its classical, European meaning, as the social order based on free markets, limited government under the rule of law, and the primacy of individual freedom. As he explains in the Foreword to the first (1956) paperback edition of his classic *The Road to Serfdom*,

> I use throughout the term 'liberal' in the original, nineteenth-century sense in which it is still current in Britain. In current American usage it often means very much the opposite of this. It has been part of the camouflage of leftish movements in this country, helped by the muddleheadedness of many who really believe in liberty, that 'liberal' has come to mean the advocacy of almost every kind of government control. I am still puzzled why those in the United States who truly believe in liberty should not only have allowed the Left to appropriate this almost indispensable term but should even have assisted by beginning to use it themselves as a term of opprobrium.[3]

We shall abide here by these strictures and continue to favour 'liberal' over the less elegant 'classical liberal' or 'libertarian', now becoming standard parlance in the United States.

Hayek came to the University of Vienna at age nineteen just after the First World War, when it was one of the three best places in the world to study economics (the others being Stockholm and Cambridge, England). Though he was enrolled as a law student, his

---

[3]F. A. Hayek, *The Road to Serfdom* (London: Routledge & Kegan Paul; Chicago: University of Chicago Press, 1944; reprinted, 1976), p. ix.

primary interests were economics and psychology, the latter due to the influence of Mach's theory of perception on Wieser and Wieser's colleague Othmar Spann, and the former stemming from the reformist ideal of Fabian socialism so typical of Hayek's generation. Like many students of economics then and since, Hayek chose that subject not for its own sake, but because he wanted to make the world a better place—the poverty of post-war Vienna serving as a daily reminder of such a need. Socialism seemed to provide a solution; then in 1922, Mises, who was not on the paid Vienna faculty but was a central figure in the economics community there, published his *Die Gemeinwirtschaft*, later translated as *Socialism*. "To none of us young men who read the book when it appeared", Hayek recalls, "the world was ever the same again" (this volume, p. 133). *Socialism*, an elaboration of Mises's pioneering article from two years before, argued that economic calculation *requires* a market for the means of production; without such a market there is no way to establish the values of those means and, consequently, no way to determine their proper uses in production. From Mises, who was briefly Hayek's superior in a temporary government office and in whose private seminar Hayek became a regular participant, Hayek was gradually convinced of the superiority of the market order.

Mises had done earlier work on monetary and banking theory, successfully applying the Austrian marginal utility principle to the value of money and then sketching a theory of industrial fluctuations based on the doctrines of the English currency school and the ideas of the Swedish economist Knut Wicksell. Hayek used this last as a starting point for his own research on fluctuations, explaining the business cycle in terms of credit expansion by banks. His work in this area earned him an invitation to lecture at the London School of Economics and Political Science and then to occupy its Tooke Chair in Economics and Statistics, which he accepted in 1931. There he found himself among a vibrant and exciting group: Lionel (later Lord) Robbins, Arnold Plant, T. E. Gregory, Dennis Robertson, John Hicks, and the young Abba Lerner, to name just a few. Hayek brought his (to them) unfamiliar views,[4] and gradually the 'Austrian' theory of the business cycle became known and accepted.

---

[4]Hicks notes, in reference to Hayek's first (1931) English book, that "*Prices and Production* was in English, but it was not English economics". Sir John Hicks, "The Hayek Story", in his *Critical Essays in Monetary Theory* (Oxford: Clarendon Press, 1967), p. 204.

Within a very few years, however, the fortunes of the Austrian school would suffer a dramatic reversal. First, the Austrian theory of capital, an integral part of the business-cycle theory, came under attack from the Italian-born Cambridge economist Piero Sraffa and the American Frank Knight, while the cycle theory itself was forgotten amid the enthusiasm for the *General Theory* of John Maynard Keynes. Second, beginning with Hayek's move to London and continuing until the early 1940s, the Austrian economists left Vienna, for personal and then for political reasons, so that a school ceased to exist there as such. Mises left Vienna in 1934 for Geneva and then New York, where he continued to work in isolation; Hayek remained at the LSE until 1950, when he joined the Committee on Social Thought at the University of Chicago. Other Austrians of Hayek's generation would become prominent in the United States—Gottfried Haberler at Harvard, Fritz Machlup and Oskar Morgenstern at Princeton, Paul Rosenstein-Rodan at the Massachusetts Institute of Technology—but their work no longer seemed to show any traces of the Menger tradition.

At Chicago Hayek once again found himself among a dazzling group: The economics department, led by Knight, Jacob Viner, Milton Friedman, and later George Stigler, was one of the best anywhere; Aaron Director at the law school would soon set up the first law and economics program; and internationally known scholars like Hannah Arendt and Bruno Bettelheim were active lecturers. But economic theory, in particular its *style* of reasoning, was rapidly changing: Paul Samuelson's *Foundations* had appeared in 1949, establishing physics as the science for economics to imitate, and Friedman's 1953 essay on 'positive economics' set a new standard for economic method. In addition Hayek had ceased to work on economic theory, concentrating on psychology, philosophy, and politics, and Austrian economics entered a prolonged eclipse. Some important work in the Austrian tradition was done during this period by two younger men who had studied with Mises at New York University: Murray Rothbard, who published his *Man, Economy, and State* in 1962, and Israel Kirzner, whose *Competition and Entrepreneurship* appeared in 1973. But for the most part the Austrian tradition lay dormant.

Then in 1974 something quite startling occurred: Hayek received a Nobel prize in economics. Due to the prestige of this award, interest in the Austrian school was revived; coincidentally, a number of isolated scholars working in the Austrian tradition had been brought together that same year at a memorable conference in

THE FORTUNES OF LIBERALISM

South Royalton, Vermont.[5] Since then an 'Austrian revival' has continued to spread, with books, journals, and even graduate programs specialising in the Menger tradition appearing at a growing rate. And Austrian economics is slowly beginning to be noticed by the rest of the profession. Some areas in which modern Austrian views are starting to exert influence include banking theory, advertising and its relation to market structure, and the reinterpretation of the socialist calculation debate;[6] furthermore, the literature of the last fifteen years or so on the economics of incomplete information and the theory of incentives may be considered an outgrowth of Hayek's work on dispersed knowledge and prices as signals, though such a debt is often forgotten.[7]

There is another reason for contemporary economists to be interested in Hayek. Today the analysis of the welfare properties of the market is framed as a two-sided debate: The defenders of free markets are the 'new classical' economists, whose theories depend on the assumptions of hyper-rational human agents with 'rational expectations' and instantaneous market clearing; the skeptics, usually carrying some sort of 'Keynesian' label, view expectations as more problematic and prices as slow to adjust. Hayek, in stark contrast, bases a defence of the market not on human rationality, but on human ignorance! "[T]he whole argument for freedom, or the greater part of the argument for freedom, rests on the fact of our

[5]The proceedings of that conference were published as *The Foundations of Modern Austrian Economics*, ed. Edwin G. Dolan (Kansas City: Sheed & Ward, 1976). A follow-up volume appeared two years later: *New Directions in Austrian Economics*, ed. Louis M. Spadaro (Kansas City: Sheed Andrews & McMeel, 1978).

[6]For example, Lawrence H. White, *Free Banking in Britain: Theory, Experience, and Debate, 1800-1845* (Cambridge: Cambridge University Press, 1984), and George A. Selgin, *The Theory of Free Banking: Money Supply Under Competitive Note Issue* (Totowa, N.J.: Rowman & Littlefield, 1988); Robert B. Ekelund, Jr., and David S. Saurman, *Advertising and the Market Process* (San Francisco: Pacific Institute for Public Policy Research, 1988); and Don Lavoie, *Rivalry and Central Planning: The Socialist Calculation Debate Reconsidered* (Cambridge: Cambridge University Press, 1985).

[7]See, for example, the excerpt from the *New Palgrave* dictionary published as *Allocation, Information and Markets* (London: Macmillan, 1989). It is also curious that the emerging literature on 'coordination failures' in macroeconomics, pioneered by the theorists Peter Diamond and Martin Weitzman, makes no reference to Hayek, though the problem of coordination is an explicit theme in his writings (hence Gerald P. O'Driscoll's study *Economics as a Coordination Problem: The Contributions of Friedrich A. Hayek* (Kansas City: Sheed Andrews & McMeel, 1977)). For a summary of this literature see Russell Cooper and Andrew John, "Coordinating Coordination Failures in Keynesian Models", *Quarterly Journal of Economics*, vol. 103, August 1989, pp. 441–463.

ignorance and not on the fact of our knowledge."[8] Hayek's agents are *rule followers*, responding to price signals within a system selected by a process of evolution—a spontaneous order, rather than a system deliberately chosen; yet their actions bring unintended benefits for the system as a whole, benefits that *could not* have been rationally predicted. This is quite strange to the modern economist, for whom evolution and spontaneity play little if any role.[9]

Hayek's work is also different from the new classical economists' in another regard: It is broader, integrating economic theory into a wide social philosophy, encompassing political, legal, and moral aspects of the social order. The new classicals, instead, are purely theorists and have not attracted a broadly based following. Leonard Rapping, himself one of the first 'rational expectations' economists, notes that "[m]any of the young and idealistic are attracted by the concepts of freedom and justice, not efficiency and abundance. Aside from their contributions to economic theory, Friedman and Hayek wrote powerful defences of capitalism as a system that promotes liberal democracy and individual freedom. This attracted to their ideas many adherents outside of economics. The new classicals have no such agenda."[10] Indeed, the students of Austrian economics often have a wide range of interests, and the interdisciplinary flavour of the Austrian tradition surely helps explain its appeal.

Clearly the Austrian revival owes as much to Hayek as to anyone. But are Hayek's writings really 'Austrian economics'—part of a

---

[8]From Hayek's remarks at a conference organised by the Congress for Cultural Freedom and published as *Science and Freedom* (London: Martin Secker & Warburg, 1955), p. 53.

[9]The interpretation of economic behaviour as 'routines' or rules of thumb, developed by Richard Nelson and Sydney Winter in their *Evolutionary Theory of Economic Change* (Cambridge, Mass.: Harvard University Press, 1982), bears some relation to Hayek's idea of rule-following agents. It is also true that the equilibrium concepts of modern game theory partly reflect the notion of 'plan coordination' mentioned before, in the sense of finding sets of mutually consistent 'strategies', and that the theory of repeated games yields significant insights into the evolution of cooperative behaviour. Game theory, however, does not explain how cooperative action comes to be selected; it shows only that strategies of repeated cooperation can be mutual best responses. A standard reference on such matters is Robert Axelrod, *The Evolution of Cooperation* (New York: Basic Books, 1984). For an application with an Austrian flavour, see Bruce L. Benson, *The Enterprise of Law: Justice Without the State* (San Francisco: Pacific Institute for Public Policy Research, 1990).

[10]In a review of Kevin D. Hoover, *The New Classical Macroeconomics: A Skeptical Inquiry* (New York and Oxford: Basil Blackwell, 1988), in the *Journal of Economic Literature*, vol. 28, March 1990, pp. 71–73, esp. p. 73.

separate, recognisable tradition—or should we regard them, instead, as an original, deeply personal contribution?[11] Some observers charge that Hayek's later work, particularly after he began to turn away from technical economics, shows more influence of his friend Sir Karl Popper than of Menger or Mises: One critic speaks of "Hayek I" and "Hayek II", while another writes on "Hayek's Transformation".[12]

Though this is to some extent merely a matter of labels, there are some substantive issues involved. One is whether or not it is useful to distinguish between schools of thought within a discipline at all. Hayek himself is of two minds on this. In the first chapter of this volume, written in 1968 for the *International Encyclopaedia of the Social Sciences*, he describes his own generation of the Austrian school with the following:

> But if this fourth generation in style of thinking and in interests still shows the Vienna tradition clearly, nonetheless it can hardly any longer be seen as a separate school in the sense of representing particular doctrines. A school has its greatest success when it ceases as such to exist because its leading ideals have become a part of the general dominant teaching. The Vienna school has to a great extent come to enjoy such a success. (This volume, p. 52)[13]

[11]Wieser's have generally been considered a personal contribution, by Hayek himself and others. For a contrary view, see Robert B. Ekelund, Jr., "Wieser's *Social Economics*: A Link to Modern Austrian Theory?", *Austrian Economics Newsletter*, vol. 6, Fall 1986, pp. 1–2, 4, 9–11.

[12]For Hayeks I and II see T. W. Hutchinson, "Austrians on Philosophy and Method (since Menger)", in his *The Politics and Philosophy of Economics: Marxians, Keynesians, and Austrians* (New York and London: New York University Press, 1984), pp. 203–232, esp. pp. 210–219; for the 'transformation' see Bruce J. Caldwell, "Hayek's Transformation", *History of Political Economy*, vol. 20, no. 4, 1988, pp. 513–541.

[13]It is significant that those neoclassical economists who see any truth in the Austrians' writings tend to argue similarly that the latter are merely saying the same things as everyone else but in a different language (i.e., Austrians generally reason verbally rather than mathematically). Mises himself once said nearly this, in the following remarkable statement: "We usually speak of the Austrian and the Anglo-American schools [following William Stanley Jevons] and the school of Lausanne [following Léon Walras]. . . .[yet in fact] these three schools of thought differ only in their mode of expressing the same fundamental idea and . . . are divided more by their terminology and by peculiarities of presentation than by the substance of their teachings." Mises, *Epistemological Problems of Economics* (New York and London: New York University Press, 1981; first published 1933), p. 214. Mises would later abandon this view, as have recent scholars of the Menger-Jevons-Walras 'marginalist revolution'. On this see the references in this volume, chapters 1 and 2.

By the mid-1980s, however, he seemed to have changed his mind, writing of an Austrian school with a distinct identity, working mainly in opposition to Keynesian macroeconomics, which continues to exist today.[14] Present-day Austrians are also divided on this point: some are highly conscious of their Austrian heritage, wearing it as a badge of honour, while others avoid any labels, maintaining the dictum that there is no 'Austrian economics', only good and bad economics. Whether these are matters of deeply held beliefs, or simply related to persuading the profession at large to take Austrian ideas seriously, is difficult to say.

Of special interest here, though, is the exact nature of Hayek's relationship with Mises. Undoubtedly no economist has had a greater impact on Hayek's thinking than Mises—not even Wieser, from whom Hayek learned his craft but who died in 1927 when Hayek was still a young man; Hayek's words in chapter 4 of this volume make this plain enough. In addition, Mises clearly considered Hayek the brightest of his generation: Margit von Mises recalls of her husband's seminar in New York that "Lu met every new student hopeful that one of them might develop into a second Hayek."[15] Yet, as Hayek reminds us, he was from the beginning always something less than a pure follower: "Although I owe [Mises] a decisive stimulus at a crucial point of my intellectual development, and continuous inspiration throughout a decade, I have perhaps most profited from his teaching because I was not initially his student at the university, the innocent young man who took his word for gospel, but came to him as a trained economist, trained in a parallel branch of Austrian economics [the Wieser branch] from which he gradually, but never completely, won me over."[16]

There are two frequently discussed areas of disagreement between Hayek and Mises: the socialist calculation debate, and Mises's 'apriorist' methodology. The issue on socialism is whether a socialist economy is "impossible", as Mises charged in 1920, or simply less efficient or more difficult to implement. Hayek now maintains that Mises's "central thesis was not, as it is sometimes misleadingly put, that socialism is impossible, but that it cannot achieve an efficient

[14]See this volume, chapter 1, Addendum.
[15]Margit von Mises, *My Years with Ludwig von Mises*, second enlarged edition (Cedar Falls, Iowa: Center for Futures Education, 1984), p. 133.
[16]From a lecture delivered at Hillsdale College, Hillsdale, Michigan, on November 8, 1977, published in revised form as "Coping with Ignorance", in *Imprimis*, vol. 7, no. 7, July 1978, pp. 1–6, and reprinted in *Champions of Freedom* (Hillsdale, Mich.: Hillsdale College Press, 1979).

utilisation of resources" (this volume, p. 127). That interpretation is itself subject to dispute. Hayek is arguing here against the standard view on economic calculation, found for instance in Schumpeter's *Capitalism, Socialism, and Democracy* or Abram Bergson's "Socialist Economics".[17] This view holds that Mises's original statement of the impossiblity of economic calculation under socialism was refuted by Oskar Lange, Abba Lerner, and Fred Taylor, and that later modifications by Hayek and Robbins amounted to an admission that a socialist economy is possible *in theory* but difficult in practice because knowledge is decentralised and incentives are weak. Hayek's response in the cited text, that Mises's actual position has been widely misunderstood, receives support from the primary revisionist historian of the calculation debate, Don Lavoie, who states that the "central arguments advanced by Hayek and Robbins did not constitute a retreat from Mises's position, but rather a clarification, redirecting the challenge to the later versions of central planning. . . . Although comments by both Hayek and Robbins about the computational difficulties of the [later versions] were responsible for misleading interpretations of their arguments, in fact their main contributions were fully consistent with Mises's challenge".[18] Israel Kirzner similarly contends that Mises's and Hayek's positions should be viewed together as an early attempt to elaborate the Austrian 'entrepreneurial-discovery' view of the market process.[19]

Second, there is Mises's insistence that economic theory (unlike history) is a purely deductive, wholly a priori exercise requiring no empirical confirmation of its propositions. It is clear that Hayek was uncomfortable with this opinion, sometimes arguing that Mises's position was actually more moderate, and at other times simply distancing himself from his mentor. The secondary literature contains some debate as to whether or not Hayek's seminal 1937 article "Economics and Knowledge" represents a decisive break with Mises in favor of a Popperian 'falsificationist' approach, one holding that empirical evidence can be used to falsify a theory (though not to

---

[17]Schumpeter, op. cit., pp. 172–186; Bergson, in Howard S. Ellis, ed., *A Survey of Contemporary Economics*, vol. 1 (Homewood, Ill.: Richard D. Irwin, 1948).

[18]Lavoie, op. cit., p. 21.

[19]Israel M. Kirzner, "The Socialist Calculation Debate: Lessons for Austrians", *Review of Austrian Economics*, vol. 2, 1988, pp. 1–18. See also a recent contribution by Joseph T. Salerno arguing by contrast *for* a part of the standard view—that Mises's original calculation problem is distinct from the discovery-process problem emphasised by Lavoie and Kirzner. Joseph T. Salerno, "Ludwig von Mises as Social Rationalist", *ibid.*, vol. 4, 1990, pp. 26–54.

'verify' it by induction).[20] This article contended that while the economic analysis of *individual* action could be strictly a priori, the study of multi-person exchange requires assumptions about the process of learning and the transmission of knowledge, themselves empirical matters. Hayek himself reports that beginning in 1937, "[a]gainst [Mises's 'extreme apriorism'] the present writer, then largely unaware that he was merely developing a rather neglected part of the Mengerian tradition, contended that while it was true that the pure logic of choice by which the Austrian theory inter-preted individual action was indeed purely deductive, as soon as the explanation moved to the interpersonal activities of the market, the crucial processes were those by which information was transmitted among individuals, and as such were purely empirical (Mises never explicitly rejected this criticism but no longer was prepared to reconstruct his by then fully developed system)" (this volume, p. 56). It is also true that Hayek first read Popper in the early 1930s, and that by at least 1941 he was showing open (but subtle) signs of moving away from the Mises position.[21] Popper's influence begins to appear where Hayek's interests move from the theory of value to the theory of knowledge; it has been suggested that Hayek's critique of central planning depends in part on the Popperian notion of the unpredictable consequences of a theory—planning fails because we cannot know in advance the full implications of the knowledge we already have.[22]

We must also note that Hayek's later emphasis on evolution and spontaneous order is not shared by Mises, although there are elements of this line of thought in Menger. A clue to this difference is in Hayek's statement that "Mises himself was still much more a

[20]For the case that 1937 is in fact a crucial turning point see Hutchinson, op. cit., p. 215, and Caldwell, op. cit., p. 528; for a denial see John Gray, *Hayek on Liberty* (second edition, Oxford: Basil Blackwell, 1986), pp. 16–21, and Roger W. Garrison and Israel M. Kirzner, "Hayek, Friedrich August von", in *The New Palgrave: A Dictionary of Economics* (London: Macmillan, 1987), vol. 2, pp. 609–614, esp. p. 610. Hayek himself, in recent interviews with W. W. Bartley, III, and others, has sup-ported the former interpretation, maintaining that it was indeed Mises he had hoped to persuade in the 1937 article. If true, Hayek's attempt was remarkably subtle, for Mises apparently welcomed Hayek's argument, unaware that it was directed at him.

[21]Bruce Caldwell describes Hayek's 1941 review of the German version of Mises's *magnum opus*, reprinted in this volume, chapter 4, as "cryptic", noting the faintness of Hayek's praise. "Compared to what others have said about *Human Action*, Hayek's review is extremely favourable. It is lukewarm when we remember Hayek's special relationship with Mises". Caldwell, op. cit., p. 529.

[22]On this point see W. W. Bartley III, *Unfathomed Knowledge, Unmeasured Wealth* (LaSalle, Ill.: Open Court, 1990).

child of the rationalist tradition of the Enlightenment and of continental, rather than of English, liberalism . . . than I am myself."[23] This is a reference to the 'two types of liberalism' to which Hayek frequently alludes: the continental rationalist or utilitarian tradition, which emphasises reason and man's ability to shape his surroundings, and the English common-law tradition, which stresses the limits to reason and the spontaneous forces of evolution. As Hayek writes in 1978, five years after Mises's death:

> One of my differences is over a statement of Mises on basic philosophy over which I always felt a little uneasy. But only now can I articulate why I was uncomfortable with it. Mises asserts in this passage that liberalism "regards all social cooperation as an emanation of rationally recognised utility, in which all power is based on public opinion, and can undertake no course of action that would hinder the free decision of thinking men". It is the first part of this statement only which I now think is wrong. The extreme rationalism of this passage, which as a child of his time he could not escape from, and which he perhaps never fully abandoned, now seems to me factually mistaken. It certainly was not rational insight into its general benefits that led to the spreading of the market economy. It seems to me that the thrust of Mises's teaching is to show that we have *not* adopted freedom because we understood what benefits it would bring: that we have *not* designed, and certainly were not intelligent enough to design, the order which we now have learnt partly to understand. . . . Man has *chosen* it only in the sense that he has learnt to prefer something that already operated, and through greater understanding has been able to improve the conditions for its operation. (This volume, p. 146)

Hayek fears that the 'extreme rationalism' of the continental view leads to what he calls the 'error of constructivism'—the idea that no social institution can be beneficial unless it is the result of man's deliberate design. This, he feels, underlies the socialist vision: Since markets are not created, a deliberately organised artificial system imposed, as it were, from above, ought to be able to outperform any decentralised and natural one.[24]

As a result, the modern Austrian school may have become split into opposing camps: the 'strict Misesians', who are 'social rational-

[23]In "Coping with Ignorance", op. cit.

[24]It is interesting that most of modern welfare economics is thoroughly 'constructivist'; it proceeds by first solving an economic problem for the optimal 'central planner's solution', and then tries to see if the market outcome can replicate the benevolent dictator's plan.

ists' and practise 'extreme apriorism', and the 'Hayekians', who emphasise spontaneous order and the limits to rationality. (There is also a third group, the 'radical subjectivists', who follow G. L. S. Shackle and Ludwig Lachmann and deny the possiblity of *any* order in economic affairs.) These differences have not yet been resolved, as the nature of the Mises-Hayek relationship is not fully understood. How all of this affects the continuing vitality of the school, it should be added, remains to be seen.

The year 1871, when Menger published his *Grundsätze* and the Austrian school was born, is significant in another respect: It was the year of Bismarck's creation of the German Reich. Hayek was deeply interested in the fortunes of Germany after the Second World War; the prospects for a rebirth of liberalism on the international scene, he believed, depended critically on the rehabilitation of the German intellectual community. The essays in Part II of this volume demonstrate that concern.

Hayek was convinced of the need for an international scholarly organisation of liberals, and to that end he arranged the 1947 meeting which became the Mont Pèlerin Society. His concern came in part from the role the economics profession had played in the war. For the first time, professional economists had joined the ranks of government planning bureaus en masse—to control prices, as with the United States Office of Price Administration, led by Leon Henderson and later John Kenneth Galbraith; or to study military procurement (what became known as 'operations research') with Columbia University's Statistical Research Group; or to provide various consulting services. This was thoroughly unprecedented, and for liberals quite alarming. (Hayek, though a naturalised Briton, was excluded by the fact of Austrian birth from British efforts.)

The intellectual climate of this period is captured by the economists' reaction to Minister Ludwig Erhard's decision to free prices and wages in newly created West Germany. Galbraith in 1948 assured his colleagues that "[t]here has never been the slightest possibility of getting German recovery by the wholesale repeal [of controls and regulations]." Walter Heller, later the chairman of John F. Kennedy's Council of Economic Advisers, added two years later that "[t]he positive use of fiscal and monetary measures [which I support] is, to be sure, not in harmony with the orthodox, free-market policies espoused by the current administration of the West

German Federal Republic."[25] And Hayek recalls Erhard's own contemporary account: "He [Erhard] himself has gleefully told me how the very Sunday on which the famous decree about the freeing of all prices accompanying the introduction of the new German mark was to be published, the top American military commander, General Clay, called him and told him on the telephone: 'Professor Erhard, my advisers tell me you are making a great mistake', whereupon, according to his own report, Erhard replied: 'So my advisers also tell me'" (this volume, pp. 197–198).[26]

Against all this Hayek gathered for the first Mont Pèlerin meeting a remarkable group of liberals, mostly people previously working in isolation. The group included internationally known scholars in economics, history, political science, and philosophy (four of the economists there have since received Nobel prizes); two of the participants, Walter Eucken and Wilhelm Röpke, were among the chief architects of the miraculous post-war recovery of the German Federal Republic. Hayek's purpose was to encourage the flourishing of liberal scholarship, in the hope that public opinion would follow. "For it is a real problem", he observes, "that many people hold the illusion that freedom can be imposed from above, instead of by creating the preconditions with which people are given the possiblity to shape their own fate" (this volume, p. 191).

The effects of Hayek's efforts are deep and long lasting: Not only has the Society itself continued to exist, but newer organisations with similar purposes have been founded, especially since the Austrian revival. These include the Institute of Economic Affairs in London; the Institute for Humane Studies at George Mason University in Fairfax, Virginia; the Cato Institute in Washington, D.C.; and the Ludwig von Mises Institute at Auburn University in Alabama. All these groups have contributed decisively to the revival of liberal thought in the United States and Europe.

For an example of this liberal revival, we need look no farther than the 1989 absorption of what was formerly East Germany into West Germany; this represents a 'rediscovery of freedom' in eastern

---

[25]John Kenneth Galbraith, "The German Economy", in Seymour E. Harris, ed., *Foreign Economic Policy for the United States* (Cambridge, Mass.: Harvard University Press, 1948); Walter Heller, "The Role of Fiscal-Monetary Policy in German Economic Recovery", *American Economic Review*, vol. 40, May 1950, pp. 531–547. These references, and a number of other similar examples, are provided in T. W. Hutchinson, "Walter Eucken and the German Social-Market Economy", in his *The Politics and Philosophy of Economics*, op. cit., pp. 155–175.

[26]Today's intellectual climate is very different. For evidence see Amity Shales, "Germany Needs Another Erhard", *The Wall Street Journal*, April 13, 1991, p. A18.

Germany, forty years after Hayek's efforts helped establish the same in the western part. And while it would be presumptuous to say that Hayek was prescient, chapters 8, 10, and 11 of this volume contain numerous insights about the nature of the German nation and people that are relevant to the events there of today.

Hayek has quoted approvingly the famous passage from Keynes's *General Theory* about the influence of abstract ideas on real-world events. "[T]he ideas of economists and political philosophers, both when they are right and when they are wrong, are more powerful than is commonly understood. Indeed the world is ruled by little else."[27] Hayek's writings in this volume do much to confirm this truth.

Peter G. Klein

[27]John Maynard Keynes, *The General Theory of Employment Interest and Money* (London: Macmillan, 1936), p. 383.

PART I

THE AUSTRIAN SCHOOL OF ECONOMICS

THE ECONOMICS OF THE 1920s
AS SEEN FROM VIENNA[1]

Although I believe that the sponsors of these lectures rather wished me to do some reminiscing, I have deliberately chosen until now topics which precluded this. It is a dangerous habit to acquire, and when one begins to discover that to most of one's audience things one remembers are unfamiliar and uninteresting, it is difficult to know where to stop. I have myself in the past not been the most patient of listeners to such recollections and now even regret that, when I first visited this country forty years ago and an old stockbroker who had discovered that I was interested in economic crises insisted on talking to me about his experiences in the crisis of 1873, I was not intelligent enough to ask him the right questions but rather regarded him as a bore. I don't know why I should expect you to be any more patient, particularly as I have discovered that once one opens the floodgates all sorts of memories tend to slip through which throw more light on the vanity of the speaker than on any matter of wider interest.

On the other hand, as a student of the history of economics I have often spent much effort in vain endeavours to reconstruct the intellectual atmospheres in which past discussions took place and wished that the participants had left some account of their relations with their contemporaries, and especially that they had done so at a time when their recollections were still tolerably reliable. Now as I stand before you committed to the task I can well understand why most men were reluctant to do so: It is, I am afraid, almost inevitable that in such an attempt one becomes somewhat egotistical, and if I speak perhaps too much about my own experiences, please remember that the fact that I can do so is my only, though perhaps

---

[1][This chapter, which has not been previously published, is one of five lectures delivered by Hayek at the University of Chicago in October 1963, under the sponsorship of the Charles O. Walgreen Foundation. It should be noted that Hayek had intended to revise the lecture before publication but was unable to do so. It is reproduced here in its original form. -Ed.]

19

insufficient, justification for talking at all about this subject. I have no doubt that if I ever prepare these lectures for publication, what I have put down for these talks will need a good deal of pruning. But this oral presentation is after all largely a talk to old friends and so I will let myself go.

The University of Vienna, which I entered late in 1918 as a raw youth fresh from the war, and particularly the economics part of its law faculty, was an extraordinarily lively place. Though material conditions were most difficult and the political situation highly uncertain, this had at first little influence on the intellectual level preserved from pre-war days. I do not want here to consider the question why the University of Vienna, which until the 1860s had not been particularly distinguished, then for a period of sixty or seventy years became one of the intellectually most creative anywhere and produced distinct internationally known schools of thought in a great variety of fields: philosophy and psychology, law and economics, anthropology and linguistics, to name only those closest to our interests. I am not clear myself what the explanation is—or whether such a phenomenon can really be fully explained. I will merely record that the rise of the place to eminence coincides precisely with the victory of political liberalism in that part of the world and that this eminence did not long survive the predominance of liberal thought.

It is possible that immediately after the First [World] War, though some of the great men of the pre-war period had already gone and there were, at least at first, serious gaps in the faculty, the intellectual fermentation among the young was even greater than before. In part this may have been due to the fact, so conspicuous after the Second [World] War, that the student body was of a more mature age, and partly that the experience of the war and its aftermath had produced a keen interest in social and political problems. Though some of the older men of course were mainly anxious to qualify for a profession as rapidly as possible, among the younger ones the wasted years of war service had rather created an unusual determination to make full use of the opportunities to which we had so long been looking forward.

In part it was of course the circumstances of the time that many of the issues and problems were in those years intensely discussed in Vienna which only somewhat later became topical in the Western world, with the result that in the course of my migrations I had again and again the feeling that "I have been here before".[2] The nearness of the communist revolution—Budapest, only a few hours away, had for a few months a communist government in which some of the intellectual leaders of Marxism were active who soon appeared as refugees at Vienna—the sudden academic respectability of Marxism, the rapid expansion of what we have since learned to call the welfare state, the then-new conception of the 'planned economy', and above all the experience of an inflation of a degree which no living European remembered, determined very largely the topics of discussion. But some of the purely intellectual currents which since have swept the Western world were already at their height in Vienna at the time. I will mention only psychoanalysis and the beginning of the tradition of logical positivism, which dominated all philosophical discussion.

I must, however, try to concentrate here on the development of economic theory, and perhaps the most remarkable circumstance is how much the interest at the University, at a time when so many urgent practical issues presented themselves, centred upon the purest of pure economics. Here the effects of the marginalist revolution,[3] which did not lie much farther back than the time about which I am speaking does now, were still clearly felt. Of the great men who had brought it about only Wieser[4] was still active. Both Böhm-Bawerk[5] and Philippovich,[6] the two most influential teachers of the pre-war period, the first in theory and the second mainly in problems of policy, had died early during the war. Carl Menger[7] was still alive, but a very old man who had retired fifteen years earlier and was to be seen only on rare occasions. He was to us

[2][Hayek refers to his travels to London, where he spent most of the 1930s and 1940s as Tooke Professor of Economics and Statistics at the London School of Economics; to Chicago, where he was Professor of Social and Moral Sciences at the University of Chicago from 1950 to 1962; and to Freiburg, West Germany, where he has been Professor (now Emeritus) at the University of Freiburg since 1962. -Ed.]

[3][I.e., the near-simultaneous 'discovery' of the marginal utility principle by Carl Menger and William Stanley Jevons in 1871, and Léon Walras in 1874. See the discussion in this volume, chapters 1 and 2. -Ed.]

[4][Hayek's teacher Friedrich von Wieser (1851–1926). See this volume, chapter 3. -Ed.]

[5][Eugen von Böhm-Bawerk (1851–1914), former Austrian minister of finance and Wieser's brother-in-law. See this volume, chapters 1 and 2. -Ed.]

[6][Eugen Philippovich von Philippsberg (1858–1917). -Ed.]

[7][Carl Menger (1840–1921), founder of the Austrian school of economics. See this volume, chapter 2. -Ed.]

young men more a myth than a reality, particularly as his book[8] had become a great rarity which was practically unobtainable as the copies had even disappeared from the libraries. Few of the men whom we met still had direct contact with him. The live memory which we encountered everywhere among our seniors was that of the Böhm-Bawerk seminar, which evidently had been the centre for all those most interested in economics in the pre-war days. Our female contemporaries, on the other hand, were all full of Max Weber,[9] who for a short semester had taught at Vienna just before the war ended and we men came back.

Wieser, the last living link with the great past, seemed to most of us at first a somewhat aloof and inapproachable grand-seigneur. He had only just returned to the University after serving as Minister of Commerce in one of the last imperial governments. He lectured on the lines of his *Social Economics*,[10] published just before the outbreak of war—the only systematic treatise on economic theory which the Austrian school[11] had produced and which he seemed to know more or less by heart. It was not a lively but, as pure lectures go, a most impressive and aesthetically satisfying performance, meant mainly for the law students for whom this one survey of economic theory would be their only contact with the subject. Only those who took all their courage in their hands and approached the majestic figure after the lecture might discover that this would elicit the most kindly and helpful interest and produce an invitation to his small seminar or even to a meal at his home.

There were at first two other full-time teachers of economics, a Marxist economic historian[12] and soon a young, philosophically inclined new professor, Othmar Spann, who at first evoked considerable enthusiasm among the students. He had some helpful things to

---

[8][I.e., Menger's *Grundsätze der Volkswirtschaftslehre* (Vienna: W. Braumüller, 1871), translated by James Dingwall and Bert F. Hoselitz as *Principles of Economics* (Glencoe, Ill.: The Free Press, 1950; reprinted, New York and London: New York University Press, 1981). -Ed.]

[9][Max Weber (1864–1920), German sociologist and author of *The Protestant Ethic and the Spirit of Capitalism* (London: Allen & Unwin, 1930), first published in German in 1904–5. -Ed.]

[10][Friedrich von Wieser, *Theorie der Gesellschaftlichen Wirtschaft* (Tübingen: J. C. B. Mohr, 1914), translated as *Social Economics* (London: Allen & Unwin, 1927; reprinted, New York: Augustus M. Kelley, 1967). -Ed.]

[11][I.e., the first and second generations of the Austrian school, meaning Menger, Böhm-Bawerk, Wieser, and their contemporaries. -Ed.]

[12][This was Carl Grünberg (1861–1940), who later became the first director of the Marxist Frankfurt Institute of Social Research. -Ed.]

say on the logic of the means-ends relationship but soon moved into regions of philosophy which to most of us seemed to have little to do with economics.[13] But his little textbook on the history of economics,[14] reputedly modelled on Menger's lectures on the subject, was for most of us the first introduction to this field.

Though a new degree in the political and economic sciences had just been created, most of us were still working for the law degree in which economics was only a small part and any professional competence we had largely to acquire by our own reading and from the teaching of men for whom this was a part-time labour of love. The most important of them was of course Ludwig von Mises,[15] but I myself came to know him well only comparatively late and I shall return to him later.

I must say here, however, a few words about the Central European, and particularly Austrian, university organisation, the peculiarities of which are rarely understood and which, in spite of all their defects, contributed not a little to that close contact between the full-time academics and the amateurs, in the best sense of the word, which was so characteristic of the atmosphere of Vienna. The number of full-time teachers at the university, full and associate professors (Ordinaries and Extra-ordinaries), was at all times small, and these positions were normally reached only comparatively late in life, rarely in a man's thirties and more often in his forties or even fifties. To be eligible for such an appointment one had, however, to obtain earlier, usually a few years after one's doctor's degree, a licence to teach as a *Privatdozent*, a position which carried no salary beyond a share in the negligible fees the students paid for the particular courses. In the experimental subjects, where one could do research only at some institute, these *Privatdozenten* usually also held paid assistantships at these institutes which might just enable them to devote themselves entirely to scientific work. But in all the non-experimental fields, like mathematics, law and economics, history, languages, and philosophy, nothing of the sort was available.

---

[13][Othmar Spann (1878–1950) was the founder of 'universalist' economics, a movement emphasising social 'wholes' as against the 'atomistic' individualism of the classical school. See Edgar Salin, "Economics: Romantic and Universalist", *Encyclopedia of the Social Sciences*, vol. 5 (New York: Macmillan, 1957), pp. 385–387, and Earlene Craver, "The Emigration of the Austrian Economists", *History of Political Economy*, vol. 18, no. 1, 1986, pp. 1–32, esp. pp. 5–7 and 9–10. -Ed.]

[14][Othmar Spann, *Die Haupttheorien der Volkswirtschaftslehre* (Leipzig: Quelle & Meyer, 1911). By 1949 the book had reached its 25th edition. -Ed.]

[15][On Mises (1881–1973) see this volume, chapter 4. -Ed.]

And unless one had an independent income, which before the First World War a fair proportion of the class going in for academic work had but after the great inflation scarcely anyone had, there was no other possibility than to take some other job for a livelihood and do one's research and a little teaching in one's spare time. In the law faculties, which you will remember included economics, the most frequent choice was to become a civil servant or, the most attractive position, an officer of the various trade or industrial organisations, or a practising lawyer; and in the arts it was usually teaching at a secondary school which had to bridge the gap until at last the hoped-for professorship came, if it came at all—the number of *Privatdozenten* was always much larger than the number of professorships. Perhaps more than half of those who had aspired to an academic career thus remained mere part-time teachers on a voluntary basis all their lives, teaching whatever they were interested in but drawing practically no income from this. To the outsider and particularly to the foreign observer this situation was largely disguised by the fact that after a few years the mere title of Professor was conferred on the *Privatdozenten*, which altered however nothing in their position. In some subjects, it is true, such as medicine and law, the prestige of the title might confer considerable pecuniary advantages and a doctor or lawyer might charge considerably higher fees if he could call himself "professor". It was only in this sense that, for example, Sigmund Freud was ever a professor at the University of Vienna.

This is not to say that some of these men did not as teachers have an influence quite as great as any of the regular professors. The two or three hours a week for which they would usually lecture or hold discussion classes would, if they were gifted teachers, sometimes have more effect than the performances of the regular professors—though the fact that the latter had the monopoly of the degree examinations inevitably reduced the influence of the former.

In law and economics, at any rate, this system had not only the advantage that all university teachers had had more or less long periods of experience in practical work but also that it generally created close contacts between the academic world and the professions. In fact a very much larger proportion of the most gifted graduates than in the end ever got to qualifying as *Privatdozenten* would long keep this possibility in mind and be doing a certain amount of scientific work on the side. And this served to preserve a tradition of the *Privatgelehrte*, the private scholar, which in the nineteenth century had been of considerable importance—perhaps not of as great an importance in Austria as it had been in England, but still of some significance. In our field an interesting instance from the 1880s is the authors of one of the great contributions to mathematical economics which came from Vienna, the *Researches on the Theory of Price* by Rudolf Auspitz and Richard Lieben,[16] of whom the first was a sugar manufacturer and the second a banker. There were still a few figures of this kind about in the period after the First [World] War, of whom at least the financier Karl Schlesinger, who had written an interesting book on money[17] and invented the term 'oligopoly', regularly took part in our discussion. Two or three others of the leading businessmen and a few high officials who had earlier made themselves names as economists were during those disturbed post-war years too occupied to take more than an occasional part in current scientific activities.

But on the main platform for current economic discussions at Vienna at that time, a small informal club called the *National-ökonomische Gesellschaft*,[18] which had barely survived the war and after an interruption was revived, I think those non-academics and non-professionals were always a majority. But while this was the only group where old and young, academic and non-academic, met some five or six times a year for discussing a set paper, for us younger men other more regular opportunities for discussion outside the university were more important. For most of the period between the two wars the most important of these was what was known as the Mises *Privatseminar*, though it was really entirely outside the university. These were fortnightly informal meetings held in the evening at Mises's office at the Chamber of Commerce and invariably continued far into the night at some coffeehouse. They must have started about 1922 and I believe continued until Mises left Vienna in 1934—I cannot say exactly, since I was not in either at the beginning or at the end.[19] But from about 1924 to 1931, assisted by the

---

[16][Rudolf Auspitz and Richard Lieben, *Untersuchungen über die Theorie des Preises* (Leipzig: Duncker & Humblot, 1889). -Ed.]

[17][Karl Schlesinger, *Theorie der Geld- und Kreditwirtschaft* (Munich: Duncker & Humblot, 1914). A partial translation appears as "Basic Principles of the Money Economy" in *International Economic Papers*, vol. 9, 1959, pp. 20–38. -Ed.]

[18][The National Economic Association or the Vienna Economic Society. On the *Gesellschaft* see Craver, op. cit., pp. 17–18. -Ed.]

[19][The *Privatseminar* in fact began in 1920 and ended in 1934. See Mises's own account in his *Notes and Recollections*, translated by Hans F. Sennholz (South Holland, Ill.: Libertarian Press, 1978), pp. 97–100. -Ed.]

circumstance that Mises had got Haberler[20] and myself jobs in the same building, and Haberler, as assistant librarian, continued the work started by Mises of turning the library of the Chamber of Commerce into the best economics library in Vienna, this Chamber of Commerce building and the meetings held there were at least as much the centre of economic discussion in Vienna as the University.

There were three or four special circumstances which gave these discussions in the Mises circle their peculiar interest. Mises was of course as acutely interested in the basic problems of marginal-utility analysis, which almost exclusively dominated discussion at the University, as anybody else. But such questions as the reconciliation of the marginal-productivity analysis with the theory of imputation of utility, which was, for instance, my chief interest in the early 1920s, or all the other refinements of marginal-utility analysis which you find set out at length in Rosenstein-Rodan's article on *Grenznutzen* (marginal utility) in the *Handwörterbuch der Staatswissenschaften*,[21] were not to such an extent an exclusive interest as they were at the University under Wieser and his successor Hans Mayer.[22] In the first instance, Mises had already in 1912 published his *Theory of Money*[23] and I scarcely exaggerate when I say that during the great inflation he was the only person in Vienna, or perhaps in the German-speaking world, who really understood what was happening. He had also introduced and developed in that book some of the Wicksellian ideas[24] and thereby provided the foundations of a theory of crises and depressions. He had more recently, just after the end of the war, published a little known but highly interesting book on the borderline problems of economics, politics, and sociology[25] and was

[20][Gottfried von Haberler (1900–) later became Professor of Economics at Harvard University and is presently Resident Scholar at the American Enterprise Institute. -Ed.]

[21][Paul N. Rosenstein-Rodan, "Grenznutzen", *Handwörterbuch der Staatswissenschaften*, vol. 4 (fourth edition, Jena: Gustav Fischer, 1927). -Ed.]

[22][Hans Mayer (1879–1955). -Ed.]

[23][Ludwig von Mises, *Theorie des Geldes und der Umlaufsmittel* (Munich and Leipzig: Duncker & Humblot, 1912), translated by H. E. Batson as *The Theory of Money and Credit* (London: Jonathan Cape, 1934; reprinted, Indianapolis, Ind.: LibertyClassics, 1981). -Ed.]

[24][I.e., Knut Wicksell's (1851–1926) theory of the 'natural' rate of interest. -Ed.]

[25][Ludwig von Mises, *Nation, Staat und Wirtschaft: Beiträge zur Politik und Geschichte der Zeit* (Vienna: Manz'sche Verlags- und Universitätsbuchhandlung, 1919), translated and edited by Leland B. Yeager as *Nation, State, and Economy: Contributions to the Politics and History of Our Time* (New York and London: New York University Press, 1983). -Ed.]

soon to bring out his great book on *Socialism*[26] which, by raising the problem of the possibility of rational calculation without a market, provided one of the main topics for current discussion.[27] He was almost alone—at least among men of his own generation (there were still a few older men like Gustav Cassel,[28] of whom this was also true) who were prepared to defend the principles of the free market to their last consequences. And he combined even at that time this passionate interest in what we now call libertarian principles with a strong interest in those methodological and philosophical foundations of economics which have become so characteristic of his later work. It was the latter circumstance which made the Mises seminar so attractive for many who not only did not share his politics but were also little interested in technical economics. But it was the regular presence of such men as Felix Kaufmann,[29] who was mainly a philosopher, or Alfred Schutz,[30] who was mainly a sociologist, and a few others, about whom I shall speak presently, who gave these discussions their special character.

Before I say more about the group in which these discussions took place I want to say a few words about the source of that intransigent liberalism of which in his generation Mises was really unique and almost completely isolated—at least among authors of the German tongue. He is certainly not, as it may seem to some of

[26][Ludwig von Mises, *Die Gemeinwirtschaft: Untersuchungen über den Sozialismus* (Jena: Gustav Fischer, 1922), translated by J. Kahane as *Socialism: An Economic and Sociological Analysis* (London: Jonathan Cape, 1936; reprinted, Indianapolis, Ind.: LibertyClassics, 1981). -Ed.]

[27][Other participants in Mises's seminar, however, recall that there was little discussion of economic calculation under socialism, because "Mises rightfully believed there was no one there to persuade". See Craver, op. cit., p. 15. -Ed.]

[28][Gustav Cassel (1866–1944) taught for many years at the University of Stockholm, where his students included future Nobel laureates in economics Bertil Ohlin and Gunnar Myrdal (with whom Hayek shared the 1974 prize). His most important theoretical works are "Grundriß einer elementaren Preislehre", *Zeitschrift für die gesamte Staatswissenschaften*, vol. 55, 1899; *The Nature and Necessity of Interest* (London: Macmillan, 1903); and *Theoretische Sozialökonomie* [1918], translated as *Theory of Social Economy* (London: T. F. Unwin, 1923; revised edition, London: E. Benn, 1932). -Ed.]

[29][Felix Kaufmann (1895–1949), a student of the philosopher Hans Kelsen, taught at the University of Vienna and the New School for Social Research. He authored *Methodology of the Social Sciences* (London and New York: Oxford University Press, 1944). See Alfred Schutz's tribute in *Social Research*, vol. 17, March 1950, pp. 1–7. -Ed.]

[30][Alfred Schutz (1899–1959) left Vienna in 1939 for New York, where he taught with Kaufmann at the New School. His most famous work is *Der Sinnhafte Aufbau der sozialen Welt* (Vienna: J. Springer, 1932), translated as *The Phenomenology of the Social World* (Evanston, Ill.: Northwestern University Press, 1967). -Ed.]

the younger generations, simply a relic of an older age, because there is something like a whole generation between him and the last consistent classical liberals. And it is known that at the time when he started his studies he was at least as much under the influence of the then-current ideals of social reform as any other young men of his time. It is true that Carl Menger, who still taught when Mises began his studies (though I do not believe that Mises ever attended his lectures[31]), was on the whole still a classical liberal. But, though the fourth book of Menger's famous book on method[32] contains some of the most important contributions to what I have previously called a theory of spontaneous growth providing the foundations for a policy of freedom, he was never a dogmatic or aggressive liberal.[33] In the next generation Böhm-Bawerk, Wieser, and Philippovich would certainly have called themselves liberal, and I happen to know that in the case of the first two men their general political outlook, as that of so many continental liberals of their generation, was essentially that which we find expressed in T. B. Macaulay's essays,[34] which both men had closely studied. But in the case of

[31][Mises confirms that he knew nothing of Menger before discovering the *Grundsätze* in 1903, three years after entering the University of Vienna, and did not meet Menger until many years later. Mises, *Notes and Recollections*, op. cit., p. 33. -Ed.]

[32][Carl Menger, *Untersuchungen über der Sozialwissenschaften und der Politischen Oekonomie insbesondere* (Leipzig: Duncker & Humblot, 1883), translated as *Problems of Economics and Sociology* (Urbana, Ill.: University of Illinois Press, 1963; reprinted, with the title *Investigations into the Method of the Social Sciences with Special Reference to Economics*, New York and London: New York University Press, 1985). Hayek actually means Book 3. Terence Hutchinson notes that this part was the main reason for the English translation of the *Untersuchungen*. See T. W. Hutchinson, "Some Themes from Investigations into Method", in J. R. Hicks and W. Weber, eds, *Carl Menger and the Austrian School of Economics* (Oxford: Clarendon Press, 1973), pp. 15–37, revised and republished as "Carl Menger on Philosophy and Method" in Hutchinson, *The Politics and Philosophy of Economics: Marxians, Keynesians and Austrians* (New York and London: New York University Press, 1981), pp. 176–202, esp. p. 183. -Ed.]

[33][On Menger's political views see now Erich Streissler, "Carl Menger on Economic Policy: The Lectures to Crown Prince Rudolph", in Bruce J. Caldwell, ed., *Carl Menger and his Legacy in Economics*, annual supplement to *History of Political Economy*, vol. 22 (Durham, N.C., and London: Duke University Press, 1990), pp. 107–130. -Ed.]

[34][Thomas Babbington Macaulay (1800–1859), later Lord Macaulay, was an English historian and critic. This is a reference to Macaulay's essays in the *Edinburgh Review*, probably in particular the January 1830 essay "Southey's Colloquies on Society", which contains the following oft-quoted passage: "Our rulers will best promote the improvement of the nation by strictly confining themselves to their own legitimate duties, by leaving capital to find its most lucrative course, commodities their fair price, industry and intelligence their natural reward, idleness and folly their natural punishment, by maintaining peace, by defending property, by diminishing the

Wieser and still more in that of Philippovich this liberalism already included a good deal of argument for control, certainly so far as problems of the labour market and social policy are concerned: Philippovich indeed was rather more a Fabian than a liberal in the classical sense. Böhm-Bawerk may have been an exception and have remained a true liberal throughout, and his last essay on "Control and Economic Law"[35] may even be regarded as the beginning of the liberal revival. But Mises had broken away and deliberately stood apart as an isolated intransigent liberal, and for his gradual building up of a new liberal doctrine he had to go on a voyage of discovery to the nineteenth-century English literature, since the current German literature would scarcely have enabled him to discover what the principles of liberalism really were. At the time of which I am speaking he had, however, already discovered kindred spirits in Edwin Cannan[36] and Theodore Gregory[37] at London and it is from this time in the early 1920s that the contacts between the Austrian and the London liberal groups date.

Mises's liberalism not only involved him in a running controversy with the strong group of Marxist intellectuals in Vienna—some of whose leading lights had indeed been his schoolmates and who, through Otto Neurath,[38] had very great influence on the group of neo-positivist philosophers of the 'Vienna circle' which was then forming; it was also unpalatable to the large group of middle-of-the-road liberals which then probably included the majority of the intellectually active young men. Or, strictly speaking, all of us who were not Marxists in the beginning belonged to that group and only

---

price of law, and by observing strict economy in every department of the state. Let the Government do this: The People will assuredly do the rest." In Macaulay's *Critical and Historical Essays* (second edition, London: Longman, Brown, Green, and Longmans, 1843), vol. 1, pp. 217–269, esp. p. 269. -Ed.]

[35][Eugen von Böhm-Bawerk, "Macht oder ökonomisches Gesetz?", *Zeitschrift für Volkswirtschaft, Sozialpolitik und Verwaltung*, vol. 23, 1914, pp. 205–271, in Böhm-Bawerk's *Gesammelte Schriften*, vol. 1 (Vienna: Hölder-Pichler-Tempsky, 1924). Translated by John Richard Mez as "Control or Economic Law?", in *Shorter Classics of Böhm-Bawerk* (South Holland, Ill.: Libertarian Press, 1962), pp. 139–199. -Ed.]

[36][Edwin Cannan (1861–1935) was Professor at the London School of Economics and Political Science from 1907 to 1925. On Cannan see Hayek's obituary "Edwin Cannan", in the *Zeitschrift für Nationalökonomie*, vol. 6, 1935, pp. 246–250. -Ed.]

[37][Theodore Emanuel Gugenheim Gregory (1890–1970) was Lecturer and Professor at the London School of Economics from 1913 to 1937. -Ed.]

[38][Otto Neurath (1882–1945), the Marxian philosopher and sociologist, was a member of the 'Vienna circle' along with Moritz Schlick and Rudolf Carnap. Neurath is chiefly remembered for the invention of isotypes, pictograph symbols used in education, and for the planning of the *International Encyclopedia of Unified Science*. -Ed.]

some of us were slowly and gradually won over to [Mises's] point of view. Even in the *Privatseminar*, I suspect, the majority was long half-socialist at heart, and even more kept away because they resented the constant return of the discussion to the principles of liberalism—though the systematic asking of what would happen if the state did not interfere was one of the chief sources of the strength of these discussions.

Before I say more about the milieu in which my own generation formed its views I must say a few words about some men intermediate between it and the generation of Schumpeter[39] and Mises, three men whose work deserves to be better known than it is but who all died comparatively early. None of them was ever a full-time economist yet their contributions to technical economics are considerable. There was in the first instance Richard Strigl,[40] whom we all regarded as the destined and legitimate successor to the chair at Vienna and who indeed would have been the best qualified to continue the tradition if he had lived. His study of the theory of wages[41] is one of the most distinguished in the field and he also made important contributions to the theory of capital. Though he had long been a *Privatdozent* and had been given the title of professor, his main occupation was as an official in an industrial commission which directed the labour exchanges and similar matters. Then there was Ewald Schams,[42] the only one of our whole group who had been a student of Schumpeter's at Graz and probably also the only one who was intimately familiar with the work of Walras and Pareto.[43] His essays on the method and logical character of economic theory are little gems, showing all the tidiness and precision of the passionate butterfly collector that he was—in addition to being a legal counsellor in one of the sections of the Federal Chancellery. The third of this group was the brilliant Leo Schönfeld (who later changed his name to Leo Illy),[44] so busy in his profession as an

[39][Joseph A. Schumpeter (1883–1950), Professor at the Universities of Graz and Bonn and later Harvard University, is author of *Capitalism, Socialism and Democracy* (London: Allen & Unwin, 1942) and the *History of Economic Analysis* (New York: Oxford University Press, 1954). On Schumpeter see this volume, chapter 5. -Ed.]

[40][On Strigl (1891–1942) see this volume, chapter 6. -Ed.]

[41][Richard von Strigl, *Angewandte Lohntheorie: Untersuchungen über die wirtschaftlichen Grundlagen der Sozialpolitik* (Leipzig and Vienna: Franz Deuticke, 1926). Hayek's review of this book is reprinted as an Addendum to this volume, chapter 6. -Ed.]

[42][On Schams (1899–1955) see this volume, chapter 6. -Ed.]

[43][Léon Walras (1834–1910) and Vilfredo Pareto (1848–1923) were pioneers in mathematical economics at the University of Lausanne in Switzerland. -Ed.]

[44][Leo Illy (Leo Schönfeld) (1888–1952). -Ed.]

accountant that we saw him only rarely, but the author of the last major treatise on the traditional central interest of the Austrian school, the theory of subjective value.[45]

When I now turn to the men of my own generation, the diversity of their occupations, before they all became professors in the United States, was even greater. Felix Kaufmann, philosopher, legal theorist, logician, and mathematician, was head of the Vienna office of a large oil company. Alfred Schutz, the sociologist, was secretary of an association of small banks, Fritz Machlup[46] a cardboard manufacturer; Friedrich Engel-Jánosi, the historian, produced wooden flooring; J. H. Fürth, later of the Federal Reserve Board, and Walter Fröhlich, later at Marquette, were practising lawyers. None of these, in the formal course of events, would ever have been full-time university teachers and few of them ever taught at all at the University before they left Vienna. Yet all of them were quite as important in the formation of a common body of views as the relative professionals like myself, who after four years in the civil service was fortunate enough to become director of an economic research institute,[47] or Oskar Morgenstern,[48] who soon became my associate and eventually successor, or Haberler, whose occupation I have already mentioned, or Rosenstein-Rodan,[49] who had an assistantship at the University and with Morgenstern edited the *Zeitschrift für Nationalökonomie*. It will be easy to see that in this circle the discussion, even if it was on technical economics, rarely remained on pure economics. Kaufmann's influence as the link to the legal positivists of the Kelsen *Kreis* and the logical positivism of Schlick and his circle was particularly important, and it was he who taught us all the rudiments of the modern philosophy of science and of symbolic

[45][Leo Illy (Leo Schönfeld), *Das Gesetz des Grenznutzens* (Vienna: Springer, 1948). -Ed.]

[46][Machlup (1902–1983) would later teach at the University of Buffalo and Princeton University. -Ed.]

[47][The *Österreichische Konjunkturforschungsinstitut* or Austrian Institute for Business-Cycle Research, founded by Mises in 1926 as an independent centre for empirical research. A substantial grant from the Rockefeller Foundation in 1930 at the urging of Mises's friend Jon Van Sickle helped secure the Institute's survival. See Craver, op. cit., pp. 19–20. -Ed.]

[48][Morgenstern (1902–1977) followed Hayek as director of the Institute and became the last of this generation to remain in Vienna. After the *Anschluß* in 1938 he accepted a professorship at Princeton University, where he remained until 1970. His work at Princeton with John von Neumann resulted in their *Theory of Games and Economic Behavior* (Princeton, N. J.: Princeton University Press, 1944). -Ed.]

[49][Paul N. Rosenstein-Rodan (1902–1985), who would later teach at University College, London, and at the Massachusetts Institute of Technology. -Ed.]

logic. Through Schutz we all became familiar with Max Weber and Husserl's phenomenology (which I, however, never understood, though Kaufmann's unique expository talents assisted Schutz in this).

What made this a relatively closely-tied group was not least that in the circumstances of the early post-war period it had perforce to be pretty self-contained and had to rely very much on its own resources. But it was not only the special circumstances of the time which for a few years made even access to current foreign literature difficult and travel almost impossible. It is perhaps difficult to realise today how little personal contact or intellectual exchange yet existed between the scientists of different countries fifty or even forty years ago. Though they might occasionally correspond, I believe that before the First [World] War few of the leading economists of the different countries had ever met face to face. There had been some first deliberate efforts to remedy this in the years immediately preceding that war. One of these was the first exchange of visiting professors between American and Continental universities; the fact that one of the first, if not the very first, Austrian exchange professor was Schumpeter, who came to Harvard in 1913, is of some significance. I think it must have been largely due to this that in the early post-war period the work of the American theorists John Bates Clark,[50] Thomas Nixon Carver,[51] Irving Fisher,[52] Frank Fetter,[53] and Herbert Joseph Davenport[54] was more familiar to us in Vienna than that of any other foreign economists except perhaps the Swedes. A pre-war visit of Wicksell to Vienna was remembered as an event and Gustav Cassel, of course, was in the years immediately after the war the most famous of all living economists, lecturing and writing in the newspapers in all European countries—as much overrated then as he is underrated now. But while we wel-

---

[50][John Bates Clark (1847–1938) was Professor at Columbia University and an author of the marginal-productivity theory of distribution. For a note on Clark see the first Addendum below. -Ed.]

[51][Thomas Nixon Carver (1865–1961) was Professor of Political Economy at Harvard University. -Ed.]

[52][Irving Fisher (1867–1947) was a Yale University economist and author of seminal works on interest theory and the purchasing power of money. -Ed.]

[53][Frank Albert Fetter (1863–1949) taught at Cornell and Princeton Universities; he is sometimes confused with his son, the economic historian Frank Whitson Fetter. On Frank A. Fetter's influence on later Austrian economists see Murray N. Rothbard's introduction to Fetter's *Capital, Interest and Rent* (Kansas City, Mo.: Sheed, Andrews & McMeel, 1977), pp. 1–24. -Ed.]

[54][Herbert Joseph Davenport (1861–1931) was Professor at the Universities of Chicago and Missouri and Cornell University. -Ed.]

comed the fact that his simplified version of Walras brought about a revival of interest in economic theory in Germany, he did not have much to offer to us.

But to return for a moment to the pre-war situation. How exceptional a personal meeting between economists of different countries, and still more across the seas, then still was, was shown by the lively recollection Wieser had preserved of the one exception: a meeting which not long before the war the Carnegie Foundation for International Peace had organised in Switzerland to discuss a series of publications which it planned. And I must not omit here the episode of the accidental meeting of Alfred Marshall and some of the Austrians which Mrs. Marshall recounts in her recollections[55] and which I will tell as I heard it from Wieser—even if some of you will have heard me tell the story before. The Marshalls and the Wiesers had for some time, I believe, been spending their summer holidays in the same village in a valley of the Dolomites, then part of Austria. But although they soon discovered each other's identity, both were rather shy men and no great talkers and hence made no attempt to make each other's acquaintance. Then one day Böhm-Bawerk, I believe in company of a third member of the Austrian school, came to visit his brother-in-law Wieser, and, being an enthusiastic and brilliant talker (who somewhat resented his brother-in-law's reluctance to talk economics with him), he took the occasion to introduce himself to Marshall, with whom, I believe, he had had some earlier correspondence. Mrs. Marshall then gave the tea party which she mentions and of which a photograph exists. It was apparently all very pleasant and amiable. But in the following year both the Marshalls and the Wiesers independently chose another place for their holidays where they could work undisturbed and without meeting another economist.

Speaking about great conversationalists among economists reminds me that you may wonder why I have not yet said more about Schumpeter—certainly the most brilliant talker among economists I have known with the sole exception of Keynes, with whom he had many other things in common, not least a puckish itch *pour épater le bourgeois* and a certain pretence to omniscience and a tendency to

---

[55][Mary Paley Marshall, *What I Remember* (Cambridge: Cambridge University Press, 1947). The described episode is on p. 48. Alfred Marshall (1842–1924) was Professor of Political Economy at Cambridge University. -Ed.]

bluff which went far beyond their astounding knowledge.[56] So far as Schumpeter is concerned, the fact is that during the few post-war years he lived at Vienna he had scarcely any contact with the economists and saw little even of those who had been his contemporaries in the Böhm-Bawerk seminar. Of course his two pre-war books and his essay on money[57] were familiar to all of us. But we hardly saw him and some of his pronouncements on current affairs had earned him a reputation as an *enfant terrible* among economists. He had then the misfortune that during a short spell as minister of finance during the height of the inflation[58] he had to put his name under a decree which confirmed that debts incurred in good crowns could legally be discharged by the same amount of depreciated crowns, that *"Krone ist Krone"* as the phrase ran, with the result that I believe to the present day the average Austrian of my generation gets red in the face when the name of Schumpeter is mentioned. He then became president of one of the smaller banking houses at Vienna, which had greatly prospered during the inflation but went broke completely soon afterwards, and after that he returned to academic life at Bonn in Germany. I should add that though he was admired but not much liked by his seniors and contemporaries, all who knew the details of his financial involvements spoke most highly of the manner in which he behaved after the collapse of the bank over which he presided to those who had suffered in the affair.

I only met him once during that period and since the occasion is connected with the resumption and rapid extension of international contacts after the war, I will mention it. Just a little over forty years ago I had decided that a visit to the United States was essential to an aspiring economist and somehow managed to scrape together the funds for the journey and to obtain a half-promise for a job if I made my way over there. Wieser then asked Schumpeter to give me letters of introduction to his friends in the States. So I visited

[56][Schumpeter "is said to have made a vow to become the best economist, horseman, and lover in Vienna, and later to have remarked that he had never fully achieved that degree of mastery on a horse". George J. Stigler, *Memoirs of an Unregulated Economist* (New York: Basic Books, 1988), p. 100. -Ed.]

[57][Joseph A. Schumpeter, *Das Wesen und der Hauptinhalt der theoretischen Nationalökonomie* (Leipzig: Duncker & Humblot, 1908); *Theorie der wirtschaftlichen Entwicklung* (Leipzig: Duncker & Humblot, 1912), translated by Redvers Opie as *The Theory of Economic Development* (Cambridge, Mass.: Harvard University Press, 1934; reprinted, New York: Oxford University Press, 1961); and "Das Sozialprodukt und die Rechenpfennige", *Archiv für Sozialwissenschaft und Socialpolitik*, vol. 44, 1917. -Ed.]

[58][March 15 to October 17, 1919. -Ed.]

Schumpeter in his magnificent office—bank presidents' offices tend to become more and more grandiose as you move East, and Schumpeter's might have been in Bucharest instead of in Vienna—and he supplied me with a set of most kind introductory letters to all the great American economists, veritable ambassadorial letters, so large in size that I had to have a special folder made to get them uncrumpled to their destination. But they did prove true 'open sesames'—as probably the first Central European economist to visit the States after the war I was received and treated much beyond my deserts by John Bates Clark, Seligman,[59] Seager,[60] Mitchell,[61] and H. P. Willis[62] at New York, T. Carver at Harvard (I missed Taussig[63] on a short visit), Irving Fisher at Yale, and Jacob Hollander at Johns Hopkins.[64] It was owing to these introductions that I was allowed to read the last paper in J. B. Clark's last seminar—not on a theoretical subject, but on economic conditions in Central Europe, and last but not least, that, when my expectations of a job failed and my small funds were used up, I never had to start on the job as a dishwasher in a Sixth Avenue restaurant which I had already taken but was found an assistantship with Jeremiah W. Jenks at New York University (or rather the Alexander Hamilton Institute) which enabled me to devote my time to more intellectual matters. A year later the first Rockefeller fellowships—or at least the first for ex-enemy allies—were granted, and the ever-increasing flow of European students to this country [the United States] started which has made such contacts an everyday affair.

I must confess that from my predominantly theoretical interest the first impression of American economics was disappointing. I soon discovered that the great names which were household words to me were regarded as old-fashioned men by my American contemporaries, that work on their lines had moved no further than I knew already, and that the one name by which the eager young men

---

[59][E. R. A. Seligman (1861–1939) was Professor at Columbia University from 1885 to 1931. -Ed.]

[60][Henry Rogers Seager (1870–1930) was Professor at Columbia University. -Ed.]

[61][Wesley Clair Mitchell (1874–1948) was Professor at Columbia University and Director of the New School for Social Research. On Mitchell see this chapter, second Addendum. -Ed.]

[62][Henry Parker Willis (1874–1937) was then consulting economist with the Federal Reserve Board. -Ed.]

[63][Frank William Taussig (1859–1940) was Harvard University professor from 1885 to 1935. -Ed.]

[64][Jacob Harry Hollander (1871–1940) was the discoverer and editor of Ricardo's *Letters* and Ricardo's *Notes on Malthus*. -Ed.]

swore was the only one I had not known until Schumpeter gave me a letter of introduction addressed to him, Wesley Clair Mitchell. Indeed business cycles and institutionalism were the two main topics of discussion. It was the year in which *The Trend of Economics*, intended to provide a program for the institutionalist school, had been brought out by Rexford Guy Tugwell.[65] And one of the first things the visiting economist was urged to do was to go to the New School for Social Research to hear Thorstein Veblen mumble sarcastically and largely inaudibly to a group of admiring old ladies—a curiously unsatisfactory experience.[66] Probably the most instructive and solid part of current discussion was that on central bank policy, turning largely around the important 1923 Report of the Federal Reserve Board. 'Stabilisation' was the general catchword under which all these problems were discussed. What intrigued me most about these problems, and has intrigued me ever since, was how much a stabilisation of the price level, or any other observable magnitude, would really secure an elimination of those disequilibrating forces which came from money. But the only paper I wrote at the time was an attempt to demonstrate that one could not at the same time stabilise the external and the internal value of money. I never published it because, before I could get it into decent enough English to submit it to an editor, Keynes's *Tract on Monetary Reform*[67] was published in which he made the same point. I believe it struck most economists at that time as an entirely new consideration, though you may be surprised how late such a relatively simple circumstance came to be generally understood.

Great fascination of course was exercised at the time by the attempts at economic forecasting, particularly the economic barometers of the Harvard Economic Service, and, however questionable it all appears in retrospect, acquaintance with them and the whole technique of dealing with economic time series was the greatest practical advantage we returnees from the United States derived, I am a little ashamed to confess, for our professional careers. But it did produce the solid advantage that it forced us to familiarise

[65][R. G. Tugwell, ed., *The Trend of Economics* (New York: Alfred A. Knopf, 1924). Hayek's 1933 essay "The Trend of Economic Thinking", reprinted in vol. 3 of *The Collected Works of F. A. Hayek*, may be an allusion to Tugwell's anthology. -Ed.]

[66][Thorstein Veblen (1857–1929) was author of *The Theory of the Leisure Class* (New York: Macmillan, 1899). -Ed.]

[67][John Maynard Keynes, *A Tract on Monetary Reform* (London: Macmillan, 1923), reprinted as vol. 4 of *The Collected Writings of John Maynard Keynes* (London: Macmillan and St. Martin's Press, for the Royal Economic Society, 1971). -Ed.]

ourselves with the modern techniques of economic statistics which were still practically unknown in Europe.

There can be no doubt that it was this experience on my American visit which turned me and soon many of the other visitors to this country to the problems of the relations between monetary theory and the trade cycle. Perhaps the now-forgotten but at the time much-discussed 'underconsumption' theories of Foster and Catchings offered to the theoretician the most interesting starting point.[68] But I found them, and the critiques which had been submitted for a prize for the best adverse criticism of their work, no more satisfactory than the outcome of the more empirical work of Mitchell, which seemed to raise more questions than it answered. It all sent me rather back to Wicksell and Mises and made me attempt to build on the foundations they had laid a fully explicit account of the successive phases of the business cycle, in which we then still all believed. It was this work which occupied me most of the seven years I remained in Vienna after my return. In a moment when I thought I had the solution in my hands I was emboldened to give a concise sketch in *Prices and Production*.[69] But I soon became aware that the theory of capital on which I had built was much too oversimplified to carry the burden of the superstructure I had tried to build on it. The result was that I had to devote most of the next decade to providing a more satisfactory theory of capital than that I had to work with. I am afraid it still seems to me the part of economic theory which is in the least satisfactory state. But I am

---

[68][William Trufant Foster and Waddill Catchings, *Profits*, Publications of the Pollak Foundation for Economic Research, no. 8 (Boston: Houghton Mifflin, 1925); idem, *Business Without A Buyer*, no. 10 of the same series (Boston: Houghton Mifflin, 1927; second edition, 1928); and idem, *The Road to Plenty*, no. 11 of the Pollak series (Boston: Houghton Mifflin, 1928). Theories of underconsumption attribute business fluctuations to changes in the ratio of consumption demand to output (a doctrine similar, but not identical, to the Keynesian notion of insufficient aggregate demand). Hayek's *Road to Serfdom* (Chicago: University of Chicago Press, and London: Routledge & Kegan Paul, 1944) may be an allusion to the title of this latter volume. On Foster and Catchings see Hayek's article "Gibt es einen 'Widersinn des Sparens'? Eine Kritik der Krisentheorie von W. T. Foster und W. Catchings mit einigen Bemerkungen zur Lehre von den Beziehungen zwischen Geld und Kapital", *Zeitschrift für Nationalökonomie*, vol. 1, 1929, pp. 387–429, translated by Nicholas Kaldor and Georg Tugendhat as "The Paradox of Saving", in *Economica*, vol. 11, 1931, pp. 125–169, reprinted in *Profits, Interest and Investment* (London: Routledge, 1939; reprinted, Clifton, N. J.: Augustus M. Kelley, 1969), pp. 199–263. -Ed.]

[69][F. A. Hayek, *Prices and Production* (London: Routledge & Sons, 1931; second revised edition, London: Routledge & Kegan Paul, 1935). -Ed.]

already beyond the point of time which I meant to reach in today's lecture.

There does not seem very much to say about the second half of the 1920s. It may be merely my own preoccupation as the head of a new business-cycle research institute which makes me think that watching the American boom and wondering how long it would last was the prime concern. Reparation payments and the transfer problem were the other sources of main theoretical interest, but I have never taken an active interest in international trade theory, and Haberler's book[70] is of course the representative product of discussion at that time. But the general effort of theorists was probably moving towards an integration of the different schools. We in Vienna of any note were busy very early with merely absorbing the flood of new ideas which were coming in from elsewhere, mainly from England—Hawtrey,[71] one of the most advanced writers—but increasingly also from the United States.

Addendum: John Bates Clark (1847–1938)[72]

When John Bates Clark died on March 23, 1938, at the age of ninety-one, he had become to the younger economists on this side of the Atlantic[73] an almost legendary figure and to some he seems to be known mainly as a kind of modern Bastiat,[74] a last believer in the natural harmony of the economic forces. This is not the place to defend him against this misinterpretation. And of his great achievement in the realm of economic theory, the development and definite establishment of marginal productivity analysis, which places him among the founders of modern economic theory, it will be for the future historian of economic thought to speak. But we all should be grateful for this charming memorial to John Bates Clark the man, one of the most lovable and wise among the teachers of his generation, as one who

---

[70][Gottfried von Haberler, *Der internationale Handel: Theorie der weltwirtschaftlichen Zusammenhänge sowie Darstellung und Analyse der Außenhandelspolitik* (Berlin: J. Springer, 1933), translated as *The Theory of International Trade* (London: W. Dodge, 1936; New York: Macmillan, 1937). -Ed.]

[71][Ralph George Hawtrey (1879–1975) was an economist with the British Treasury and author of *Currency and Credit* (London: Longmans, 1919) and *Trade and Credit* (London: Longmans, 1928). -Ed.]

[72][Review of *John Bates Clark: A Memorial* (privately printed by Columbia University Press, 1938), published in *Economica*, N.S., vol. 6, 1939, pp. 223–224. -Ed.]

[73][I.e., in Britain. -Ed.]

[74][Frédéric Bastiat (1801–1850), French economist and essayist. On Bastiat see chapter 15 of *The Trend of Economic Thinking*, being vol. 3 of *The Collected Works of F. A. Hayek*. -Ed.]

knew him well during his last year of active teaching can testify. Many must be those who owe him a deep debt of gratitude for the generous way in which he befriended and guided them in the early steps of their scientific careers. And to those who never knew him this modest sketch of his life and activities will give a vivid view of one of the really great figures in our subject.

Perhaps this is the proper occasion to make a small contribution to the biography of J. B. Clark by reprinting the following letter which happens to be in the possession of the reviewer. It was written soon after the appearance of the late Robert Zuckerkandl's *Theorie des Preises mit besonderer Berücksichtigung der Lehre* (Leipzig: Stein, 1889) and enclosed with it was a copy of the *New Englander*, no. 161, July 1881, containing J. B. Clark's article on "The Philosophy of Value":

Smith College, Northampton, Mass. Jan. 14th, 1890.

Dear Sir,

I am at present deriving profit and pleasure from the reading of your admirable book on the *Theory of Price*. I take the liberty of sending to you an early publication of mine on Value. At the time of the publication, in 1881, I was a young teacher in one of our western colleges; and I actually thought that I was the original discoverer of the principles expressed in the article. The analysis was written quite a long time before it was published.

Yours very truly,
J. B. Clark.

Herrn Dr. Robert Zuckerkandl,
Vienna.

P.S.—Nothing gives me greater pleasure than to render full honour to the eminent thinkers, mainly Austrians, who were earlier in this field than myself, and who have carried their analysis to greater lengths.

It may be added, perhaps, that in spite of the well-known lively controversy on the theory of capital, personal relations between J. B. Clark and the Austrians, when at last they were established just before the war, were most cordial, and that at least some of the members of the second or third generation of the Austrian school owed nearly as much to the teaching of J. B. Clark as to their immediate teachers.

Addendum: Wesley Clair Mitchell (1874–1948)[75]

With the death of Wesley Clair Mitchell at the age of seventy-four, American economics has lost one of its most distinguished figures and, perhaps, the most representative one. Apart from his important contributions to particular problems, he probably contributed more than any other economist of his generation to shape the general approach to the subject which during the last thirty years[76] has been distinctive of much of the work done in the United States.

Trained originally in Chicago in the orthodox classical tradition, represented by J. L. Laughlin, Mitchell came soon under the decisive influences of Thorstein Veblen and John Dewey. Although he made himself thoroughly familiar with contemporary economic theory, and through a great part of his career as a teacher devoted his main course of lectures to a discussion of its development, he regarded its usefulness as somewhat limited, and devoted his efforts to the development of a different approach which seemed to him more in the spirit of empirical science, and for which he drew largely on the inspiration of Veblen, Dewey, and the German historical school. It was from these efforts of his more than from those of any other man that there arose that 'institutionalist' school of economics which in the 1920s found its most active protagonists at Columbia University, where Mitchell had taught since 1914, and in the 1930s exercised great influence on the economic policies of President Roosevelt.

Mitchell's research work was devoted almost entirely to problems on the borderline of economics and statistics. After two studies on the monetary problems of the "Greenback" period, published in 1903 and 1908, he turned to the investigation of the problem of industrial fluctuations, and in 1913 brought out his monumental work on *Business Cycles,*[77] which rapidly became a classic, and which has probably influenced development in this field during the following twenty years more than any other work. The subject remained Mitchell's central interest, to which most of his technical work was devoted for the remainder of his life. His further contributions to it consist as much in the work of a devoted group of collaborators and

---

[75][Published as "Wesley Clair Mitchell, 1874–1948" in the *Journal of the Royal Statistical Society*, Series A (General), vol. 111, 1948, pp. 254–255. Hayek came to know Mitchell in New York in 1923, when he attended his lectures at Columbia University. It was from Mitchell that he first heard the doctrine, which Hayek later dubbed "constructivism", according to which "since man has himself created the institutions of society and civilisation, he must also be able to alter them at will so as to satisfy his desires or wishes". See Hayek's brief discussion of Mitchell in *New Studies in Philosophy, Politics, Economics and the History of Ideas* (Chicago: University of Chicago Press; London: Routledge & Kegan Paul, 1978), p. 3, n 3. Emil Kauder mentions the correspondence between Mitchell and Hayek in his *History of Marginal Utility Theory* (Princeton: Princeton University Press, 1965). -Ed.]

[76][Hayek is writing in 1948. -Ed.]

[77][Wesley Clair Mitchell, *Business Cycles* (Berkeley, Calif.: University of California Press, 1913). -Ed.]

pupils, whom he inspired and assisted, and in the research organisation he created, as in his own later publications. The National Bureau of Economic Research in New York, which he founded after the First [World] War, is probably much the most successful institution of its kind anywhere. In addition to directing all its activities for twenty-five years, Mitchell took special charge of the series of special studies which aimed at superseding his early single-handed effort by a more comprehensive survey of the whole problem of cyclical fluctuations. A first volume of the new great work he had planned appeared in the series of publications of the Bureau in 1927, under the title *Business Cycles: The Problem and its Setting*.[78] A second volume, *Measuring Business Cycles*,[79] produced jointly with Dr. A. F. Burns, later his successor as Director of the Bureau,[80] appeared only in 1946. A further volume which was to sum up the main conclusion of a quarter-century's work in this field was said to be practically completed some time before Mitchell's death.[81]

Mitchell's interests and activities were, however, far more extensive than this sketch of his persistent main aim would suggest. For many years public duties claimed much of his time. And although he will probably be mainly remembered for his pathbreaking work in a special field, his interests and general outlook were almost as much that of a philosopher as of a specialist. The character and significance of the social sciences and their function in society were at least as persistent a problem to him as those of the special field in which he himself experimented with new techniques. A collection of his essays published in 1937 under the title *The Backward Art of Spending Money*[82] gives perhaps the best impression of the range of his interests, and of the character of his methodological views. Equally, a volume of essays by his pupils and admirers published in his honour two years earlier under the title[83] [see note] gives some indication of the influence of his ideas. Even to one who knew Mitchell only slightly it is not difficult to see how this influence must have been magnified by the power of his personality, and by the example of single-minded devotion to a scientific ideal.

[78][Wesley Clair Mitchell, *Business Cycles: The Problem and its Setting* (New York: National Bureau of Economic Research, 1927. -Ed.]

[79][Arthur F. Burns and Wesley Clair Mitchell, *Measuring Business Cycles* (New York: National Bureau of Economic Research, 1946). -Ed.]

[80][Arthur Frank Burns (1904–1987), also later Chairman of the Federal Reserve Board, 1970–78. -Ed.]

[81][Published posthumously as *What Happens During Business Cycles: A Progress Report* (New York: National Bureau of Economic Research, 1951). -Ed.]

[82][Wesley Clair Mitchell, *The Backward Art of Spending Money, and Other Essays* (New York: McGraw-Hill, 1937. -Ed.]

[83][*Economic Essays in Honor of Wesley Clair Mitchell* (New York: Columbia University Press, 1935). In the original version of this article the title of the Mitchell volume was misidentified as "On the Changing Structure of Economic Life", which is in fact the title of one of the essays in the volume. -Ed.]

ONE

THE AUSTRIAN SCHOOL OF ECONOMICS[1]

Value Theory before 1871

The 'marginal[ist] revolution' of the 1870s is generally recognised as a major step in the advance of economic theory. Those who have been able to start with its established results often find it difficult to comprehend why an obvious and simple idea, which had occurred to many earlier thinkers, should have exercised such a great effect when W. S. Jevons, Carl Menger, and Léon Walras independently rediscovered it at about the same time[2] and, particularly, why the tradition founded by Menger should so profoundly have affected economic theory for two generations. To account for this it is

[1][Published as "Economic Thought: The Austrian School" in the *International Encyclopedia of the Social Sciences* (London: Macmillan; New York: The Free Press, 1968), vol. 4, pp. 458–462. A slightly different version of the essay was published in 1965 as "Wiener Schule" in *Handwörterbuch der Sozialwissenschaften*, vol. 12 (Stuttgart: Gustav Fischer; Tübingen: J. C. B. Mohr (Paul Siebeck); Göttingen: Vandenhoeck & Ruprecht, 1965). The version published here restores a few paragraphs and phrases from the earlier essay that were later omitted. Hayek had also begun around 1982 to draft an essay on the Austrian school for *The New Palgrave: A Dictionary of Economics*, ed. John Eatwell, Murray Milgate, and Peter Newman (London: Macmillan, 1987), but the essay was never completed. The unfinished sketch was used by Professor Israel M. Kirzner of New York University as a source for his essay which did appear as the "Austrian School of Economics" in the *New Palgrave*, vol. 1, pp. 145–150. For the most part Hayek's draft for the new dictionary repeats material in the chapters in Part I of this volume, but one section, surveying the period since this chapter was written, has been included here as an Addendum. In addition, a few paragraphs and phrases from the *New Palgrave* sketch that bring out new information or emphasis have been added as footnotes to the text in this chapter and chapter 4. -Ed.]

[2]Menger and Jevons in 1871 and Walras in 1874. [Carl Menger (1840–1921) is the subject of chapter 2 below. William Stanley Jevons (1835-1882) was Professor of Logic and Moral Philosophy at Owens College, Manchester, and author of *The Theory of Political Economy* (London and New York: Macmillan, 1871). Léon Walras (1834-1910) was Professor at the Academy (later University) of Lausanne in Switzerland from 1870 to 1892 and the founder of modern general equilibrium theory. Recent scholarship on the marginalist revolution has tended to emphasise the differences, rather than the similarities, between Menger, Jevons, and Walras. In particular see Erich Streissler, "To What Extent Was the Austrian School Marginalist?", *History of Political Economy*, vol. 4, Fall 1972, pp. 426–441, and William Jaffé, "Menger, Jevons and Walras De-homogenized", *Economic Inquiry*, vol. 14, December 1976, pp. 511–524. -Ed.]

necessary to elaborate on the distinction that is commonly but inadequately expressed as a contrast between 'objective' and 'subjective' theories of value.

Since value is evidently an attribute possessed by certain things or services, it was natural to seek its determinants in some property or properties of the particular objects that possess it. This procedure had proved successful in the physical sciences, and the expectation that objects having the same value should have also other 'intrinsic' properties in common therefore seemed reasonable. Of course it had often been seen that the decisive factor might be something discoverable not in the object itself but rather in the relations of men to the object. Ever since the medieval scholastic philosophers (and even Aristotle), it had been pointed out again and again that to possess value an object must be useful and scarce.[3] But this idea was rarely followed through systematically (though an exception must be made for the greatest of the early anticipators of modern theory, Ferdinando Galiani in his *Della moneta* of 1750[4]) and never to the point of realising that what was relevant was not merely man's relation to a particular thing or a class of things but the position of the thing in the whole means-end structure—the whole scheme by which men decide how to allocate the resources at their disposal among their different endeavours.

It was largely from approaching the problem of value through patient analysis of the character of economic choice in the various types of possible relations between different means and different ends that there ultimately emerged the explanation of value that made the work of Menger and his pupils so immediately effective. Although the answers supplied by Jevons and Walras to the old value paradox were no less correct, they were concealed from most contemporary economists by the mathematical notation employed. Moreover, these authors treated the solution of the utility paradox as merely a preliminary step to be gotten quickly out of the way in order to get on with the main business, the explanation of value in

---

[3][On the contributions of the late scholastics, particularly the sixteenth- and seventeenth-century school of Salamanca in Spain, and their place as forerunners of Austrian economics, see Alejandro Chafuen's fine study with the unfortunate title, *Christians for Freedom: Late-Scholastic Economics* (San Francisco: Ignatius Press, 1986). See also Raymond de Roover, *Business, Banking and Economic Thought in Late Medieval and Early Modern Europe* (Chicago: University of Chicago Press, 1974). -Ed.]

[4]Ferdinando Galiani, *Della moneta* (Naples: G. Raimondi, 1750). [Translated by Peter R. Toscano as *On Money* (Ann Arbor, Mich.: Published for the Department of Economics, University of Chicago, by University Microfilms International, 1977). -Ed.]

exchange. The Austrians, on the other hand, made the full analysis of the conditions of valuation, independent of the possibility of exchange, so much their central task that later they had to defend themselves against the misunderstanding that they believed marginal utility provided a direct explanation of price.[5] Of course, the subjective value that it explains is merely a first step to the second stage, the theory of price.

On the Continent the utility-*cum*-scarcity approach had, since Galiani, remained an important tradition and considerable insight had been achieved in such works as E. B. de Condillac's *Le commerce et le gouvernement*, 1776,[6] Louis Say's *Considérations sur l'industrie*, 1822,[7] Auguste Walras's *De la nature de la richesse*, 1831,[8] Jules Dupuit's *De la mesure de l'utilité des travaux publics*, 1844,[9] and finally in the remarkable but at the time completely overlooked work of H. H. Gossen, *Entwicklung der Gesetze des menschlichen Verkehrs*, 1854.[10] In England, on the other hand, the generally much more highly developed classical political economy had become wedded to an 'objective' labour theory of value, and the utility tradition persisted only as a sort of undercurrent of protest, which reached a high

---

[5][On this see this volume, pp. 73–748. -Ed.]

[6]Etienne Bonnot de Condillac, *Le commerce et la gouvernement, ouvrage élémentaire, par l'abbé de Condillac* (Amsterdam: n.p., 1776).

[7]Louis Auguste Say, *Considerations sur l'industrie et la législation* (Paris: J. P. Aillaud, 1822). [Louis Auguste Say (1774–1840) was a sugar merchant and the brother of Jean-Baptiste Say. -Ed.]

[8]Auguste Walras, *De la nature de la richesse* (Paris: Furne, 1832). [Antoine Auguste Walras (1801–1866) was Professor of Philosophy at the Royal Colleges of Lille and Caen and the father of Léon Walras. -Ed.]

[9]Jules Dupuit, *De la mesure de l'utilité des travaux publics* (Paris: Imprimerie de Poupart-Davyl, 1844). [Translated and reprinted in Kenneth Arrow and Tibor Scitovsky, eds, *Readings in Welfare Economics* (Homewood, Ill.: R. D. Irwin, for the American Economic Association, 1969). On Dupuit (1804–1866) see chapter 15 of F. A. Hayek, *The Trend of Economic Thinking*, being vol. 3 of *The Collected Works of F. A. Hayek*. -Ed.]

[10]Hermann Heinrich Gossen, *Entwicklung der Gesetze des menschlichen Verkehrs*, new edition (Berlin: R. L. Praeger, 1889). [Translated by Rudolph C. Blitz as *The Laws of Human Relations and the Rules of Human Action Derived Therefrom*, with an introductory essay by Nicholas Georgescu-Roegen (Cambridge, Mass.: MIT Press, 1983). See Hayek's discussion of Gossen (1810–1858) in chapter 15 of *The Trend of Economic Thinking*, op. cit. In his unfinished essay for the *New Palgrave* dictionary (see footnote 1 above) Hayek adds to this list F. B. W. Hermann's *Staatswirtschaftliche Untersuchungen* (Munich: A. Weber, 1832) and Hans von Mangoldt's *Grundriß der Volkswirtschaftlehre* (Stuttgart: J. Maier, 1863), noting that "[i]n Germany as well as in France the Ricardian labour theory of value had never achieved the same dominance" as in Britain. -Ed.]

point in 1834 with W. F. Lloyd's *The Notion of Value*.[11] It was fully swamped when as late as 1848 J. S. Mill in his *Principles of Political Economy* not only re-expounded the classical position but calmly asserted, "Happily, there is nothing in the laws of value which remains for the present or any future writer to clear up; the theory of the subject is complete".[12]

Menger and the Origins of the School

While W. S. Jevons (who with his preliminary sketch of a theory of value based on "final utility" had anticipated Menger by nine years[13]) was writing in direct opposition to dominant doctrine and had little more than Benthamite utilitarianism to draw upon, both Menger and Walras were able to build on a rich literary tradition favorable to the utility approach. But in Vienna, where Menger worked, there was little interest in economic theory. At that time economics was taught at the University of Vienna by Germans of chiefly sociological interests.[14] The rapid rise of a distinct Austrian school of economic theory was thus entirely owing to Menger's work —though it did coincide with the university's rise to great eminence in a number of other fields, which for some fifty or sixty years made it an intellectual centre of great influence.[15]

[11]William Forster Lloyd, *A Lecture on the Notion of Value* (London: Roake and Varty; Oxford: J. H. Parker, 1834).

[12]John Stuart Mill, *Principles of Political Economy, with Some of Their Applications to Social Philosophy* (Boston: Little & Brown, 1848), book 3, chapter 1, section 1. [In *The Collected Works of John Stuart Mill*, vol. 3 (Toronto: University of Toronto Press, and London: Routledge & Kegan Paul, 1965), p. 456. -Ed.]

[13][I.e., Jevons's "Brief Account of a General Mathematical Theory of Political Economy", a paper read to the British Association, Section F, Cambridge, October 1862; published in the *Journal of the Statistical Society of London*, vol. 29, 1866, pp. 282–287, and reprinted as an Appendix to later editions of Jevons's *Theory of Political Economy*. -Ed.]

[14][In his unfinished essay for the *New Palgrave*, however, Hayek cites an unpublished 1982 Oxford Ph.D. thesis by Klaus H. Hennings suggesting that one of these German professors, Albert E. F. Schäffle (1831–1903), may have been the one to encourage Böhm-Bawerk and Wieser as students to pursue Menger's ideas.]

[15][In his *New Palgrave* draft Hayek writes: "In view of the remarkable number of 'Austrian' or 'Viennese' schools that became internationally known during the early part of this century, it should be pointed out that in general these had little in common and in some instances developed rather in conflict with each other. This was clearly the case with the relation between the Austrian economic tradition and the schools of logical and legal positivism. There was also no connexion between the economic and psychoanalytical schools which developed there, while the Austrian

Carl Menger was a civil servant in the prime minister's office at Vienna when at the age of thirty-one he published his first and decisive work, *Principles of Economics*.[16] It was the first part of an intended treatise, the rest of which never appeared. It dealt with the general conditions that create economic activity, value, exchange, price, and money. What made it so effective was that the explanation of value it offered arose from an analysis of the conditions determining the distribution of scarce goods among competing uses and of the way in which different goods competed or cooperated for the satisfaction of different needs—in short, what has been called above the 'means-ends structure'. It is this analysis that precedes the theory of value proper. Friedrich von Wieser was to develop this systematically into a *vorwerttheoretische* part of economic theory that made the Austrian form of marginal utility analysis so suitable as a basis of further development. From this analysis springs most of what is known today as the logic of choice, or the 'economic calculus'.

Menger's exposition is generally characterised more by painstaking detail and relentless pursuit of the important points than by elegance or the use of graphic terms to express his conclusions. Though always clear, it is laboured, and it is doubtful whether his doctrines would ever have had wide appeal in the form in which he stated them. However, he had the good fortune of finding at once avid and gifted readers in two young men who had left the University of Vienna some time before Menger became a professor there. They decided to make the fulfillment of his teaching their lifework. It was mainly through the work of Eugen von Böhm-Bawerk and Friedrich von Wieser, classmates and later brothers-in-law, that Menger's ideas were developed and spread.[17] Gradually during the

---

economists and Marxists were of course in constant opposition." See also this volume, pp. 20–21. -Ed.]

[16]Carl Menger, *Grundsätze der Volkswirtschaftslehre*, op. cit. [The title page bears the subtitle] "Erster, Allgemeiner Teil" (First, General Part). It was soon sold out and became quite difficult to obtain.

[17]Menger became *außerordentlicher Professor* at the University of Vienna in 1873 and *Ordinarius* in 1879. Böhm-Bawerk and Wieser, approximately eleven years younger than he, did their habilitations with him in Vienna in the early 1880s. [Böhm-Bawerk (1851–1914) held a chair at Innsbruck and was Austrian finance minister on three occasions before accepting a professorship at Vienna where he conducted a famous seminar on economic theory. His best-known works are *Kapital und Kapitalzins* [1884–1912], translated by George D. Huncke and Hans F. Sennholz as *Capital and Interest*, 3 vols (South Holland, Ill.: Libertarian Press, 1959), and "Zum Abschluß des Marxschen Systems", in *Staatswissenschaftliche Arbeiten, Festgaben für Karl Knies* (Berlin: Haering, 1896), translated as *Karl Marx and the Close of His System*

1880s, when their most influential works appeared, they were joined by others working in the universities or elsewhere in Austria. Of these, Emil Sax (1845–1927), Robert Zuckerkandl (1856–1926), Johann von Komorzynski (1843–1912), Viktor Mataja (1857–1933), and Robert Meyer (1855–1914) particularly deserve mention. Somewhat later came Hermann von Schullern zu Schrattenhofen (1861–1931) and Richard Schüller (1871–1972).

The year 1889, in which the greatest number of important publications of the group were concentrated, also saw the appearance of an important theoretical treatise by two Viennese businessmen, Rudolf Auspitz and Richard Lieben, *Untersuchungen über die Theorie des Preises*.[18] This can, however, only with qualifications be included in the works of the Austrian school. It moved on parallel but wholly independent lines and with its highly mathematical exposition was too difficult for most contemporary economists, so that its importance was recognised only much later.

Of great importance for spreading the teachings of the school, especially in Germany, was the fact that another Viennese professor, Eugen von Philippovich von Philippsberg (1858–1917), though not himself an active theoretician, incorporated the marginal utility doctrine into a very successful textbook, *Grundriß der politischen Ökonomie*.[19] For some twenty years after publication this remained the most widely used textbook in Germany and almost the only channel through which the marginal utility doctrine became known there.[20] In other foreign countries, especially England, the United States, Italy, the Netherlands, and the Scandinavian countries, the basic economic publications of the Austrians became known sooner,

---

(London: Fisher Unwin, 1898) and reprinted in Paul Sweezy, ed., *Karl Marx and the Close of His System and Böhm-Bawerk's Criticism of Marx* (New York: Augustus M. Kelley, 1949). On Wieser (1851–1926), who assumed Menger's chair after the latter retired in 1903, see this volume, chapter 3. -Ed.]

[18]Rudolf Auspitz and Richard Lieben, *Untersuchungen über die Theorie des Preises* (Leipzig: Duncker & Humblot, 1889).

[19]Eugen Philippovich von Philippsberg, *Grundriß der politischen Ökonomie* (Freiburg: J. C. B. Mohr, 1893). Philippsberg was *Ordinarius* at the University of Vienna from 1893 to 1917. [See Hayek's essay on Philippsberg in the *International Encyclopedia of the Social Sciences*, op. cit., vol. 11, p. 116. -Ed.]

[20][Textbooks were of particular importance in nineteenth-century Germany because academic economists tended to express their ideas in this form rather than by publishing monographs, which was the preferred practice in Britain. See Erich Streissler, "The Influence of German Economics on the Work of Menger and Marshall", in *Carl Menger and his Legacy in Economics*, op. cit., pp. 31–68, esp. p. 32. -Ed.]

partly in English translations.[21] Probably the most important foreign adherent was an exact contemporary of Böhm-Bawerk and Wieser, the Swede Knut Wicksell. Although he was also greatly indebted to Walras, Wicksell could write in 1921 that "since Ricardo's *Principles* there has been no other book—not even excepting Jevons's brilliant but somewhat aphoristic and Walras's unfortunately difficult work—which has had such a great influence on the development of economics as Menger's *Grundsätze*".[22]

Development by Böhm-Bawerk and Wieser

In the theoretical development of Menger's ideas the most important steps were Wieser's interpretation of costs as sacrificed utility (or 'opportunity costs', as the concept later came to be called) and the theory of the determination of the value of the factors of production by 'imputation' (*Zurechnung*). (This later term and the term *Grenznutzen*—'marginal utility'—were introduced by Wieser.) In the field of value theory proper Böhm-Bawerk contributed mainly by the lucidity of his exposition and the great skill of his polemics. His most important original contribution was his theory of capital and interest, which was by no means accepted by all members of the school.[23] In general it may be said that the school never developed a strict orthodoxy but that the development of Menger's idea by its different members shows distinct differences. This applies

[21][In the *New Palgrave* draft Hayek singles out the following as exponents of the new Austrian theory of value: James Bonar and William Smart in England; Irving Fisher, Frank A. Fetter, T. N. Carver, and Herbert J. Davenport in the United States; Maffeo Pantaleoni in Italy; Charles Rist in France; N. G. Pierson in Holland; and Knut Wicksell in Sweden. -Ed.]

[22][Wicksell (1851–1926) is known as a pioneer in capital and interest theory and the monetary theory of the business cycle. He is credited with the distinction, so crucial to the Austrian theory of industrial fluctuations, between the 'natural' and 'bank' rates of interest. The quotation is from Wicksell's essay "Carl Menger" in *Ekonomisk Tidskrift*, 1921, pp. 113–124, in *Selected Papers on Economic Theory*, ed. Erik Lindahl (Cambridge, Mass.: Harvard University Press, 1958), p. 191. -Ed.]

[23][Menger is said to have called Böhm-Bawerk's theory of capital "one of the greatest errors ever committed" (quoted in Joseph Schumpeter, *History of Economic Analysis* (New York: Oxford University Press, 1954), p. 847, note 8). On Menger's disagreement with Böhm-Bawerk see A. M. Endres, "The Origins of Böhm-Bawerk's 'Greatest Error': Theoretical Points of Separation from Menger", *Journal of Institutional and Theoretical Economics*, vol. 143, 1987, pp. 291–309, and Roger W. Garrison, "Austrian Capital Theory: The Early Controversies", in *Carl Menger and his Legacy in Economics*, op. cit., pp. 133–154. -Ed.]

particularly to Böhm-Bawerk and Wieser, who in many respects represented very different intellectual types[24] and whose endeavours marked the starting points of two distinguishable traditions within the school. Böhm-Bawerk was a particularly consistent logical reasoner, a masterly debater, and at the same time, a man of great practical experience (he was three times Austrian minister of finance). He was able to ground his work on a thorough command of the whole of economic literature, and he was always ready to take issue with other views. He therefore kept closer in many ways to Menger's foundation than Wieser, who after the initial stimulus received from Menger, very much pursued his own ways. Wieser's work in consequence has a highly personal character, and though in some respects (e.g., in the analysis of the role of different degrees of monopoly) he anticipated later development, in others, such as his insistence on the calculability and interpersonal comparability of utility, he developed in directions that had later to be abandoned. His *Social Economics*,[25] which constitutes the only complete systematisation of the economic theory of the earlier Menger school, therefore cannot be regarded as representative but nonetheless constitutes a distinctly personal achievement.

Controversy with the Historical School

Carl Menger was a very effective teacher, and through his numerous pupils and his participation in the contemporary discussion of economic and financial policy he exercised considerable influence on Austrian public life. If after his first work, his literary contributions to pure theory, except in the field of money, are few, this is to be ascribed mainly to his involvement in the *Methodenstreit*, his dispute about method with the leader of the younger German historical school, Gustav Schmoller.[26] That Menger's book had remained

---

[24][These two intellectual types are discussed in Hayek's essay "Two Types of Mind", chapter 3 of *The Trend of Economic Thinking*, being vol. 3 of *The Collected Works of F. A. Hayek*. -Ed.]

[25]Friedrich von Wieser, *Theorie der gesellschaftliche Wirtschaft*, his contribution to *Grundriß der Sozialökonomik* (Tübingen: J. C. B. Mohr (Paul Siebeck), 1914), translated by A. Ford Hinrichs as *Social Economics* (New York: Greenberg, 1927).

[26][Gustav von Schmoller (1838–1917) was Professor at the Universities of Halle, Strasbourg, and Berlin and leader of the younger German historical school or *Kathedersozialisten* (Socialists of the Chair). On the *Methodenstreit* see Ludwig von Mises, *The Historical Setting of the Austrian School of Economics* (Auburn, Ala.: Ludwig von Mises Institute, 1984), and Samuel Bostaph, "The Methodological Debate Between Carl

practically unnoticed in Germany was chiefly owing to the fact that the dominance of the historical school had almost eliminated the teaching of economic theory from German universities. In these circumstances it was natural that it should seem urgent to Menger to vindicate the importance of theoretical research. This he undertook in his *Problems of Economics and Sociology*,[27] which in several respects became as important for the development of the Austrian school as his earlier *Grundsätze*, although in detail his methodological views were not fully accepted even within his own school. But the systematic justification of what Schumpeter was later to call "methodological individualism"[28] and the analysis of the evolution of social institutions (in which he revived ideas originally conceived by Bernard Mandeville[29] and David Hume) had a profound influence on all members of the school and, later, far beyond the limits of economics. Compared with this, the points immediately at issue with Schmoller are of lesser significance, although at the time they led to a passionate exchange of opinions to which several disciples on each side contributed. This exchange caused such a rift between the two groups that the German universities came to be filled more and more exclusively by members of the historical school and the Austrian universities by members of Menger's school.

Menger and the German Historicists", *Atlantic Economic Journal*, vol. 6, September 1978, pp. 3–16. -Ed.]

[27]Carl Menger, *Untersuchungen über die Methode der Sozialwissenschaften und der politischen Oekonomie insbesondere*, op. cit. [Now translated as *Investigations into the Method of the Social Sciences, with Special Reference to Economics*. -Ed.]

[28]Joseph A. Schumpeter, *Das Wesen und der Hauptinhalt theoretischen Nationalökonomie* (Leipzig: Duncker & Humblot, 1908). [An excerpt from this work was published in English as a pamphlet entitled *Methodological Individualism* (Brussels: Institutum Europaeum, 1980); Hayek's Preface to the pamphlet is reprinted in this volume, chapter 5. Methodological individualism, a tenet of modern neoclassical economics as well as the Austrian school, is simply the view that all social-scientific explanations must be based on the plans and decisions of individuals. "*Methodological individualism* is the view that allows *only* individuals to be the decision-makers in any explanation of social phenomena. . . . [It] does not allow explanations which involve non-individualist decision-makers such as institutions, weather or even historical destiny". Lawrence A. Boland, *The Foundations of Economic Method* (London: Allen & Unwin, 1982), p. 28. Compare also Joseph Agassi, "Methodological Individualism", in John O'Neill, ed., *Modes of Individualism and Collectivism* (London: Heinemann, 1973), pp. 185–212, and Ludwig von Mises, *Human Action: A Treatise on Economics* (third revised edition, Chicago: Henry Regnery, 1966), pp. 41–43. -Ed.]

[29][See Hayek's essay, "Dr. Bernard Mandeville", chapter 6 of *The Trend of Economic Thinking*, op. cit. -Ed.]

The Third and Fourth Generations

In 1903 Menger retired prematurely from teaching and in consequence exercised little direct influence on the formation of the third generation of the Austrian school, which grew up during the decade preceding [the First] World War. These years, during which Böhm-Bawerk, Wieser, and Philippovich were teaching at Vienna, were the period of the school's greatest fame. It was particularly Böhm-Bawerk's seminar that provided the centre of theoretical discussion and produced the leading members of the third generation. Among them, particular mention must be made of Ludwig von Mises (1881–1973),[30] who continued the tradition of Böhm-Bawerk, and Hans Mayer (1879–1955),[31] who continued that of Wieser. (Franz X. Weiss (1885–?) belonged to the stricter Böhm-Bawerk tradition.) Joseph Schumpeter (1883–1950),[32] although much indebted to Böhm-Bawerk, absorbed so many other influences (particularly that of the Lausanne school[33]) that he cannot be wholly regarded as a member of this group. The same might be said of Alfred Amonn (1883–1962), who stood close to the English classical tradition. Somewhat younger but still wholly active at Vienna were Richard von Strigl (1891–1942), Ewald Schams (1889–1955),[34] and Leo Illy (1888–1952), whose name was originally Leo Schönfeld.[35]

[30][On Mises see this volume, chapter 4. -Ed.]

[31][In his unfinished essay for the *New Palgrave* Hayek writes that Mayer "was unquestionably a highly gifted, but emotionally handicapped man who wasted much of his energy in a long battle with his professorial colleague Othmar Spann. Apart from a monumental work on the state of modern economic theory, which he edited in four volumes and entitled *Die Wirtschaftstheorie der Gegenwart* (Vienna: J. Springer, 1927–32) he left only a series of very thoughtful essays whose contents may yet have to be fully worked out." On Mayer and Spann see Craver, op. cit., pp. 5–13. -Ed.]

[32][On Schumpeter see this volume, chapter 5. -Ed.]

[33][I.e., the University of Lausanne (Switzerland) economists Walras and Pareto (see note 37 below). On the Lausanne school see Claude Ménard, "The Lausanne Tradition: Walras and Pareto", in Klaus Hennings and Warren Samuels, eds., *Neoclassical Economic Theory, 1870 to 1930* (Boston, Dordrecht, and London: Kluwer, 1990), pp. 95–136. -Ed.]

[34][On Strigl and Schams see this volume, chapter 6. -Ed.]

[35]To these names should perhaps be added that of one of the first representatives of the school in Germany (after H. Oswalt), namely, that of Wilhelm Vleugels (1893-1942). [Other well-known participants in Böhm-Bawerk's seminar included the Marxian theoreticians Otto Bauer (1881–1938) and Rudolf Hilferding (1877–1941). Hilferding would later write a famous reply to Böhm-Bawerk's *Karl Marx and the Close of his System*, namely "Böhm-Bawerk's Marx-Kritik", in vol. 1 of the series *Marx-Studien* (Vienna: I. Brand, 1904), translated by Eden and Cedar Paul as *Böhm-Bawerk's Criticism of Marx* (Glasgow: Socialist Labour Press, n.d.) and reprinted in Paul Sweezy,

The Vienna school showed its fruitfulness once again in the 1920s, when Hans Mayer and Ludwig von Mises (and for a time also still Friedrich von Wieser) were teaching in Vienna. At that time a fourth generation appeared, including an unusually large number of younger theoreticians who were to become widely known. These included Gottfried Haberler (1900–), Fritz Machlup (1902–1983), Alexander Mahr (1896–?), Oskar Morgenstern (1902–1977), Paul N. Rosenstein-Rodan (1902–1985), and the author of this article. Most of these were later most active in the United States.

But if this fourth generation in style of thinking and in interests still shows the Vienna tradition clearly, nonetheless it can hardly any longer be seen as a separate school in the sense of representing particular doctrines. A school has its greatest success when it ceases as such to exist because its leading ideals have become a part of the general dominant teaching. The Vienna school has to a great extent come to enjoy such a success. Its development has indeed led to a fusion of the thought stemming from Menger with that of W. S. Jevons (by way of Philip H. Wicksteed[36]), of Léon Walras (by way of Vilfredo Pareto[37]), and, especially, of the leading ideas of Alfred Marshall.[38] But if the total structure of modern theory, as taught today in most centres of the western world, is most strongly determined by the tradition flowing from Marshall, and even its cornerstone, value and price theory, has in recent decades undergone developments that have strongly altered its form, the latter represents a consistent continuation of the fundamental principles handed down by the Vienna school.

---

ed., *Karl Marx and the Close of His System and Böhm-Bawerk's Criticism of Marx*, op. cit. On Bauer and Hilferding see Emil Kauder, "Austro-Marxism vs. Austro-Marginalism", *History of Political Economy*, vol. 2, no. 2, 1970, pp. 398–418, and Mark E. Blum, *The Austro-Marxists* (Lexington, Ky.: University Press of Kentucky, 1985). -Ed.]

[36][Philip Henry Wicksteed (1844-1927) was a Unitarian minister, writer, and lecturer in England and author of *The Common Sense of Political Economy* (London: Macmillan, 1910; second edition, edited by Lionel Robbins, London: Routledge & Kegan Paul, 1933). -Ed.]

[37][Vilfredo Pareto (1848–1923) succeeded Walras as the chairholder in political economy at the University of Lausanne in Switzerland. -Ed.]

[38][Alfred Marshall (1842–1924) was Professor of Political Economy at Cambridge University and founder of the "Cambridge School" including himself, A. C. Pigou, and John Maynard Keynes. Marshall's textbook *Principles of Economics* went through eight editions between 1890 and 1920. -Ed.]

Addendum: In Britain and the United States[39]

Of the fourth generation developing in Mises's *Privatseminar*, which played for it a similar role to that which Böhm-Bawerk had played for the third generation, only the oldest member, the writer of this article, had still been a proper pupil and member of Wieser's last seminar. Only slightly younger and in close contact with the writer, because they had been working for years in the same building, were Gottfried von Haberler, Fritz Machlup, Oskar Morgenstern, and Paul N. Rosenstein-Rodan. Under the influence of Mises and in constant association with philosophers, sociologists and political scientists of about their own age, such as Alfred Schutz, Felix Kaufmann, and Erik Vögelin, discussions centred mainly on problems of the method and philosophical character of the social sciences.

From the beginning of the 1930s this Vienna group began to receive decisive support and an extension of its literary sources when Lionel C. Robbins, as newly appointed professor at the London School of Economics, espoused what had till then been an almost exclusively Austrian tradition. Then two new sources were to exercise considerable influence on its further development. The first of these was the one successful system of economic theory developed by the only important follower of W. S. Jevons, P. H. Wicksteed with his *Common Sense of Political Economy*,[40] and the other was the congenial summary of the current state of microeconomic theory contained in the first four chapters of the study on *Risk, Uncertainty and Profit* by Professor Frank H. Knight of Chicago.[41] It was part of the same efforts when Robbins secured the appointment in 1931 of the writer to a professorship at the London School of Economics, with the result that during the 1930s the joint Robbins-Hayek seminar became another centre at which what until then had been a mainly Austrian tradition further developed its thought.

Robbins's own most influential work, *The Nature and Significance of Economic Science*,[42] made what had been the methodological approach to microeconomic theory established by the Austrian school the generally recognised standard. Equally important is what may well be regarded as the final formulation of the marginal utility analysis by J. R. Hicks of the marginal utility analysis of value in the concept of the marginal rate of substitution, based on the indifference curve technique introduced by Irving Fisher and F. Y. Edgeworth.[43] This conception of varying rates of substitution or

[39][The following is excerpted from Hayek's unfinished essay for the *New Palgrave* dictionary of economics (see this chapter, note 1). -Ed.]

[40]Philip H. Wicksteed, *The Common Sense of Political Economy*, op. cit.

[41]Frank H. Knight, *Risk, Uncertainty and Profit* (Boston: Houghton Mifflin, 1921).

[42]Lionel Robbins, *An Essay on the Nature and Significance of Economic Science* (London: Macmillan, 1932).

[43]J. R. Hicks and R. G. D. Allen, "A Reconsideration of the Theory of Value", *Economica*, *N.S.*, vol. 1, 1934, pp. 52–76 (part I) and 196–219 (part II), and Hicks, *Value and Capital* (Oxford: Clarendon Press, 1939).

equivalence, wholly independent of any conception of measurable utility, may well be regarded as the ultimate statement of more than half a century's discussion in the tradition of the Austrian school,[44] while further refinements suggested by P. A. Samuelson[45] are hardly in the Austrian tradition.

Another distinct contribution to this branch of the Austrian tradition is well represented by the essays edited in 1973 by J. M. Buchanan and G. F. Thirlby.[46] It was also in this London group that G. L. S. Shackle[47] as well as L. M. Lachmann[48] developed the subjective tradition so that eventually they played a significant role in the American branch of the Austrian school.

Ludwig von Mises had left Vienna in 1934 for a professorship at the Graduate Institute of International Studies at the University of Geneva (Switzerland), and in 1940 under the threat of Hitler he moved on to the United States. Here the intellectual community was then as little sympathetic to such an outspoken opponent to all socialist thought as had been his potential supporters at Vienna, but he gradually rose from a kind of honourary position at the Graduate School of Business at New York University to a highly influential one.[49] For many years the term Austrian school in the United States was synonymous with Mises's disciples. The first outstanding pupils to find themselves highly respected were Murray N. Rothbard[50] and Israel M. Kirzner[51]. In the 1970s and 1980s the group

[44][Austrians have not in general, however, accepted the indifference curve technique, which assumes the constancy of the individual's preference ordering. For a well-known example see Murray N. Rothbard, "Toward a Reconstruction of Utility and Welfare Economics", in Mary Sennholz, ed., *On Freedom and Free Enterprise: Essays in Honor of Ludwig von Mises* (Princeton, N.J.: D. Van Nostrand, 1956), pp. 224–262. -Ed.]

[45]Paul A. Samuelson, *Foundations of Economic Analysis* (Cambridge, Mass.: Harvard University Press, 1947).

[46]J. M. Buchanan and G. F. Thirlby, eds, *L.S.E. Essays on Cost* (London: Weidenfeld & Nicolson, for the London School of Economics and Political Science, 1973; reprinted, New York and London: New York University Press, 1981).

[47][George L. S. Shackle (1903–), Professor (now Emeritus) at the University of Liverpool, has written several works on the theory of expectations. -Ed.]

[48][Ludwig M. Lachmann (1906–1991) studied with Shackle and Hayek at the London School of Economics in the 1930s. He later taught at the University of the Witwatersrand, Johannesburg, and New York University. His views are summarised in his books *Capital, Expectations, and the Market Process* (Kansas City: Sheed Andrews & McMeel, 1977), and *The Market as an Economic Process* (Oxford: Basil Blackwell, 1988). -Ed.]

[49][Mises's salary at NYU was paid entirely by the private William Volker Fund from 1949 until 1962 and then by a group headed by the businessman Lawrence Fertig. The Volker Fund also subsidised Hayek's post with the Committee on Social Thought at the University of Chicago. -Ed.]

[50][Murray N. Rothbard (1926–) studied at Columbia University and with Mises at New York University. He was Professor of Economics at Brooklyn Polytechnic Institute before becoming S. J. Hall Distinguished Professor of Economics at the

greatly expanded, with the present most representative work probably being done by Thomas Sowell.[52] Mises himself, however, was rather more than the earlier Austrians a strictly rationalist utilitarian, which was not entirely reconcilable with his basic subjectivism and particularly his own denial of the possibility of an interpersonal comparison of utilities, or a measurement of welfare. This deprived his epistemology and his elaborate criticism of socialism of their full effects.

Although by the third quarter of the twentieth century the Austrian school's approach had become the leading form of microeconomic theory, this approach had been to a great extent displaced as the centre of professional interest by Keynes's macroeconomics. The parallel efforts encouraged by the success of Keynes's teachings were, however, from the Austrian point of view of methodological individualism the product of an erroneous conception of what the scientific explanation of highly complex phenomena required. The Austrian school thus became for a period, and for the second time, involved in a sort of *Methodenstreit*, in which its opponents claimed to be more scientific because their findings were more empirical; that is, more directly based on observation and measurements (at that time, however, more statistical than historical). The situation was becoming rather complicated, at least in the United States, because Mises as the representative of the Austrian school had taken a somewhat extreme position in his reaction to the dominant scientistic positivism of that time. But at the same time he was also making greater concessions to rationalist utilitarianism of the Anglo-American tradition than fitted the Austrian methodological tradition. The distinctive form this had taken in his teaching was that all economic theory had a logically deductive *a priori* character.

Against this the present writer, then largely unaware that he was merely developing a rather neglected part of the Mengerian tradition, contended[53] that while it was true that the pure logic of choice by which the Austrian theory interpreted individual action was indeed purely deductive, as soon as

University of Nevada, Las Vegas, in 1986. -Ed.]

[51][Israel M. Kirzner (1930–) received his Ph.D. under Mises at New York University, where he is currently Professor of Economics and head of its Austrian Economics program. -Ed.]

[52][Thomas Sowell (1936–) is Senior Research Fellow at the Hoover Institution, Stanford University. On Sowell see Hayek's review of the former's *Knowledge and Decisions* (New York: Basic Books, 1980) in *Reason*, December 1981, pp. 47–49. -Ed.]

[53]In "Economics and Knowledge", *Economica, N.S.*, vol. 4, 1937, pp. 33–54 (reprinted in *Individualism and Economic Order* (London: Routledge & Sons, 1948)) and several later essays: "The Use of Knowledge in Society", *American Economic Review*, vol. 35, September 1945, pp. 519–530 (also in *Individualism and Economic Order*, op. cit.); "The Theory of Complex Phenomena", in Mario A. Bunge, ed., *The Critical Approach to Science and Philosophy: Essays in Honor of Karl R. Popper* (New York: The Free Press, 1964), reprinted in *Studies in Philosophy, Politics and Economics* (Chicago: University of Chicago Press; London: Routledge & Kegan Paul, 1967); and "Competition as a Discovery Procedure", in *New Studies in Philosophy, Politics, Economics and The History of Ideas* (Chicago: University of Chicago Press; London: Routledge & Kegan Paul, 1978).

the explanation moved to the interpersonal activities of the market, the crucial processes were those by which information was transmitted among individuals, and as such were purely empirical (Mises never explicitly rejected this criticism but no longer was prepared to reconstruct his by then fully developed system). . . .

The main achievement of the Austrian school's theory thereby became that it decidedly helped to clear up the differences that must inevitably exist among disciplines that deal with relatively simple phenomena, like mechanics, which necessarily were the first to be very successful and which for this reason came to be regarded as paradigms that other disciplines ought to imitate, and the sciences of highly complex phenomena, or of structures determined by a greater number of particular facts than could ever be concretely ascertained by scientific observers and containing objects of theoretical (rather than physically observable) thought—i.e., the thoughts of other persons. What had already been implicit in Adam Smith's conception of the "invisible hand", which led to the formation of an order that no individuals in the society could understand,[54] in this way became the prototype of the model on which an increasing number of attempts are based to master the problems of determining highly complex orders.

Bibliography[55]

Works by Members of the Austrian School

Alfred Amonn, *Objekt und Grundbegriffe der theoretischen Nationalökonomie* (Vienna: Deuticke, 1911; Leipzig: Deuticke, 1927).

Rudolf Auspitz and Richard Lieben, *Untersuchungen über die Theorie des Preises* (Leipzig: Duncker & Humblot, 1889). French translation, *Recherches sur la théorie du prix* (Paris: M. Giard & E. Brière, 1914).

[54][Compare Hayek's discussion in "Adam Smith: His Message in Today's Language", chapter 8 of *The Trend of Economic Thinking*, op. cit. -Ed.]

[55][This is a slightly revised version of the list prepared by Hayek for "Wiener Schule", the German version of the essay that forms this chapter (see note 1 above). Supplementary bibliographical references have been provided throughout the text of Part I of this volume. In his *New Palgrave* draft Hayek appended the following note: "This is perhaps the proper place to explain the frequent but irregular occurrence among Austrian scholars of the title 'von'. It was in the Austrian Empire often conferred on government servants and occasionally on professional or business men for special merits, rather like 'Sir' in Great Britain. In Austria, however, it was inherited by all male and unmarried female descendants. After its abolition in 1918 most bearers of this title ceased to use it themselves, but it was still generally applied to them by other persons. These names ought, therefore, unlike Dutch names beginning with 'Van', to be inserted in the alphabetical list according to the initial letter of the surname proper." -Ed.]

Eugen von Böhm-Bawerk, *Capital and Interest*, 3 vols (South Holland, Ill.: Libertarian Press, 1959). First published as *Kapital und Kapitalzins*. Volume 1: *Geschichte und Kritik der Kapitalzinstheorien* (*History and Critique of Interest Theories*) (Innsbruck: Verlag der Wagner'schen Universitätsbuchhandlung, 1884). Volume 2: *Die Positive Theorie des Kapitals* (*Positive Theory of Capital*) (Innsbruck: Verlag der Wagner'schen Universitätsbuchhandlung, 1889). Volume 3: *Further Essays on Capital and Interest*, first published as appendices to Volume 2 of the 1909–12 edition; printed as a separate volume in the fourth edition (Jena: Gustav Fischer, 1921).

Eugen von Böhm-Bawerk, *Karl Marx and the Close of His System* [1896], ed. Paul M. Sweezy (New York: Kelley, 1949).

Eugen von Böhm-Bawerk, *Control or Economic Law?* [1914] (South Holland, Ill.: Libertarian Press, 1951).

Eugen von Böhm-Bawerk, *Gesammelte Schriften*, 2 vols, ed. Franz X. Weiß (Vienna: Hölder, 1924-26).

Eugen von Böhm-Bawerk, *Rechte und Verhältnisse vom Standpunkt der volkswirtschaftlichen Güterlehre* (Innsbruck: Wagner, 1881); reprinted in *Gesammelte Schriften*, ed. F. X. Weiß (Vienna: Hölder, 1924–26).

Eugen von Böhm-Bawerk, *Grundzüge der Theorie des wirtschaftlichen Güterwertes* (Jena: Gustav Fischer, 1886; reprinted, London: London School of Economics and Political Science, 1932).

Eugen von Böhm-Bawerk, *Eugen von Böhm-Bawerks kleinere Abhandlungen über Kapital und Zins*, ed. Franz X. Weiß (Vienna: Hölder, 1926).

F. A. Hayek, "Bemerkungen zum Zurechnungsproblem", *Jahrbücher für Nationalökonomie und Statistik*, vol. 124, 1926, pp. 1–18.

Leo Illy (Leo Schönfeld), *Grenznutzen und Wirtschaftsrechnung* (Vienna: Manz, 1924).

Leo Illy (Leo Schönfeld), *Das Gesetz des Grenznutzens* (Vienna: J. Springer, 1948).

Johann von Komorzynski, *Der Werth in der isolierten Wirthschaft* (Vienna: Manz, 1889).

Viktor Mataja, *Der Unternehmergewinn* (Vienna: Hölder, 1884).

Hans Mayer, "Untersuchungen zu dem Grundgesetz der wirtschaftlichen Wertrechnung", *Zeitschrift für Volkswirtschaft und Sozialpolitik*, *N.S.*, vol. 1, 1921, pp. 431–458; vol. 2, 1922, pp. 1–23, and vol. 6, 1928.

Hans Mayer, "Der Erkenntniswert der funktionellen Preistheorie", in Hans Mayer et al., eds, *Die Wirtschaftstheorie der Gegenwart* (Vienna: Springer, 1932), vol. 2, pp. 147–239b.

Carl Menger, *The Collected Works of Carl Menger*, 4 vols, with an introduction by F. A. Hayek (London: London School of Economics and Political Science, 1933–36). These volumes, in German, include: vol. 1: *Grundsätze der Volkswirtschaftslehre* [1871]; vol. 2: *Untersuchungen über die Methode der Socialwissenschaften* [1883]; vol. 3: *Kleinere Schriften zur Methode und Geschichte der Volkswirtschaftslehre* [1884–1915]; vol. 4: *Schriften über Geldtheorie* [1889–1893].

Carl Menger, *Grundsätze der Volkswirtschaftslehre*, vol. 1 (Vienna: W. Braumüller, 1871; second edition, Vienna: Hölder-Pichler-Tempsky, 1923). Reprinted in *The Collected Works of Carl Menger*, vol. 1 (London: London School of Economics, 1934). Translated as *Principles of Economics: First General Part*, ed. James Dingwall and Bert F. Hoselitz, with an introduction by Frank H. Knight (Glencoe, Ill.: Free Press, 1950). [A reprint of the English edition was published in 1981 by New York University Press with Hayek's essay "Carl Menger", reprinted as chapter 2 in this volume, as the Introduction. -Ed.]

Carl Menger, *Problems of Economics and Sociology*, ed. with an Introduction by Louis Schneider (Urbana, Ill.: University of Illinois Press, 1963). English translation of *Untersuchungen über die Methode der Socialwissenschaften und der politischen Ökonomie insbesondere*, 1883. [Republished under the title *Investigations into the Method of the Social Sciences with Special Reference to Economics*, with a new Introduction by Lawrence H. White (New York and London: New York University Press, 1985). -Ed.]

Carl Menger, *Untersuchungen über die Methode der Sozialwissenschaften und der politischen Ökonomie insbesondere* (Leipzig: Duncker & Humblot, 1883). Reprinted in *The Collected Works of Carl Menger*, vol. 2 (London: London School of Economics, 1933).

Robert Meyer, *Das Wesen des Einkommens: Eine volkswirtschaftliche Untersuchung* (Berlin: Hertz, 1887).

Ludwig von Mises, *Theorie des Geldes und der Umlaufsmittel* (Munich: Duncker & Humblot, 1912; second edition, 1924). English translation, *The Theory of Money and Credit*, new edition, enlarged (New Haven, Conn.: Yale University Press, 1953; reprinted, Indianapolis, Ind.: Liberty*Classics*, 1981).

Ludwig von Mises, *Die Gemeinwirtschaft* (Jena: Fischer, 1922; second edition, 1932). English translation, *Socialism: An Economic and Sociological Analysis*, new edition (New Haven, Conn.: Yale University Press, 1959; reprinted, Indianapolis, Ind.: Liberty*Classics*, 1981).

Ludwig von Mises, *Grundprobleme der Nationalökonomie* (Jena: Gustav Fischer, 1933). English translation, *Epistemological Problems of Economics* (Princeton, N.J.: D. Van Nostrand, 1960; reprinted, New York and London: New York University Press, 1981).

Ludwig von Mises, *Nationalökonomie. Theorie des Handelns und Wirtschaftens* (Geneva: Editions Union, 1940).

Ludwig von Mises, *Human Action: A Treatise on Economics* (New Haven, Conn.: Yale University Press, 1949; third revised edition, Chicago: Henry Regnery, 1966).

Eugen Philippovich von Philippsberg, *Grundriß der politischen Ökonomie*, vol. 1: *Allgemeine Volkswirtschaftslehre* (Freiburg: J. C. B. Mohr, 1893).

Emil Sax, *Grundlegung der theoretischen Staatswirtschaft* (Vienna: Hölder, 1887).

Ewald Schams, "Wirtschaftslogik", Schmoller's *Jahrbuch für Gesetzgebung, Verwaltung und Volkswirtschaft im Deutschen Reiche*, vol. 58, 1934, pp. 513–533.

Leo Schönfeld: *See* Leo Illy above.

Richard Schüller, *Die klassische Nationalökonomie und ihre Gegner* (Berlin: Heymann, 1895).

Hermann von Schullern zu Schrattenhofen, *Untersuchungen über Begriff und Wesen der Grundrente* (Leipzig: Fock, 1889).

Joseph A. Schumpeter, *Das Wesen und der Hauptinhalt der theoretischen Nationalökonomie* (Leipzig: Duncker & Humblot, 1908).

Joseph A. Schumpeter, *Theorie der wirtschaftlichen Entwicklung* (Leipzig and Munich: Duncker & Humblot, 1912). English translation by Redvers Opie, *The Theory of Economic Development: An Inquiry Into Profits, Capital, Credit, Interest, and the Business Cycle*, Harvard Economic Studies, no. 46 (Cambridge, Mass.: Harvard University Press, 1934).

Richard von Strigl, *Die ökonomischen Katagorien und die Organisation der Wirtschaft* (Jena: Gustav Fischer, 1923).

Friedrich von Wieser, *Gesammelte Abhandlungen* [1876–1923], ed. with an introduction by F. A. Hayek (Tübingen: J. C. B. Mohr (Paul Siebeck), 1929).

Friedrich von Wieser, *Das Gesetz der Macht* (Vienna: Springer, 1926).

Friedrich von Wieser, *Der natürliche Wert* (Vienna: Hölder, 1889). English translation, *Natural Value*, ed. with preface and analysis by William Smart (New York: Macmillan, 1893; reprinted, New York: Kelly & Millman, 1956).

Friedrich von Wieser, *Über den Ursprung und die Hauptgesetze des wirtschaftlichen Wertes* (Vienna: Hölder, 1884).

Friedrich von Wieser, *Theorie der gesellschaftlichen Wirtschaft*, vol. 1 (Tübingen: J. C. B. Mohr, 1914; second edition, 1924. English translation, *Social Economics* (London: Allen & Unwin, 1927; reprinted, New York: Augustus M. Kelley, 1967).

Franz X. Weiß, "Die moderne Tendenz in der Lehre vom Geldwert", *Zeitschrift für Volkswirtschaft, Sozialpolitik, und Verwaltung*, vol. 19, 1910, pp. 502–560.

Robert Zuckerkandl, *Zur Theorie des Preises mit besonderer Berücksichtigung der geschichtlichen Entwicklung der Lehre* (Leipzig: Stein, 1889).

TWO

CARL MENGER (1840–1921)[1]

The history of economics is full of tales of forgotten forerunners, men whose work had no effect and was only rediscovered after

[1][This chapter, which is in most respects identical with a study of Menger that Hayek published in *Economica*, N.S., vol. 1, November 1934, pp. 393–420, and also published as an Introduction to the London School of Economics edition of Menger's collected works in 1934, has, however, been augmented by two later publications. First, excerpts have been added from Hayek's short article on Menger for the *International Encyclopedia of the Social Sciences*, ed. David L. Sills (New York: Macmillan and The Free Press, 1968), vol. 10, pp. 124–127. Much of that article repeats information introduced in the foregoing essay, but it also introduces some new discussion and information relating to the *Methodenstreit* and to Menger's contribution to microeconomics and what was later called 'methodological individualism'. These excerpts are included here in footnotes added by the editor. Hayek himself had already in 1965 corrected and augmented the essay at the time when it was published in German translation, and these additions have also been incorporated here, most also being in the form of new footnotes.

A brief historical account of the essay can be given as follows. It was first published, in English, in 1934 as an Introduction to the reprint of Menger's *Grundsätze der Volkswirtschaftslehre*, a volume which constitutes the first of a series of four reprints embodying Menger's chief published contributions to economics printed by the London School of Economics as numbers 17 to 20 of its *Series of Reprints of Scarce Works in Economics and Political Science*. These four numbers were reprinted as Carl Menger, *Gesammelte Werke* (Tübingen: J. C. B. Mohr (Paul Siebeck), 1968–70), and Hayek's introductory essay, again slightly revised and corrected, is republished in German translation in volume 1 of this latter series. It was also published in German translation somewhat earlier in H. C. Recktenwald, ed., *Lebensbilder großer National-ökonomen* (Cologne: Kiepeneuer & Witsch, 1965), pp. 347–364. Of the revised version in German, Hayek writes: "I have taken the occasion of reviewing this translation to revise the text on a few points and thereby to take account of various suggestions from friends who were so good as to read through the draft", and acknowledges the suggestions of Friedrich Engel-Jánosi, Reginald Hansen, Karl Menger, Ludwig von Mises, and Richard Schüller. As explained, the present chapter incorporates the changes made in the German revision. Hayek's Introduction was also republished in its original form in Henry William Spiegel, ed., *The Development of Economic Thought: Great Economists in Perspective* (New York: John Wiley; London: Chapman & Hall, 1952), pp. 526–553, and as the Introduction to the 1981 English edition of the *Grundsätze*, i.e., Carl Menger, *Principles of Economics*, op. cit.

Hayek's later study of Menger, "The Place of Menger's *Grundsätze* in the History of Economic Thought", is reprinted as an Addendum to this chapter. -Ed.]

their main ideas had been made popular by others, of remarkable coincidences of simultaneous discoveries, and of the peculiar fate of individual books. But there must be few instances, in economics or any other branch of knowledge, where the works of an author who revolutionised the body of an already well-developed science and who has been generally recognised to have done so, have remained so little known as those of Carl Menger. It is difficult to think of a parallel case where a work such as the *Grundsätze* has exercised a lasting and persistent influence but has yet, as a result of purely accidental circumstances, had so extremely restricted a circulation.

There can be no doubt among historians that if, during the last sixty years,[2] the Austrian school has occupied an almost unique position in the development of economic science, this is entirely due to the foundations laid by this one man. The reputation of the school in the outside world and the development of its system at important points were due to the efforts of his brilliant followers Eugen von Böhm-Bawerk and Friedrich von Wieser.[3] But it is not unduly to detract from the merits of these writers to say that [the school's] fundamental ideas belong fully and wholly to Carl Menger. If he had not found these principles, he might have remained comparatively unknown, might even have shared the fate of the many brilliant men who anticipated him and were forgotten, and almost certainly would for a long time have remained little known outside the countries of the German tongue. But what is common to the members of the Austrian school, what constitutes their peculiarity and provided the foundations for their later contributions, is their acceptance of the teaching of Carl Menger.

The independent and practically simultaneous discovery of the principle of marginal utility by William Stanley Jevons, Carl Menger, and Léon Walras is too well known to require retelling. The year 1871, in which both Jevons's *Theory of Political Economy*[4] and Menger's *Grundsätze* appeared, is now generally and with justice regarded as the beginning of the modern period in the development of economics. Jevons had outlined his fundamental ideas nine years earlier in a lecture (published in 1866)[5] which, however, attracted little attention, and Walras began to publish his contribution only in

---

[2][Hayek is writing in 1934. -Ed.]

[3][On Wieser see this volume, chapter 3. -Ed.]

[4][W. Stanley Jevons, *The Theory of Political Economy* (London: Macmillan, 1871). -Ed.]

[5][W. Stanley Jevons, "Brief Account of a General Mathematical Theory of Political Economy", op. cit. -Ed.]

1874, but the complete independence of the work of the three founders is quite certain. And indeed, although their central positions, the point in their system to which they and their contemporaries naturally attached the greatest importance, are the same, their work is so clearly distinct in general character and background that the most interesting problem is really how so different routes should have led to such similar results.[6]

To understand the intellectual background of the work of Carl Menger, a few words on the general position of economics at that time are required. Although the quarter of a century between about 1848, the date of John Stuart Mill's *Principles*,[7] and the emergence of the new school saw in many ways the greatest triumphs of the classical political economy in the applied fields, its foundations, particularly its theory of value, had become more and more discredited. Perhaps the systematic exposition in Mill's *Principles* itself, in spite or because of his complacent satisfaction about the perfected state of the theory of value, together with his later retractions on other essential points of the doctrine, did as much as anything else to show the deficiencies of the classical system. In any case, critical attacks and attempts at reconstruction multiplied in most countries.

Nowhere, however, had the decline of the classical school of economists been more rapid and complete than in Germany. Under the onslaughts of the historical school not only were the classical doctrines completely abandoned—they had never taken very firm root in that part of the world—but any attempt at theoretical analysis came to be regarded with deep distrust. This was partly due to methodological considerations. But even more it was due to an intense dislike of the practical conclusions of the classical English school—which stood in the way of the reforming zeal of the new

---

[6][In his brief essay on Menger in the *International Encyclopedia of the Social Sciences* (see this chapter, note 1), Hayek wrote of the *Grundsätze* that "in somewhat copious but always clear language, it provided a much more thorough account of the relations between utility, value, and price than is found in any of the works of Jevons and Walras, who at about the same time laid the foundation of the 'marginal[ist] revolution' in economics." In addition, recent scholarship by Erich Streissler, William Jaffé, and others has begun to question the similarities between Menger, Jevons, and Walras. See Streissler's "To What Extent Was the Austrian School Marginalist?", op. cit., and Jaffé's "Menger, Jevons and Walras De-homogenized", op. cit. Consult also Philip Mirowski, "Physics and the 'Marginalist Revolution'", in his *Against Mechanism: Protecting Economics from Science* (Totowa, N.J.: Rowman & Littlefield, 1988), pp. 11–30, esp. pp. 22–24. -Ed.]

[7][John Stuart Mill, *Principles of Political Economy* (Boston: Little & Brown, 1848). -Ed.]

group, which prided itself on the name of the 'ethical school'.[8] In England the progress of economic theory only stagnated. In Germany a second generation of historical economists grew up who had not only never become really acquainted with the one well-developed system of theory that existed, but had also learnt to regard theoretical speculations of any sort as useless if not positively harmful.

The doctrines of the classical school were probably too much discredited to provide a possible basis of reconstruction for those who were still interested in problems of theory. But there were elements in the writings of the German economists of the first half of the century which contained the germs for a possible new development.[9] One of the reasons why the classical doctrines had never firmly established themselves in Germany was that German economists had always remained conscious of certain contradictions inherent in any cost or labour theory of value. Owing, perhaps, partly to the influence of Galiani[10] and other French and Italian authors of the eighteenth century a tradition had been kept alive which refused to separate value entirely from utility. From the early years of the century into the 1850s and 1860s a succession of writers, of whom Hermann[11] was probably the outstanding and most influential figure (the wholly successful Gossen remaining unnoticed), tried to combine the ideas of utility and scarcity into an explanation of value, often coming very near to the solution provided by Menger. It is to these speculations, which to the more practical minds of the contemporary English economists must have appeared useless excursions into philosophy, that Menger owed most. A glance through the extensive footnotes in his *Grundsätze*, or the author's index

[8][This is a reference to *Sozialpolitik*, the nineteenth-century German movement for social reform. See the more complete discussion in this volume, chapter 4. -Ed.]

[9]The same is largely true of France. Even in England there was a kind of unorthodox tradition, of which the same may be said, but it was completely obscured by the dominant classical school. It is, however, important here because the work of its outstanding representative, Longfield, had through the intermediaryship of Hearn no doubt some influence on Jevons. [Mountiford Longfield (1802–1884) was an Irish jurist and economist whose *Lectures on Political Economy* (Dublin: R. Milliken, 1833) emphasised the market determinants of value rather the Ricardian (classical) 'real' or underlying costs; William Edward Hearn (1826–1888) authored *Plutology: or the Theory of the Efforts to Satisfy Human Wants* (London: Macmillan, 1864), a treatise that follows Bastiat and Herbert Spencer. -Ed.]

[10][Ferdinando Galiani (1728–1787). -Ed.]

[11][Friedrich B. W. von Hermann (1795–1868) held a chair at the University of Munich, where he authored the influential *Staatswirtschaftliche Untersuchungen* (Munich: A. Weber, 1832). -Ed.]

which has been added to the 1934 edition, will show how extraordinarily wide a knowledge he possessed of these German authors and also of the French and Italian writers, and how small a role the writers of the classical English school plays in comparison.[12]

But while Menger probably surpassed all his fellow founders of the marginal utility doctrine in the width of his knowledge of the literature—and only from a passionate book collector inspired by the example of the encyclopaedic Roscher[13] could one expect a similar knowledge at the early age the *Grundsätze* was written—there are curious gaps in the list of authors to whom he refers which go far to explain the difference of his approach from that of Jevons and Walras.[14] Particularly significant is his apparent ignorance, at the time when he wrote the *Grundsätze*, of the work of Cournot,[15] to whom all the other founders of modern economics, Walras, Mar-

---

[12] [Menger's indebtedness to the German economists of his day is stressed in Erich Streissler, "The Influence of German Economics on the Work of Menger and Marshall", op. cit. Streissler notes that five of the ten most frequently cited authors in the *Grundsätze* are German, while only one (Adam Smith) is British. Menger's book "certainly advertises its intense attachment to German economics—almost ad nauseam" (p. 33). See also this chapter, note 106. -Ed.]

[13][Wilhelm Georg Friedrich Roscher (1817–1894), Professor at the University of Leipzig and founder of the older German historical school. The *Grundsätze* is dedicated to Roscher. -Ed.]

[14]It is hardly surprising that he did not know his immediate German predecessor Herman Heinrich Gossen, but neither did Jevons or Walras when they first published their ideas. The first book which did justice at all to Gossen's work, F. A. Lange's *Die Arbeiterfrage* (second edition, Winterthur: Bleuler-Hausheer), appeared in 1870 when Menger's *Grundsätze* was probably already being set up in print. [Menger did in fact make a brief comment on Gossen in a letter to Walras in 1887, sixteen years after the publication of the *Grundsätze*. On the relationship between Gossen and his own work Menger finds "nur in einigen Punkten, nicht aber in den entscheidenden Fragen zwischen uns Übereinstimmung, bez. Ähnlichkeit der Auffassung" (agreement only on some points, but not on those decisive ones between us). See letter of January 27, 1887, in William Jaffé, *Correspondence of Léon Walras and Related Papers* (Amsterdam: North-Holland, 1965), vol. 3, p. 176 (letter 765). Emil Kauder reports that Menger had bought a copy of Gossen's book in 1886 and that he "did not approve of Gossen, rejecting his purely hedonistic approach, his emphasis on labour, and the application of mathematics in the realm of psychology". See Emil Kauder, *A History of Marginal Utility Theory* (Princeton, N.J.: Princeton University Press, 1965), p. 82. These references are provided by Erich Streissler in "The Influence of German Economics on the Work of Menger and Marshall, op. cit. -Ed.]

[15][Antoine Augustin Cournot (1801–1877), Professor of Analysis and Mechanics at the University of Lyons. -Ed.]

shall, and very possibly Jevons,[16] seem to have been directly or indirectly indebted. Even more surprising, however, is the fact that at that time Menger does not seem to have known the work of von Thünen,[17] which one would have expected him to find particularly congenial. While it can be said, therefore, that he worked in an atmosphere distinctly favourable to an analysis on utility lines, he had nothing so definite on which to build a modern theory of price as his fellows in the same field, all of whom came under the influence of Cournot, to which must be added, in the case of Walras, that of Dupuit[18] and, in the case of Marshall, that of von Thünen.

It is an interesting speculation to think what direction the development of Menger's thought would have taken if he had been acquainted with these founders of mathematical analysis. It is a curious fact that, so far as I am aware, he has nowhere commented on the value of mathematics as a tool of economic analysis.[19] There is no reason to assume that he lacked either the technical equipment or the inclination. On the contrary, his interest in the natural sciences is beyond doubt, and a strong bias in favour of their methods is evident throughout his work. And the fact that his brothers, particularly Anton, are known to have been intensely interested in mathematics, and that his son Karl became a noted mathematician, may probably be taken as evidence of a definite mathematical strain in the family. But although he knew later not only the work of Jevons and Walras, but also that of his compatriots Auspitz and Lieben, he does not even refer to the mathematical

---

[16]Sir John Hicks tells me that he has some reason to believe that [Dionysius] Lardner's diagrammatic exposition of the theory of monopoly, by which Jevons according to his own testimony was mainly influenced, derives from Cournot. On this point see Hicks's article on Léon Walras, "Léon Walras", *Econometrica*, vol. 2, 1934, pp. 338–348.

[17][Johann Heinrich von Thünen (1783–1850) was a pioneer in the theory of agriculture and the marginal productivity theory of distribution, and an early founder of mathematical economics. See his *Der Isolierte Staat in Beziehung auf Landwirtschaft und Nationalökonomie* [1826–63], translated as *The Isolated State* (Oxford and New York: Pergamon Press, 1966). -Ed.]

[18]Menger did however know the work of Léon Walras's father, A. A. Walras, whom he quotes on p. 54 of the *Grundsätze*. [P. 290 of the 1981 English edition, *Principles of Economics*, op. cit. -Ed.]

[19]But see now the two letters of Menger to Walras, dating from the years 1883 and 1884, which are printed in the *Correspondence of Léon Walras*, op. cit., vol. 1, p. 768 (letter 556), and vol. 2, p. 4 (letter 602). [See also Jaffé's "Menger, Jevons, and Walras De-homogenized", op. cit., pp. 521–522. -Ed.]

method in any of his writings on methodology.[20] Must we conclude that he felt rather sceptical about its usefulness?

Among the influences to which Menger must have been subject during the formative period of his thought there is a complete absence of influence of Austrian economists, for the simple reason that, in the earlier part of the nineteenth century in Austria, there were practically no native economists. At the universities where Menger studied, political economy was taught as part of the law curriculum, mostly by economists imported from Germany. And although Menger, like all the later Austrian economists, proceeded to the degree of Doctor of Law, there is no reason to believe that he was really stimulated by his teachers in economics.[21] This, however, leads us to his personal history.

Born on February 28, 1840, in Neu Sandec, Galicia, the territory of the present Poland, the son of a lawyer, he came from an old family of Austrian craftsmen, musicians, civil servants and army officers, who had, only a generation before, moved from the German parts of Bohemia to the Eastern provinces.[22] His mother's father,[23] a Bohemian merchant who had made a fortune during the

[20]The only exception to this statement, a review of Rudolf Auspitz and Richard Lieben, *Untersuchungen über die Theorie des Preises*, op. cit., in a daily newspaper (the *Wiener Zeitung* of July 8, 1889), can hardly be called an exception, as he expressly says that he does not want to comment there on the value of mathematical exposition of economic doctrines. The general tone of the review as well as his objection to the fact that the authors in his opinion "use the mathematical method not only as a means of exposition but as a means of research" confirms the general impression that he did not consider it as particularly useful.

[21][This is probably not correct. Streissler, in "The Influence of German Economics", op. cit., contends that Menger was in fact strongly influenced by one of his teachers in economics at the University of Prague, Peter Mischler (1821–1864). Mischler is not cited in the *Grundsätze*, but certain passages appear to have been borrowed almost verbatim from Mischler's textbook. Menger may have failed to quote Mischler because he had only the latter's lecture notes rather than his book, or because he disapproved of Mischler's political views. -Ed.]

[22][In his brief essay on Menger in the *International Encyclopedia of the Social Sciences*, Hayek describes Menger as "the descendant of a professional family that had earned the prefix 'von' (Menger himself dropped it in early adulthood). In the well-stocked library of his father, a practising lawyer, Menger and his two brothers became acquainted early with the literature on social and economic questions". -Ed.]

[23]Anton Menger, the father of Carl, was the son of another Anton Menger, who came from an old German family that had in 1623 emigrated to Eger in Bohemia, and of Anna, *née* Müller. His wife, Caroline, was the daughter of Josef Gerzabek, merchant in Hohenmaut, and of Therese, *née* Kalaus, whose ancestors can be traced in the register of baptism of Hohenmaut back into the seventeenth and eighteenth centuries respectively. [During the Nazi period it was alleged that the members of the

67

Napoleonic wars, bought a large estate in Western Galicia where Carl Menger spent a great part of his boyhood, and before 1848 still saw the conditions of semi-servitude of the peasants, which in this part of Austria had persisted longer than in any part of Europe outside Russia. With his two brothers, Anton, later the well-known writer on law and socialism, author of *The Right to the Whole Produce of Labour*,[24] and Carl's colleague at the faculty of law of the University of Vienna, and Max, in his days a well-known Austrian parliamentarian and writer on social problems, he went to the Universities of Vienna (1859–60) and Prague (1860–63). After taking his doctor's degree at the University of Cracow he devoted himself first to journalism, writing for papers in Lemberg and later in Vienna on economic questions.[25] After a few years he entered the civil service in the press department of the Austrian *Ministerratspräsidium*, an office which had always retained a very special position in the Austrian civil service and attracted many men of great talent.[26]

Wieser reports that Menger once told him that it was one of his duties to write surveys of the state of the markets for an official newspaper, the *Wiener Zeitung*, and that it was in studying the

---

Austrian school, including Menger himself, were predominantly Jewish. Hayek wrote to the *Frankfurter Zeitung* to protest their own report to this effect, and on October 13, 1936, the *Frankfurter Zeitung* published the following brief note: "Professor F. A. von Hayek, Professor of Economics in the University of London, reports to us concerning the report published in our number 511/12 of October 6 about the *Hochschule* conference of the National Socialist '*Rechtswährerbund*', that a false claim was made in a lecture held there to the effect that, among other leading members of the 'Austrian school' of economics, even its leader, Carl Menger, in particular, had been a Jew. It is to be gathered from his letter that Professor von Hayek, on the occasion of preparing a collected edition of the works of Carl Menger being sponsored by the London School of Economics, has—in the course of writing a biographical Introduction to this collected edition—established, on the basis of documents in the possession of Menger's son, that Carl Menger, both on his paternal and maternal sides, was descended from families from various places in German Bohemia which can be traced back in the church records to the seventeenth and eighteenth centuries." -Ed.]

[24][Anton Menger, *Das Recht auf der vollen Arbeitsertrag in geschichtlicher Darstellung* (Stuttgart: J. G. Cotta, 1886), translated as *The Right to the Whole Produce of Labour* (London: Macmillan, 1899). -Ed.]

[25]At this time Menger also took part in founding a daily newspaper, the *Wiener Tagblatt*, in whose place, however, the *Neue Wiener Tagblatt* soon appeared, which for many decades remained one of the most influential Viennese newspapers. Menger remained in close association with the respected editor of the latter, Moriz Szeps, and it has often been presumed that unsigned articles in this newspaper were contributed by Menger.

[26][In his brief article on Menger in the *International Encyclopedia of the Social Sciences*, Hayek describes this as a "position which was frequently a springboard to high public office." -Ed.]

market reports that he was struck by the glaring contrast between the traditional theories of price and the facts which experienced practical men considered as decisive for the determination of prices. Whether this was really the original cause which led Menger to the study of the determination of prices or whether, which seems more likely, it only gave a definite direction to studies which he had been pursuing since he had left the university, we do not know. There can be little doubt, however, that during the years intervening between about 1867–68 and the publication of the *Grundsätze* he must have worked intensely on these problems, delaying publication until his system was fully worked out in his mind.[27]

He is said to have once remarked that he wrote the *Grundsätze* in a state of morbid excitement. This can hardly mean that this book was the product of a sudden inspiration, planned and written in great haste. Few books can have been more carefully planned; rarely has the first exposition of an idea been more painstakingly developed and followed up in all its ramifications. The slender volume which appeared early in 1871 was intended as a first, introductory part of a comprehensive treatise.[28] It dealt with the fundamental questions on which he disagreed with accepted opinion with the exhaustiveness necessary to satisfy the author that he was building on absolutely firm ground. The problems treated in this "First, General Part", as it is described on the title page, were the general conditions which led to economic activity, value exchange, price, and money. From manuscript notes communicated by his son[29] more than fifty years later, in the introduction to the second edition, we know that the second part was to treat "interest, wages, rent, income, credit, and paper money", a third "applied" part the theory of production and commerce, while a fourth part was to discuss criticism of the present economic system and proposals for economic reform.

[27]The earliest manuscript notes on the theory of value which have been preserved date from the year 1867.

[28][The title page reads "Erster, Allgemeiner Teil" (First, General Part). -Ed.]

[29][Karl Menger, Jr. (1902–1985) was a mathematician and professor at the University of Vienna; he later taught at the University of Notre Dame and the Illinois Institute of Technology in Chicago. His essay on "Austrian Marginalism and Mathematical Economics" appeared in *Carl Menger and the Austrian School of Economics*, op. cit., the volume celebrating the centennial of the *Grundsätze*. -Ed.]

His main aim, as he says in the Preface,[30] was a uniform theory of price which would explain all price phenomena and in particular also interest, wages, and rent by one leading idea. But more than half of the volume is devoted to matters which only prepare the way for that main task—to the concept which gave the new school its special character, i.e., value in its subjective, personal sense. And even this is not reached before a thorough examination of the main concepts with which economic analysis has to work.

The influence of the earlier German writers with their predilection for somewhat pedantic classifications and long-winded definitions of concepts is here clearly noticeable. But in Menger's hands the time-honoured 'fundamental concepts' of the traditional German textbook assume new life. Instead of a dry enumeration and definition they become the powerful instrument of an analysis in which every step seems to result with inevitable necessity from the preceding one. And though Menger's exposition still lacks many of the more impressive phrases and elegant formulations of the writings of Böhm-Bawerk and Wieser, it is in substance hardly inferior and in many respects definitely superior to these later works.

It is not the purpose of the present essay to give a connected outline of Menger's argument.[31] But there are certain less known, somewhat surprising, aspects of his treatment which deserve special mention. The careful initial investigation of the causal relationship between human needs and the means for their satisfaction, which within the first few pages leads him to the now celebrated distinction between goods of the first, second, third, and higher orders, and the now equally familiar concept of complementarity between different goods, is typical of the particular attention which, the widespread impression to the contrary notwithstanding, the Austrian school has always given to the technical structure of production—an attention which finds its clearest systematic expression in the elaborate *vorwerttheoretischer Teil* which precedes the discussion of the

---

[30]See *Gesammelte Werke*, op. cit., vol. 1, pp. x and 143n. [Pp. 49 and 173 in the 1981 English edition, *Principles of Economics*, op. cit. Page references to this edition are in brackets following the references to *Gesammelte Werke*, vol. 1, throughout this chapter. -Ed.]

[31][For this see Hayek's essay "The Place of Menger's *Grundsätze* in the History of Economic Thought", reprinted as the Addendum to this chapter. -Ed.]

theory of value in Wieser's late work, *The Theory of Social Economy*, 1914.[32]

Even more remarkable is the prominent role which the element of time plays from the very beginning. There is a very general impression that the earlier representatives of modern economics were inclined to neglect this factor. In so far as the originators of the mathematical exposition of modern equilibrium theory[33] are concerned, this impression is probably justified. Not so with Menger. To him economic activity is essentially planning for the future, and his discussion of the period, or rather different periods, to which human forethought extends as regards different wants[34] has a definitely modern ring.

It is somewhat difficult to believe now that Menger was the first to base the distinction between free and economic goods on the idea of scarcity. But, as he himself says,[35] while the very concept was not known in the English literature, the German authors who had used it before him, and particularly Hermann, had all been trying to base the distinction on the presence or absence of cost in the sense of effort. But, very characteristically, while all of Menger's analysis is grounded on the idea of scarcity, this simple term is nowhere used. "Insufficient quantity" or "*das ökonomische Mengenverhältnis*" are the very exact but somewhat cumbersome expressions which he uses instead.

It is characteristic of his work as a whole that he attaches more importance to a careful description of a phenomenon than to giving it a short and fitting name. This frequently prevents his exposition from being as effective as might have been wished. But it also protects him against a certain one-sidedness and a tendency towards oversimplification to which a brief formula so easily leads. The classic instance of this is, of course, the fact that Menger did not originate—nor, so far as I know, ever use—the term 'marginal utility' [*Grenznutzen*] introduced by Wieser, but always explained value by the somewhat clumsy but precise phrase, "the importance which concrete goods, or quantities of goods, receive for us from the fact that we are conscious of being dependent on our disposal

---

[32][Friedrich von Wieser, *Die Theorie der gesellschaftlichen Wirtschaft*, vol. 1 (Tübingen: J. C. B. Mohr, 1914), translated as *Social Economics* (London: Allen & Unwin, 1927); reprinted, New York: Augustus M. Kelley, 1967). -Ed.]

[33][Jevons, Walras, and Vilfredo Pareto. -Ed.]

[34]See *Gesammelte Werke*, op. cit., vol. 1, pp. 34–36 [79–82].

[35]*Ibid.*, p. 70n [109, 291–292].

over them for the satisfaction of our wants", and describes the magnitude of this value as equal to the importance which attached to the least important satisfaction which is secured by a single unit of the available quantity of the commodity.[36]

Another, perhaps less important but not insignificant, instance of Menger's refusal to condense explanations in a single formula occurs even earlier in the discussion of the decreasing intensity of individual wants with increasing satisfaction. This physiological fact, which later under the name of "Gossen's law of the satisfaction of wants" was to assume a somewhat disproportionate position in the exposition of the theory of value, and was even hailed by Wieser as Menger's main discovery, takes in Menger's system the more appropriate minor position as one of the factors which enable us to arrange the different individual sensations of want in order of their importance.

On yet another and a more interesting point in connexion with the pure theory of subjective value Menger's views are remarkably modern. Although he speaks occasionally of value as measurable, his exposition makes it quite clear that by this he means no more than that the value of any one commodity can be expressed by naming another commodity of equal value. Of the figures which he uses to represent the scales of utility he says expressly that they are not intended to represent the absolute, but only the relative importance of the wants,[37] and the very examples he gives when he first introduces them makes it perfectly clear that he thinks of them not as cardinal but as ordinal figures.[38]

Next to the general principle which enabled him to base the explanation of value on utility the most important of Menger's contributions is probably the application of this principle to the case where more than one good is required to secure the satisfaction of any want. It is here that the painstaking analysis of the causal relationship between goods and wants in the opening chapters and the concepts of complementarity and of goods of different orders

[36]See *ibid.*, p. 78, and compare p. 99 [115 and 132].
[37]See *ibid.*, pp. 163–171 [183–190].
[38]See *ibid.*, p. 92 [125]. Further aspects of Menger's treatment of the general theory of value which might be mentioned are his persistent emphasis on the necessity to classify the different commodities on economic rather than technical grounds (pp. 115–117 [142–144] and the footnote to p. 130 [303–305]), his distinct anticipation of the Böhm-Bawerkian doctrine of the underestimation of future wants (pp. 122 and 127–128 [148 and 152–154]), and his careful analysis of the process by which the accumulation of capital turns gradually more and more of the originally free factors into scarce goods.

bears its fruits. Even today it is hardly recognised that Menger answered the problem of the distribution of the utility of a final product between the several cooperating commodities of a higher order—the problem of imputation as it was later called by Wieser[39]—by a fairly developed theory of marginal productivity. He distinguishes clearly between the case where the proportions in which two or more factors can be used in the production of any commodity are variable and the case where they are fixed. He answers the problem of imputation in the first case by saying that such quantities of the different factors as can be substituted for each other in order to get the same additional quantity of the product must have equal value, while in the case of fixed proportions he points out that the value of the different factors is determined by their utility in alternative uses.[40]

In this first part of his book, which is devoted to the theory of subjective value and compares well with the later exposition by Wieser, Böhm-Bawerk, and others, there is really only one major point at which Menger's exposition leaves a serious gap. A theory of value can hardly be called complete and will certainly never be quite convincing if the role that cost of production plays in determining the relative value of different commodities is not explicitly explained. At an early point of his exposition Menger indicates that he sees the problem and promises a later answer. But this promise is never fulfilled. It was left to Wieser to develop what later became known as the principle of opportunity cost or 'Wieser's Law', i.e., the principle that the other uses competing for the factors will limit the quantity available for any one line of production in such a way that the value of the product will not fall below the sum of the value which all the factors used in its production obtain in these competing uses.

It has sometimes been suggested that Menger and his school were so pleased with their discovery of the principles governing value in the economy of an individual that they were inclined to apply the same principles in an all too rapid and over-simplified way to the

[39]['Imputation' (*Zurechnung*) is the notion that explains the value of 'higher-order' goods (i.e., means of production) in terms of the value of the 'lower-order' goods (consumers' goods) they produce. For example, the value of a steel mill is determined by the (discounted) value of the finished goods—say, automobiles—made with the steel. That is, the value of the final goods is 'imputed' back to the means of production. -Ed.]

[40]*Ibid.*, pp. 138–142 [162–165].

explanation of price.[41] There may be some justification for such a suggestion so far as the works of some of Menger's followers, particularly the younger Wieser, are concerned. But it certainly cannot be said of Menger's own work. His exposition completely conforms to the rule later so much emphasised by Böhm-Bawerk, that any satisfactory explanation of price would have to consist of two distinct and separate stages of which the explanation of subjective value is only the first. It only provides the basis for an explanation of the causes and limits of exchanges between two or more persons. Menger's arrangement in the *Grundsätze* is exemplary in this respect. The chapter on exchange which precedes that on price makes the influence of value in the subjective sense on the objective exchange relationships quite clear without postulating any greater degree of correspondence than is actually justified by the assumptions.

The chapter on price itself, with its careful investigation of how the relative valuations of the individual participants in the exchange themselves will affect the ratios of exchange in the case of an isolated exchange of two individuals, under conditions of monopoly and finally under conditions of competition, is the third and probably the least known of the main contributions of the *Grundsätze*. Yet it is only in reading this chapter that one realises the essential unity of his thought, the clear aim which directs his exposition from the beginning to this crowning achievement.

On the final chapters, which deal with the effects of production for a market, the technical meaning of the term 'commodity' (*Ware*) as distinguished from the simple 'good', their different degrees of saleability leading up to the introduction and discussion of money, little need be said at this point. The ideas contained here and the fragmentary remarks on capital contained in earlier sections are the only sections of this first work which were developed further in his printed work. Although they embody contributions of lasting influ-

---

[41][Hence Georgescu-Roegen's charge that even with the opportunity-cost doctrine appended, "Menger's theory cannot explain prices. . . . Mending this gap in the theory without adulterating its characteristic rationale would require that Menger's [utility] scale be extended to include ratings of all *sets* of concrete needs [in an economy of multiple commodities]. Menger's followers, however, moved in an entirely different, easier direction. Both Wieser and Böhm-Bawerk, by a verbal legerdemain, equated *Grenznutzen* with Jevons's marginal utility, and Menger's ordinal importance rating with Jevons's cardinal utility." The complaint, in modern terms, is that Menger's preference ordering is 'lexicographic' and hence cannot be represented by a continuous demand function. Nicholas Georgescu-Roegen, "Utility", *International Encyclopedia of the Social Sciences*, op. cit., vol. 16, pp. 236–267, esp. p. 251. -Ed.]

ence, it was mainly in their later, more elaborate exposition that they became known.

The considerable space devoted here to the discussion of the contents of the *Grundsätze* is justified by the outstanding character of this work among Menger's publications and, indeed, among all the books which have laid the foundations of modern economics. It is, perhaps, appropriate to quote in this connexion the judgement of the scholar best qualified to assess the relative merits of the different variants of the modern school, of Knut Wicksell, who was the first, and hitherto the most successful, to combine what is best in the teaching of the different groups. "His fame", he says, "rests on this work and through it his name will go down to posterity, for one can safely say that since Ricardo's *Principles* there has been no book—not even excepting Jevons's brilliant if rather aphoristic achievement and Walras's unfortunately difficult work—which has exercised such great influence on the development of economics as Menger's *Grundsätze*".[42]

But the immediate reception of the book can hardly be called encouraging. None of the reviewers in the German journals seem to have realised the nature of its main contribution.[43] At home Menger's attempt to obtain, on the strength of this work, a lectureship (*Privatdozentur*) at the University of Vienna succeeded only after some difficulty. He can scarcely have known that, just before he began his lectures, there had just left the university two young men who immediately recognised that his work provided the "Archimedean point", as Wieser called it, by which the existing systems of economic theory could be lifted out of their hinges. Böhm-Bawerk and Wieser, his first and most enthusiastic disciples, were never his direct pupils, and their attempt to popularise Menger's doctrines in the seminars of the leaders of the older historical school, Knies, Roscher, and Hildebrand, was fruitless.[44] But Menger gradually

[42]Knut Wicksell, "Carl Menger", op. cit., p. 118.

[43]An exception should, perhaps, be made for Hack's review in the *Zeitschrift für die gesamte Staatswissenschaft*, vol. 28, 1872, pp. 183–184, who not only emphasised the excellence of the book and the novelty of its method of approach, but also pointed out as opposed to Menger that the economically relevant relationship between commodities and wants was not that of cause and effect but one of means and end.

[44]It might not be altogether out of place to correct a wrong impression which may be created by Alfred Marshall's assertion that between the years 1870 and 1874, when he developed the details of his theoretical position, "Böhm-Bawerk and Wieser were still lads at school or college. . . ." (*Memorials of Alfred Marshall*, ed. A. C. Pigou

succeeded in gaining considerable influence at home. Soon after his promotion to the rank of *Professor Extraordinarius* in 1873 he resigned from his position in the prime minister's office, to the great surprise of his chief, Prince Adolf Auersperg, who found it difficult to understand that anybody should want to exchange a position with prospects to satisfy the greatest ambition for an academic career.[45] But this did not yet mean Menger's final *adieu* to the world of affairs. In 1876 he was appointed one of the tutors to the ill-fated Crown Prince Rudolph, then eighteen years of age, and accompanied him during the next two years on his extensive travels through the greater part of Europe, including England, Scotland, Ireland, France, and Germany.[46] After his return he was appointed in 1879 to the chair of political economy in Vienna, and thenceforward he settled down to the secluded and quiet life of the scholar which was to be so characteristic of the second half of his long life.

By this time the doctrines of his first book—apart from a few short reviews of books he had published nothing in the intervening period—were beginning to attract wider attention. Rightly or wrongly, with Jevons and Walras it was the mathematical form rather than the substance of their teaching which appeared to be their main innovation, and which contributed the chief obstacle to their accep-

---

(London: Macmillan, 1925), p. 417). Both had left the University [of Vienna] together and entered civil service in 1872, and in 1876 were already in a position to expound in reports to Knies's seminar in Heidelberg the main elements of their later contribution. [Karl Knies (1821–1898) taught at the University of Heidelberg from 1865 to 1896; Bruno Hildebrand (1812–1878) taught at the University of Jena. -Ed.]

[45]Menger had at that time already declined the offer of professorships at the Universities of Karlsruhe (1872) and Basel (1873), and a little later also declined an offer of a professorship in the Zurich Polytechnic Institute with prospects of a simultaneous professorship at the University.

[46][Crown Prince Rudolph (1858–1889), son of Franz Joseph I (1830–1916), the Hapsburg Emperor, committed suicide in January 1889, presumably due to pessimism about the political future of Austria (though his exact motivation is unknown). The subject of Menger's teachings to Rudolph on economics and economic policy has only recently been revealed, by means of the discovery of the Crown Prince's unpublished notebooks from Menger's lectures to him. The contents of these notebooks are reported by Erich Streissler in "Carl Menger on Economic Policy: The Lectures to Crown Prince Rudolph", op. cit. Oddly enough, Rudolph appears to have been taught straightforward classical political economy—Adam Smith, as interpreted by Karl Heinrich Rau and F. W. B. Hermann—with no mention of the revolutionary ideas contained in the *Grundsätze*. Hayek also reports in his essay on Menger in the *International Encyclopedia of the Social Sciences* that Menger "seems to have assisted the crown prince in the composition of a pamphlet (anonymously published in 1878) which attempted a critical examination of the role played by the higher Austrian aristocracy. The pamphlet caused some stir when in 1906, seventeen years after the death of the archduke, his authorship was discovered". -Ed.]

tance. But there were no obstacles of this sort to an understanding of Menger's exposition of the new theory of value. During the second decade after the publication of the book, its influence began to extend with great rapidity. At the same time Menger began to acquire considerable reputation as a teacher and to attract to his lectures and seminars an increasing number of students, many of whom soon became economists of considerable reputation. In addition to those already noted, among the early members of his school his contemporaries Emil Sax and Johann von Komorzynski, and his students Robert Meyer, Robert Zuckerkandl, Gustav Gross, and—at a somewhat later date—Hermann von Schullern zu Schrattenhofen, Richard Reisch, and Richard Schüller deserve special mention.

But while at home a definite school was forming, in Germany even more than in other foreign countries economists maintained a hostile attitude. It was at this time that the younger historical school, under the leadership of Schmoller, was gaining the greatest influence in that country.[47] The *Volkswirtschaftliche Kongress*, which had preserved the classical tradition, was superseded by the newly founded *Verein für Sozialpolitik*.[48] Indeed the teaching of economic theory was more and more excluded from German universities. Thus Menger's work was neglected, not because the German economists thought that he was wrong, but because they considered the kind of analysis he attempted to be useless.

Under these conditions it was only natural that Menger should consider it more important to defend the method he had adopted against the claims of the historical school to possess the only appropriate instrument of research than to continue the work on the *Grundsätze*. It is to this situation that his second great work, the *Untersuchungen über die Methode der Sozialwissenschaften und der politischen Ökonomie insbesondere* is due.[49] It is well to remember that in

---

[47][These *Kathedersozialisten* or 'Socialists of the Chair' were Gustav Schmoller, Lujo Brentano, Karl Bücher, Adolf Held, G. F. Knapp, and their followers. -Ed.]

[48][The *Verein für Sozialpolitik* (Association for Social Policy) was dedicated to social and economic reform through legislation, in opposition to the liberal policies of groups like the *Volkswirtschaftliche Kongress*. See Franz Boese, *Geschichte des Vereins für Sozialpolitik* (Berlin: Duncker & Humblot, 1939). -Ed.]

[49][Carl Menger, *Untersuchungen über die Methode der Sozialwissenschaften und der politischen Ökonomie insbesondere* (*Investigations into the Method of the Social Sciences*), op. cit. In his article on Menger in the *International Encyclopedia of the Social Sciences* Hayek writes of this work (referring to it by its first English title), "in . . . *Problems of Economics and Sociology* . . . [Menger] undertook to vindicate the importance of theory

1875 when Menger started to work on that book, and even in 1883 when it was published, the rich crop of works by his disciples which definitely established the position of the school had not yet begun to mature, and that he might well have thought that it would be wasted effort to continue while the question of principle was not decided.

---

in the social sciences. This was an effort that seemed necessary to him in view of the complete indifference or even hostility which most of his German colleagues, influenced by the antitheoretical attitude of the younger historical school in economics, had shown towards his attempt in the *Principles* to reconstruct economic theory.

"To understand the aim of the *Problems* and the nature of the great controversy to which it gave rise, it is necessary to appreciate the character of the school against which it was directed. The 'younger historical school' is somewhat misnamed: unlike von Savigny and the older historical school of jurisprudence, or even Roscher and the 'older historical school' in economics, this 'younger' school was not interested in history as the study of unique events but regarded historical study as the empirical approach to an eventual theoretical explanation of social institutions. Through the study of historical development it hoped to arrive at the laws of development of social wholes, from which, in turn, could be deduced the historical necessities governing each phase of this development. This was the sort of positivist-empiricist approach which was later adopted by American institutionalists (differing from similar, more recent efforts only in that it made little use of statistical technique), and which is better described (as by Popper) as historicism. [Compare K. R. Popper, *The Poverty of Historicism* (London: Routledge & Kegan Paul, 1957). -Ed.]

"It was against this use of history as a means of discovering empirical laws that Menger undertook to defend what he considered to be the proper function of theory—reconstructing the structure of social wholes from their parts by the procedure called methodological individualism by Schumpeter, or the 'compositive method' by Menger himself. It is essentially what today is called micro-theory. Menger was greatly interested in history and the genesis of institutions, and he was anxious mainly to emphasise the different nature of the task of theory and the task of history proper and to prevent a confusion of their methods. The distinction, as he elaborated it, considerably influenced the later work of [Heinrich] Rickert and Max Weber. Perhaps the most important part of his discussion was the clear recognition, first, that the object of all social theory is the tracing of what are now usually called the unintended consequences of individual actions (Menger's term was the *unbeabsichtigte Resultante*), and second, that in this effort the genetic and the functional aspects could not be separated (*Untersuchungen*, op. cit., 1963 English edition, pp. 163, 180, 182, 188). In expounding and illustrating this view he went far beyond the limit of economics and dealt particularly with the genesis of law.

"The nature of the dispute has often been confused by the fact that Menger, in arguing against what he regarded as the dominant pseudo-historical school in economics, maintained ideas which had reached him through the historical school in law. These ideas can be traced back to Mandeville, David Hume, and the later eighteenth-century Scottish philosophers, although the degree to which Menger was directly acquainted with these eighteenth-century sources is not clear. It is worth noting that Menger always had a great interest in the history of economic theory and used it with much didactic skill in his lectures as an introduction to the problems of modern economic theory." -Ed.]

In their way the *Untersuchungen* are hardly less an achievement than the *Grundsätze*. As a polemic against the claims of the historical school to an exclusive right to treat economic problems the book can hardly be surpassed. Whether the merits of its positive exposition of the nature of theoretical analysis can be rated as high is, perhaps, not quite certain. If this were, indeed, Menger's main claim to fame, there might be something in the suggestion occasionally heard among Menger's admirers that it was unfortunate that he was drawn away from his works on the concrete problems of economics. This is not to mean that what he said on the character of the theoretical or abstract method is not of very great importance or that it had not very great influence. Probably it did more than any other single book to make clear the peculiar character of the scientific method in the social sciences, and it had a very considerable effect on professional 'methodologists' among German philosophers. But to me, at any rate, its main interest to the economist in our days seems to lie in the extraordinary insight into the nature of social phenomena which is revealed incidentally in the discussion of problems mentioned to exemplify different methods of approach, and in the light shed by his discussion of the development of the concepts with which the social sciences have to work. Discussions of somewhat obsolete views, as that of the organic or perhaps better physiological interpretation of social phenomena, give him an opportunity for an elucidation of the origin and character of social institutions which might, with advantage, be read by present-day economists and sociologists.[50]

Of the central contentions of the book only one may be singled out for further comment: his emphasis on the necessity of a strictly individualistic or, as he generally says, atomistic method of analysis. It has been said of him by one of his most distinguished followers that "he himself always remained an individualist in the sense of the classical economists. His successors ceased to be so". It is doubtful whether this statement is true of more than one or two instances. But in any case it fails signally to give Menger full credit for the method he actually employed. What with the classical economists had remained something of a mixture between an ethical postulate and a methodological tool was developed by him systematically in the latter direction. And if emphasis on the subjective element has

[50][For more on the *Untersuchungen* see T. W. Hutchinson, "Some Themes from Investigations into Method", op. cit. -Ed.]

been fuller and more convincing in the writings of the members of the Austrian school than in those of any other of the founders of modern economics, this is largely due to Menger's brilliant vindication in this book.

Menger had failed to arouse the German economists with his first book. But he could not complain of neglect of his second. The direct attack on what was the only approved doctrine attracted immediate attention and provoked, among other hostile reviews, a magisterial rebuke from Gustav Schmoller, the head of the school—a rebuke couched in a tone more than usually offensive.[51] Menger accepted the challenge and replied in a passionate pamphlet, *Irrthümer des Historismus in der deutschen Nationalökonomie*,[52] written in the form of letters to a friend, in which he ruthlessly demolished Schmoller's position. The pamphlet adds little in substance to the *Untersuchungen*. But it is the best instance of the extraordinary power and brilliance of expression which Menger could achieve when he was engaged not on building up an academic and complicated argument but on driving home the points of a straightforward debate.

The encounter between the masters was soon imitated by their disciples. A degree of hostility not often equalled in scientific controversy was created. The crowning offence from the Austrian point of view was given by Schmoller himself who, on the appearance of Menger's pamphlet, took the probably unprecedented step of announcing in his journal that, although he had received a copy of the book for review, he was unable to review it because he had immediately returned it to the author, and of reprinting the insulting letter with which the returned copy had been accompanied.[53]

---

[51]Gustav Schmoller, "Zur Methodologie der Staats- und Sozialwissenschaften", in *Jahrbuch für Gesetzgebung, Verwaltung und Volkswirtschaft im deutschen Reich*, 1883. In the reprint of this article in Schmoller, *Zur Literaturgeschichte der Staats- und Sozialwissenschaften* (Leipzig: Duncker & Humblot, 1888), the most offensive passages have been mitigated.

[52][*Irrthümer des Historismus in der deutschen Nationalökonomie* (Vienna: A. Hölder, 1884). -Ed.]

[53]"The editor of the *Jahrbuch* is not in a position to review this book since he immediately returned it to its author with the following message: 'Dear Sir, I have received in the post your work, *The Errors of Historicism in German Economics*. It bears the printed notice, "From the author", so that I have to thank you personally for sending it. It was brought to my attention some time ago, from various sides, that this would, in essence, be an attack on me, and an initial glance at the first page confirms as much to me. Much as I recognise your good will in concerning yourself with me and with enlightening me, I believe that I should remain true to my principles regarding such literary armed conflict. Hence I must disclose these to you

It is necessary to realise fully the passion which this controversy aroused, and what the break with the ruling school in Germany meant to Menger and his followers, if we are to understand why the problem of the adequate methods remained the dominating concern of most of Menger's later life. Schmoller, indeed, went so far as to declare publicly that members of the 'abstract' school were unfit to fill a teaching position in a German university, and his influence was quite sufficient to make this equivalent to a complete exclusion of all adherents to Menger's doctrines from academic positions in Germany. Even thirty years after the close of the controversy Germany was still less affected by the new ideas now triumphant elsewhere than any other important country in the world.[54]

In spite of these attacks, however, in the six years from 1884 to 1889 there appeared in rapid succession the books which finally established the reputation of the Austrian School the world over. Böhm-Bawerk, indeed, had already in 1881 published his small but important study on *Rechte und Verhältnisse vom Standpunkt der wirtschaftlichen Güterlehre*,[55] but it was only with the simultaneous publications of the first part of his work on capital, the *Geschichte und Kritik der Kapitalzinstheorien*,[56] and of Wieser's *Über den Ursprung und Hauptgesetze des wirtschaftlichen Wertes*[57] in 1884 that it became apparent how powerful a support to Menger's doctrines had arisen in this quarter. Of these two works Wieser's was undoubtedly the more important for the further development of Menger's fundamental

---

and recommend that you too follow them; they save one much time and irritation. I throw all such personal attacks unread into the furnace or the waste basket, especially when I expect from the author concerned no further benefit for myself. So I never enter into any attempt to bore the public by continuing literary feuds in the polemical manner of many German professors. I do not, however, wish to be so rude to you as to destroy a little book that is so nicely fitted out. Hence I am returning it to you herewith with the obligatory thanks and with the request that you make better use of it elsewhere. For any further assaults I shall moreover always remain grateful to you. For "In much enmity there is much honour". Yours faithfully, G. Schmoller'".

[54][For more on the *Methodenstreit* see the references in this volume, chapter 1, esp. pp. 53–55. -Ed.]

[55][Eugen von Böhm-Bawerk, *Rechte und Verhältnisse vom Standpunkt der wirtschaftlichen Güterlehre* (Innsbruck: Wagner, 1881), reprinted in his *Gesammelte Schriften*, ed. F. X. Weiß (Vienna: A. Hölder, 1924–26). -Ed.]

[56][Eugen von Böhm-Bawerk, *Geschichte und Kritik der Kapitalzinstheorien* (Innsbruck: Wagner, 1884), translated as *History and Critique of Interest Theories*, vol. 1 of Böhm-Bawerk, *Capital and Interest* (South Holland, Ill.: Libertarian Press, 1959). -Ed.]

[57][Friedrich von Wieser, *Über den Ursprung und die Hauptgesetze des wirtschaftlichen Wertes* (Vienna: A. Hölder, 1884). -Ed.]

ideas, since it contained the essential application to the cost phenomenon, now known as Wieser's law of cost, to which reference
has already been made. But two years later appeared Böhm-Bawerk's *Grundzüge einer Theorie des wirtschaftlichen Güterwertes*[58] which,
although it adds little except by way of casuistic elaboration to the
work of Menger and Wieser, by the great lucidity and force of its
argument has probably done more than any other single work to
popularise the marginal utility doctrine. In the year 1884 two of
Menger's immediate pupils, Viktor Mataja and Gustav Gross, had
published their interesting books on profits, and Emil Sax contributed a small but acute study on the question of method in which he
supported Menger in his fundamental attitude but criticised him on
some points of detail.[59] In 1887 Sax made his main contribution to
the development of the Austrian school by the publication of his
Grundlegung der theoretischen Staatswirtschaft,[60] the first and most
exhaustive attempt to apply the marginal utility principle to the
problems of public finance, and in the same year another of
Menger's early students, Robert Meyer, entered the field with his
investigation of the somewhat cognate problem of the nature of
income.[61]

But the richest crop was that of the year 1889. In this year was
published Böhm-Bawerk's *Positive Theorie des Kapitalzinses*,[62] Wieser's
Natürlicher Wert,[63] Zuckerkandl's *Zur Theorie des Preises*,[64] Komorzynski's *Wert in der isolierten Wirtschaft*,[65] Sax's *Neueste Fortschritte der*

---

[58]Originally a series of articles in Conrad's *Jahrbücher für Nationalökonomie und
Statistik*, 1886, it has been reprinted as number 11 of the *Series of Reprints of Scarce
Tracts in Economics and Political Science*, published by the London School of Economics,
1932.

[59]Viktor Mataja, *Der Unternehmergewinn* (Vienna: A. Hölder, 1884); G. Groß, *Die
Lehre vom Unternehmergewinn* (Leipzig: Duncker & Humblot, 1884); Emil Sax, *Das
Wesen und die Aufgaben der Nationalökonomie* (Vienna: A. Hölder, 1884).

[60][Emil Sax, *Grundlegung der theoretischen Staatswirtschaft* (Vienna: A. Hölder, 1887).
-Ed.]

[61]Robert Meyer, *Das Wesen des Einkommens* (Berlin: Hertz, 1887).

[62][Eugen von Böhm-Bawerk, *Positive Theorie des Kapitalzinses* (Innsbruck: Wagner,
1889), translated as *Positive Theory of Capital*, vol. 2 of Böhm-Bawerk, *Capital and
Interest*, op. cit. -Ed.]

[63][Friedrich von Wieser, *Der natürlicher Wert* (Vienna: A. Hölder, 1889), translated
as *Natural Value*, ed. William Smart (New York: Macmillan, 1893; reprinted, New
York: Augustus M. Kelley, 1956). -Ed.]

[64][Robert Zuckerkandl, *Zur Theorie des Preises mit besonderer Berücksichtigung der
geschichtlichen Entwicklung der Lehre* (Leipzig: Stein, 1889). -Ed.]

[65][Johann von Komorzynski, *Der Wert in der isolierten Wirtschaft* (Vienna: Manz,
1889). -Ed.]

nationalökonomischen Theorie,[66] and Schullern-Schrattenhofen's *Untersuchungen über Begriff und Wesen der Grundrente*.[67] In the following years numerous adherents also appeared among the Czech, Polish, and Hungarian economists of the Austro-Hungarian monarchy.

Perhaps the most successful early exposition of the doctrines of the Austrian school in a foreign language was, however, Maffeo Pantaleoni's *Pure Economics*, which appeared first in the same year.[68] Of other Italian economists L. Cossa, A. Graziani, and G. Mazzola accepted most or all of Menger's doctrines. Similar success attended these doctrines in Holland where the acceptance by the great Dutch economist, N. G. Pierson, of the marginal utility doctrine in his textbook (1884–90), published later in English under the title *Principles of Economics*,[69] also had considerable influence. In France Charles Gide, E. Villey, Charles Secrétan, and M. Block spread the new doctrine, and in the United States S. N. Patten and Professor Richard Ely had received it with great sympathy. Even the first edition of Alfred Marshall's *Principles*,[70] which appeared in 1890, showed a considerably stronger influence of Menger and his group than readers of the later editions of that great work would suspect.[71]

---

[66][Emil Sax, *Die neuesten Fortschritte der nationalökonomischen Theorie* (Leipzig: Duncker & Humblot, 1889). -Ed.]

[67][Hermann von Schullern zu Schrattenhofen, *Untersuchungen über Begriff und Wesen der Grundrenten* (Leipzig: Fock, 1889). -Ed.] In the same year two other Viennese economists, Rudolf Auspitz and Richard Lieben, published their *Untersuchungen über die Theorie des Preises*, op. cit., still one of the most important works of mathematical economics. But although they were strongly influenced by the work of Menger and his group, they built rather on the foundations laid by Cournot and Thünen, Gossen, Jevons, and Walras than on the work of their compatriots.

[68]Maffeo Pantaleoni, *Principii di Economia Pura* (Florence: G. Barbera, 1889; second edition, 1894; English translation, London: Macmillan, 1898). An unjust remark in the Italian edition accusing Menger of plagiarism of Cournot, Gossen, [Richard] Jennings, and Jevons was eliminated in the English edition and Pantaleoni later made amends by editing, with an introduction from his pen, an Italian translation of the *Grundsätze*, namely Carl Menger, *Principii fondamentali di economia pura, con prefazioni di Maffeo Pantaleoni* (Imola: P. Galeati, 1909, first published as a supplement to the *Giornale degli Economisti* in 1906 and 1907 without the preface of Pantaleoni). The preface is also reprinted in the Italian translation of the second edition of the *Grundsätze* (to be mentioned below) which was published at Bari, 1925.

[69][Nikolaas Gerard Pierson, *Leerboek der Staathuishoudkunde* (Haarlem: F. Bohn, 1884–90), translated by A. A. Wotzel as *Principles of Economics* (London and New York: Macmillan, 1902–12). -Ed.]

[70][Alfred Marshall, *Principles of Economics* (London: Macmillan, 1890). -Ed.]

[71]This is confirmed also by the detailed marginal notes by Marshall in his own copy of the *Grundsätze*, which is preserved in the Marshall Library in Cambridge. [In his brief article on Menger in the *International Encyclopedia of the Social Sciences* (see

And in the next few years William Smart and James Bonar, who had already earlier shown their adherence to the school, widely popularised the work of the Austrian school in the English-speaking world.[72] But, and this brings us back to the special position of Menger's work, it was now not so much his writings as those of his pupils which continuously gained in popularity. The main reason for this was simply that Menger's *Grundsätze* had for some time been out of print and difficult to procure, and that Menger refused to permit either a reprint or a translation. He hoped to replace it soon by a much more elaborate 'system' of economics and was, in any case, unwilling to have the work republished without considerable revision. But other tasks claimed his prior attention, and for years led to a continual postponement of this plan.

Menger's direct controversy with Schmoller had come to an abrupt end in 1884. But the *Methodenstreit* was carried on by others, and the problems involved continued to claim his main attention. The next occasion which induced him to make a public pronouncement on these questions was the publication, in 1885 and 1886, of a new edition of Schönberg's *Handbuch der politischen Ökonomie*, a collective work in which a number of German economists, most of them not convinced adherents to the historical school, had combined to produce a systematic exposition of the whole field of political economy. Menger reviewed the work for a Viennese legal journal in an article which also appeared as a separate pamphlet under the title *Zur Kritik der politischen Ökonomie*.[73] Its second half is largely devoted to the discussion of the classification of the different disciplines commonly grouped together under the name of political economy, a theme which, two years later, he treated more exhaustively in another article entitled *Grundzüge einer Klassifikation der Wirtschafts-*

---

this chapter, note 1), Hayek writes of Menger: "His work also had an effect on the only important rival school of the period—the neoclassical Cambridge tradition. At an early stage, Alfred Marshall, founder of the Cambridge school, had evidently studied Menger's work much more assiduously than is suggested by the few references to Menger (most of which were dropped from later editions) in Marshall's *Principles*". -Ed.]

[72]Cf. particularly J. Bonar, "The Austrian Economists and their View of Value", *Quarterly Journal of Economics*, vol. 3, October 1888, pp. 1–31, and "The Positive Theory of Capital", *ibid.*, vol. 3, April 1889, pp. 336–351.

[73]See *Gesammelte Werke*, op. cit., vol. 3, pp. 99–131. The original review article appeared in Grünhut's *Zeitschrift für das Privat- und öffentliche Recht der Gegenwart*, vol. 14, the separate pamphlet, Vienna: A. Hölder, 1887.

wissenschaften.[74] In the intervening year, however, he published one of his two further contributions to the substance—as distinguished from the methodology—of economic theory, his important study, *Zur Theorie des Kapitals.*[75]

It is pretty certain that we owe this article to the fact that Menger did not quite agree with the definition of the term capital which was implied in the first, historical part of Böhm-Bawerk's *Capital and Interest.* The discussion is not polemical. Böhm-Bawerk's book is mentioned only to commend it. But its main aim is clearly to rehabilitate the abstract concept of capital as the money value of the property devoted to acquisitive purposes against the Smithian concept of the 'produced means of production'. His main argument, that the distinction of the historical origin of a commodity is irrelevant from an economic point of view, as well as his emphasis on the necessity of clearly distinguishing between the rent obtained from already existing instruments of production and interest proper, refer to points which, even today, have not yet received quite the attention they deserve.[76]

It was at about the same time, in 1889, that Menger was almost persuaded by his friends not to postpone further the publication of a new edition of the *Grundsätze.* But although he actually wrote a new preface to that new edition (excerpts from which were printed more than thirty years later by his son in the introduction to the actual second edition[77]), nevertheless publication was again postponed. Soon after a new set of publications emerged, which absorbed his main attention and occupied him for the next two years.

---

[74]See *Gesammelte Werke,* op. cit., vol. 3, pp. 185–218, and the *Jahrbücher für Nationalökonomie und Statistik,* 1889.

[75]See *Gesammelte Werke,* op. cit., vol. 3, pp. 133–183, and the *Jahrbücher für Nationalökonomie und Statistik,* 1888. An abridged French translation by Charles Secrétan appeared in the same year in the *Revue d'Economie Politique* under the title "Contribution à la théorie du capital".

[76][On Böhm-Bawerk's views on capital see Ludwig von Mises, *Human Action: A Treatise on Economics* (third revised edition, Chicago: H. Regnery, 1966), pp. 479–489; Ludwig M. Lachmann, *Capital and its Structure* (London: Bell, 1956; reprinted, Kansas City, Mo.: Sheed Andrews & McMeel, 1978), pp. 81–85; Roger W. Garrison, "A Subjectivist Theory of a Capital-Using Economy", in Gerald P. O'Driscoll and Mario J. Rizzo, *The Economics of Time and Ignorance* (Oxford and New York: Basil Blackwell, 1985), pp. 160–187, esp. pp. 181–184; and the references cited in this volume, chapter 1, footnote 23. -Ed.]

[77][Carl Menger, *Grundsätze der Volkswirtschaftslehre, zweite Auflage, mit einem Geleitwort von Richard Schüller, aus dem Nachlaß herausgeben von Karl Menger* (Vienna and Leipzig: Hölder-Pichler-Tempsky, 1923. -Ed.]

Towards the end of the 1880s the perennial Austrian currency problem had assumed a form where a drastic final reform seemed to become both possible and necessary. In 1878 and 1879 the fall of the price of silver had first brought the depreciated paper currency back to its silver parity and soon afterwards made it necessary to discontinue the free coinage of silver; since then the Austrian paper money had gradually appreciated in terms of silver and fluctuated in terms of gold. The situation during that period—in many respects one of the most interesting in monetary history—was more and more regarded as unsatisfactory, and as the financial position of Austria seemed for the first time for a long period strong enough to promise a period of stability, the government was generally expected to take matters in hand. Moreover, the treaty concluded with Hungary in 1887 actually provided that a commission should immediately be appointed to discuss the preparatory measures necessary to make the resumption of specie payments possible. After considerable delay, due to the usual political difficulties between the two parts of the dual monarchy, the commission, or rather commissions, one for Austria and one for Hungary, were appointed and met in March 1892, in Vienna and Budapest respectively.

The discussions of the Austrian *Währungs-Enquete-Commission*, of which Menger was the most eminent member, are of considerable interest quite apart from the special historical situation with which they had to deal. As the basis of their transactions the Austrian Ministry of Finance had prepared with extraordinary care three voluminous memoranda, which contain probably the most complete collection available of documentary material for monetary history of the preceding period which has appeared in any publication.[78] Among the members besides Menger there were other well-known economists, such as Sax, Richard Lieben, and Mataja, and a number of journalists, bankers and industrialists, such as Benedikt, Hertzka, and Taussig, all of whom had a more than ordinary knowledge of monetary problems, while Böhm-Bawerk, then in the Ministry of Finance, was one of the government representatives and vice-chairman. The task of the commission was not to prepare a report, but to hear and discuss the views of its members on a number of

---

[78]*Denkschrift über den Gang der Währungsfrage seit dem Jahre 1867*; *Denkschrift über das Papiergeldwesen der österreichisch-ungarischen Monarchie*; *Statistische Tabellen zur Währungsfrage der österreichisch-ungarischen Monarchie*. All published by the k.k. Finanzministerium, Vienna, 1892.

questions put to them by the government.[79] These questions concerned the basis of the future currency, the retention, in the case of the adoption of the gold standard, of the existing silver and paper circulation, the ratio of exchange between the existing paper florin and gold, and the nature of the new unit to be adopted.

Menger's mastery of the problem, no less than his gift of clear exposition, gave him immediately a leading position in the commission and his statements attracted the widest attention. It even achieved what, for an economist, was perhaps the unique distinction of causing a temporary slump on the stock exchange. His contribution consisted not so much in his discussion of the general question of the choice of the standard—here he agreed with practically all the members of the commission that the adoption of the gold standard was the only practical course—but in his careful discussion on the practical problems of the exact parity to be chosen and the moment of time to be selected for the transition. It is mainly for his evaluation of these practical difficulties connected with any transition to a new standard of currency, and the survey of the different considerations that have to be taken into account, that his evidence is rightly celebrated. It is of extraordinarily topical interest today, where similar problems have to be faced by almost all countries.[80]

The work on this commission, the first of a series of contributions to monetary problems, was the final and mature product of several years of concentration on these questions. The results of these were published in rapid succession in the course of the same year—a year during which there appeared a greater number of publications from Menger's hand than at any other period of his life. The results of his investigations into the special problems of Austria appeared as two separate pamphlets. The first, entitled *Beiträge zur Währungsfrage*

---

[79]Cf. *Stenographische Protokolle über die vom 8. bis 17 März 1892 abgehaltenen Sitzungen der nach Wien einberufenen Währungs-Enquete-Commission* (Vienna: k.k. Hof- und Staatsdruckerei, 1892). Shortly before the commission met Menger had already outlined the main problems in a public lecture, "Von unserer Valuta", which appeared in the *Allgemeine Juristen Zeitung*, nos. 12 and 13, 1892.

[80]It is unfortunately impossible, within the scope of this essay, to devote to this important episode in currency history the space it deserves because of its close connexion with Menger and his school and because of the general interest of the problems which were discussed. It would be well worth a special study and it is very regrettable that no history of the discussions and measures of that period exists. In addition to the official publications mentioned before, the writings of Menger provide the most important materials for such a study.

in Osterreich-Ungarn,[81] and dealing with the history and the peculiarities of the Austrian currency problem and the general question of the standard to be adopted, is a revised reprint of a series of articles which appeared earlier in the year in Conrad's *Jahrbücher* under a different title.[82] The second, called *Der Übergang zur Goldwährung, Untersuchungen über die Wertprobleme der österreichisch-ungarischen Valutareform*,[83] treats essentially the technical problems connected with the adoption of a gold standard, particularly the choice of the appropriate parity and the factors likely to affect the value of the currency once the transition had been made.

But the same year also saw the publication of a much more general treatment of the problem of money which was not directly concerned with the special question of the day, and which must be ranked as the third and last of Menger's main contributions to economic theory. This was the article on money in volume 3 of the first edition of the *Handwörterbuch der Staatswissenschaften*, which was then in the process of publication.[84] It was his preoccupation with the extensive investigations carried out in connexion with the preparation of this elaborate exposition of the general theory of money, investigations which must have occupied him for the preceding two or three years, which brought it about that the beginning of the discussion of the special Austrian problems found Menger so singularly equipped to deal with them. He had, of course, always been strongly interested in monetary problems. The last chapter of the *Grundsätze* and parts of the *Untersuchungen über die Methode* contain important contributions, particularly on the question of the origin of money. It should also be noted that, among the numerous review articles which Menger used to write for daily newspapers, particularly in his early years, there are two in 1873 which deal in great detail with J. E. Cairnes's *Essays* on the effects of the gold discoveries: In some respects Menger's later views are closely related to those of Cairnes.[85] But while Menger's earlier contributions, particularly the introduction of the concepts of the different degrees

---

[81]See *Gesammelte Werke*, op. cit., vol. 4, pp. 125–187.

[82]"Die Valutaregulierung in Osterreich-Ungarn", Conrad's *Jahrbücher für Nationalökonomie und Statistik*, 1892.

[83]See *Gesammelte Werke*, op. cit., vol. 4, pp. 189–224.

[84]See *ibid.*, vol. 4, pp. 1–116.

[85]These articles appeared in the *Wiener Abendpost* (a supplement to the *Wiener Zeitung*) of April 30 and June 19, 1873. As is the case with all the early journalistic work of Menger, they are anonymous. [The reference to Cairnes is to his *Essays Towards a Solution of the Gold Problem*, published as *Essays in Political Economy, Theoretical and Applied* (London: Macmillan, 1873). -Ed.]

of 'saleability' of commodities as the basis for the understanding of the functions of money, would have secured him an honourable position in the history of monetary doctrines, it was only in this last major publication that he made his main contribution to the central problem of the value of money. Until the work of Professor Mises twenty years later,[86] the direct continuation of Menger's work, this article remained the main contribution of the Austrian school to the theory of money. It is worth while dwelling a little on the nature of this contribution, for it is a matter on which there is still much misunderstanding. It is often thought that the Austrian contribution consists only of a somewhat mechanical attempt to apply the marginal utility principle to the problem of the value of money. But this is not so. The main Austrian achievement in this field is the consistent application to the theory of money of the peculiar subjective or individualistic approach which, indeed, underlies the marginal utility analysis, but which has a much wider and more universal significance. Such an achievement springs directly from Menger. His exposition of the meaning of the different concepts of the value of money, the causes of changes and the possibility of a measurement of this value, as well as his discussion of the factors determining the demand for money, all seem to me to represent a most significant advance beyond the traditional treatment of the quantity theory in terms of aggregates and averages. And even where, as in the case of his familiar distinction between the 'inner' and the 'outer' value (*innerer und äußerer Tauschwert*) of money, the actual terms employed are somewhat misleading—the distinction does not, as would appear from the terms, refer to different kinds of value but to the different forces which affect prices—the underlying concept of the problem is extraordinarily modern.[87]

With the publications of the year 1892[88] the list of Menger's major works which appeared during his lifetime comes to an abrupt end. During the remaining three decades of his life he published only occasional small articles, a complete list of which will be found in

[86][Ludwig von Mises, *Theorie des Geldes und der Umlaufsmittel*, op. cit. -Ed.]

[87][For an interpretation of Menger's theory of money as a disequilibrium theory under uncertainty, see Erich Streissler, "Menger's Theory of Money and Uncertainty", in Hicks and Weber, op. cit., pp. 164–189. -Ed.]

[88]In addition to those already mentioned there appeared in the same year a French article, "La Monnaie Mesure de la Valeur", in the *Revue d'Economie Politique*, vol. 6, 1892, and an English article, "On the Origin of Money", in the *Economic Journal*, vol. 2, 1892, pp. 239–255.

the bibliography of his writings at the end of the last volume of his collected works.[89] For a few years these publications were still mainly concerned with money. Of these, his lecture on *Das Goldagio und der heutige Stand der Valutareform* [1893],[90] his article on money and coinage in Austria since 1857 in the *Österreichische Staatswörterbuch* [1897], and particularly the thoroughly revised edition of his article on money in volume four of the second edition of the *Handwörterbuch der Staatswissenschaften* [1900],[91] ought to be specially mentioned. The latter publications are mainly of the character of reviews, biographical notes or introductions to works published by his pupils. His last published article[92] is an obituary of his disciple Böhm-Bawerk, who died in 1914.

The reason for this apparent inactivity is clear. Menger now wanted to concentrate entirely on the major tasks which he had set himself—the long-postponed systematic work on economics, and beyond this a comprehensive treatise on the character and methods of the social sciences in general. It was to the completion of this work that his main energy was devoted and in the late 1890s he looked forward to a publication in the near future and considerable parts were ready in a definite form. But his interests and the scope of the proposed work continued to expand to wider and wider circles. He found it necessary to go far in the study of other disciplines. Philosophy, psychology, and ethnography[93] claimed more and more of his time, and the publication of the work was again and again postponed. In 1903 he went so far as to resign from his chair at the comparatively early age of sixty-three in order to be able to devote himself entirely to his work.[94] But he was never satisfied and seems to have continued to work on it in the increasing seclusion of his old age until he died in 1921 at the advanced age of eighty-one. An inspection of his manuscript has shown that, at one time, considerable part of the work must have been ready for publication. But

[89][I.e., the LSE reprint edition described in this chapter, note 1.]

[90]See *Gesammelte Werke*, op. cit., vol. 4, pp. 308–324.

[91]The reprint of the same article in vol. 4 of the third edition of the *Handwörterbuch* [1909] contains only small stylistic changes compared with the second edition.

[92]["Eugen von Böhm-Bawerk", *Almanach der kaiserlichen Akademie der Wissenschaften*, 1915, in *Gesammelte Werke*, op. cit., vol. 3, pp. 293–307. -Ed.]

[93]In an assessment of Menger's influence it should be noted that his ideas were introduced into anthropology by Richard Thurnwald, one of his students.

[94]In consequence, almost all of the later representatives of the Austrian school [the 'third generation'], e.g., Professors Hans Mayer, Ludwig von Mises, and Joseph Schumpeter, were not direct pupils of Menger but of Böhm-Bawerk or Wieser.

even after his powers had begun to fail, he continued to revise and rearrange the manuscripts to such an extent that any attempt to reconstruct this would be a very difficult, if not an impossible task. Some of the material dealing with the subject matter of the *Grundsätze* and partly intended for a new edition of this work has been incorporated by his son in a second edition of this work, published in 1923.[95] Much more, however, remains in the form of voluminous but fragmentary and disordered manuscripts, which only the prolonged and patient efforts of a very skilful editor could make accessible. For the present, at any rate, the results of the work of Menger's later years must be regarded as lost.[96]

For one who can hardly claim to have known Carl Menger in person it is a hazardous undertaking to add to this sketch of his scientific career an appreciation of his character and personality. But as so little about him is generally known to the present generation of economists, and since there is no comprehensive literary portrait available,[97] an attempt to piece together some of the impressions recorded by his friends and students, or preserved by the oral tradition in Vienna, may not be altogether out of place. Such impressions naturally relate to the second half of his life, to the period when he had ceased to be in active contact with the world of affairs, and when he had already taken to the quiet and retired life of the scholar, divided only between his teaching and his research.

The impression left on a young man by one of those rare occasions when the almost legendary figure became accessible is well reproduced in the well-known engraving of F. Schmutzer. It is possible, indeed, that one's image of Menger owes as much to this masterly portrait as to memory. The massive, well-modelled head,

---

[95]Carl Menger, *Grundsätze der Volkswirtschaftslehre, Zweite Auflage mit einem Geleitwort von Richard Schüller aus dem Nachlaß herausgegeben von Karl Menger*, op. cit. A full discussion of the changes and additions made in this edition will be found in F. X. Weiß, "Zur zweiten Auflage von Carl Mengers Grundsätzen", *Zeitschrift für Volkswirtschaft und Sozialpolitik*, N.S., vol. 4, 1924.

[96][Shortly before his death in 1985, Karl Menger, Jr., had nearly completed a biography of his father, and the Menger family have, on his instructions, entrusted the completion of the manuscript to Professor Albert Zlabinger, Director of the Carl Menger Institute in Vienna. In addition, a collection of Carl Menger's papers has recently been acquired by Duke University. -Ed.]

[97]Of shorter sketches those by F. von Wieser in the *Neue österreichische Biographie* (Vienna: Amalthea, 1923), and by R. Zuckerkandl in the *Zeitschrift für Volkswirtschaft, Sozialpolitik und Verwaltung*, vol. 19, 1911, ought to be specially mentioned.

with the colossal forehead and the strong but clear lines there delineated are not easily forgotten. Of medium height,[98] with a wealth of hair and full beard, in his prime Menger must have been a man of extraordinarily impressive appearance.

In the years after his retirement it became a tradition that young economists entering upon an academic career undertook the pilgrimage to his home. They would be genially received by Menger among his books and drawn into conversation about the life which he had known so well, and from which he had withdrawn after it had given him all he had wanted. In a detached way he preserved a keen interest in economics and university life to the end and when, in later years, failing eyesight had defeated the indefatigable reader, he would expect to be informed by the visitor about the work he had done. In these late years he gave the impression of a man who, after a long active life, continued his pursuits not to carry out any duty or self-imposed task, but for the sheer intellectual pleasure of moving in the element which had become his own. In his later life, perhaps, he conformed somewhat to the popular conception of the scholar who has no contact with real life. But this was not due to any limitation of his outlook. It was the result of a deliberate choice at a mature age and after rich and varied experience.

For Menger had lacked neither the opportunity nor the external signs of distinction to make him a most influential figure in public life, if he had cared. In 1900 he had been made a life member of the upper chamber of the Austrian Parliament. But he did not care sufficiently to take a very active part in its deliberations. To him the world was a subject for study much more than for action, and it was for this reason only that he had intensely enjoyed watching it at close range. In his written work one can search in vain for any expressions of his political views.[99] Actually, he tended to conserva-

---

[98][The original text read "tall". In his German revision of this article in 1968, Hayek wrote: "It deserves to be mentioned that the only factual alteration I have made in the text concerns the single point on which I believed myself able to testify from my own experience. I had in the original English text described Carl Menger as tall, and that was certainly the impression that that dignified figure left on me as he strode by me at a ceremony of the University of Vienna. But all who knew him better later assured me that he was barely of medium height". -Ed.]

[99][But see now Streissler, "Carl Menger on Economic Policy: The Lectures to Crown Prince Rudolph", op. cit. Streissler reports that Rudolph's notes "show Menger to have been a classical liberal of the purest water with a much smaller agenda for the state in mind than even Adam Smith" (p. 110). See also this chapter, note 46. -Ed.]

tism or liberalism of the old type. He was not without sympathy for the movement for social reform, but social enthusiasm would never interfere with his cold reasoning. In this, as in other respects, he seems to have presented a curious contrast to his more passionate brother Anton.[100] Hence it is mainly as one of the most successful teachers at the university that Menger is best remembered by generations of students,[101] and that he has indirectly had enormous

[100]The two brothers were regular members of a group which met in the 1880s and 1890s almost daily in a coffeehouse opposite the University and which consisted originally mainly of journalists and businessmen, but later increasingly of Carl Menger's former pupils and students. It was through this circle that, at least until his retirement from the university, he mainly retained contact with, and exercised some influence on, current affairs. The contrast between the two brothers is well described by one of his most distinguished pupils, Rudolf Sieghart. Cf. the latter's *Die letzten Jahrzehnte einer Großmacht* (Berlin: Ullstein, 1932), p. 21: "Wahrlich ein seltsames und seltenes Brüderpaar die beiden Menger: Carl, Begründer der österreichischen Schule der Nationalökonomie, Entdecker des wirtschaftspsychologischen Gesetzes vom Grenznutzen, Lehrer des Kronprinzen Rudolf, in den Anfängen seiner Laufbahn auch Journalist, die grosse Welt kennend wenn auch fliehend, seine Wissenschaft revolutionierend, aber als Politiker eher konservativ; auf der anderen Seite Anton, weltfremd, seinem eigenen Fach, dem bürgerlichen Recht und Zivilprozess, bei glänzender Beherrschung der Materie immer mehr abgewandt, dafür zunehmend mit sozialen Problemen und ihrer Lösung durch den Staat befasst, glühend eingenommen von den Fragen des Sozialismus. Carl völlig klar, jederman verständlich, nach Ranke's Art abgeklärt; Anton schwieriger zu verfolgen, aber sozialen Problemen in allen ihren Erscheinungsformen–im bürgerlichen Recht, in Wirtschaft und Staat—zugewandt. Ich habe von Carl Menger die nationalökonomische Methode gelernt, aber die Probleme, die ich mir stellte, kamen aus Anton Mengers Hand." ["The two Mengers were in truth an odd and unusual pair of brothers: on the one hand Carl, founder of the Austrian school of economics and discoverer of the psychoeconomic principle of marginal utility, a teacher of Crown Prince Rudolph, and a journalist in his early days as well, familiar with the big world yet eager to escape it, a revolutionary in his field, though politically rather conservative; on the other hand Anton, unworldly, progressively less interested in his own field, civil law and civil procedure, and increasingly concerned with social problems and the state's role in their solution, passionately involved in the problem of socialism. Here was Carl, a master of clear exposition and popular writing, dispassionate in Ranke's manner; and there was Anton, less accessible in his writings, but attracted to social problems in all their manifestations—civil law, the economy, and political life. It was Carl Menger from whom I learned economic methodology, but as to the problems that preoccupied me, these reflected Anton Menger's influence." Translation by G.H.]

[101]The number of men who at one time or another belonged to the more intimate circle of Menger's pupils and later made a mark in Austrian public life is extraordinarily large. To mention only a few of those who have also contributed some form to the technical literature of economics, the names of Karl Adler, Stefan Bauer, Moriz Dub, Markus Ettinger, Max Garr, Viktor Grätz, I. von Gruber-Menninger, A. Krasny, G. Kunwald, Wilhelm Rosenberg, Hermann Schwarzwald, E. Schwiedland, Rudolf Sieghart, Ernst Seidler, and Richard Thurnwald may be added

influence on Austrian public life.[102] All reports agree in the praise of his transparent lucidity of exposition. The following account of his impression by a young American economist who attended Menger's lectures in the winter 1892–93 may be reproduced here as representative: "Professor Menger carries his fifty-three years lightly enough. In lecturing he rarely uses his notes except to verify a quotation or a date. His ideas seem to come to him as he speaks and are expressed in language so clear and simple, and emphasised with gestures so appropriate, that it is a pleasure to follow him. The student feels that he is being led instead of driven, and when a conclusion is reached it comes into his mind not as something from without, but as the obvious consequence of his own mental process. It is said that those who attend Professor Menger's lectures regularly need no other preparation for their final examination in political economy, and I can readily believe it. I have seldom, if ever, heard a lecturer who possessed the same talent for combining clearness and simplicity of statement with philosophical breadth of view. His lectures are seldom 'over the heads' of his dullest students, and yet always contain instruction for the brightest."[103] All his students retain a particularly vivid memory of the sympathetic and thorough treatment of the history of economic doctrines, and mimeographed copies of his lectures on public finance were still sought after by the student twenty years after he had retired, as the best preparation for the examinations.

His great gifts as a teacher were, however, best shown in his seminar, where a select circle of advanced students and many men who had long ago taken their doctor's degree assembled. Sometimes, when practical questions were discussed, the seminar was organised on parliamentary lines with appointed main speakers *pro* and *contra* a measure. More frequently, however, a carefully prepared paper by one of the members was the basis of long discussions. Menger left the students to do most of the talking, but he took infinite pains in assisting in the preparation of the papers. Not

---

to those mentioned earlier in the text.

[102]However, through his brother Max, who for many years belonged to the Council of the Austrian Reich, and through various coffeehouse acquaintances, Menger exercised a considerable influence throughout a lengthy period on the economic and political views of the German-liberal deputies to the house of representatives.

[103]Henry R. Seager, "Economics at Berlin and Vienna", *Journal of Political Economy*, vol. 1, 1893, pp. 236–262, esp. p. 255, republished in the author's *Labor and other Economic Essays* (New York: Harper, 1931).

only would he put his library completely at the disposal of the students, and even bought for them books specially needed, but he would go through the manuscript with them many times, discussing not only the main question and the organisation of the paper, but even "teaching them elocution and the technique of breathing".[104]

For newcomers it was, at first, difficult to get into closer contact with Menger. But once he had recognised a special talent and received the student into the select circle of the seminar he would spare no pains to help him on with his work. The contact between Menger and his seminar was not confined to academic discussions. He frequently invited the seminar to a Sunday excursion into the country or asked individual students to accompany him on his fishing expeditions. Fishing, in fact, was the only pastime in which he indulged. Even here he approached the subject in the scientific spirit he brought to everything else, trying to master every detail of its technique and to be familiar with its literature.

It would be difficult to think of Menger as having a real passion which was not in some way connected with the dominating purpose of his life, the study of economics. Outside the direct study of his subject, however, there was a further preoccupation hardly less absorbing, the collection and preservation of his library. So far as its economics section is concerned this library must be ranked as one of the three or four greatest libraries ever formed by a private collector.[105] But it comprised by no means only economics, and its collections of ethnography and philosophy were nearly as rich. After his death the greater part of this library, including all economics and ethnography, went to Japan and is now preserved as a separate part of the library of the school of economics in Tokyo (today Hitotsubashi University). That part of the published catalogue which deals with economics alone contains more than 20,000 entries.[106]

---

[104]Cf. Viktor Grätz, "Carl Menger", *Neues Wiener Tagblatt*, February 17, 1921.

[105][In his brief article on Menger published in *The International Encyclopedia of the Social Sciences*, Hayek writes that in 1911 Menger estimated the size of his library at something like 25,000 volumes. -Ed.]

[106]*Katalog der Carl Menger-Bibliothek in der Handelsuniversität Tokyo*, Erster Teil, Sozialwissenschaften (Tokyo: Bibliothek der Handelsuniversität, 1926), and *Katalog der Carl Menger-Bibliothek in der Hitotsubashi Universität*, vol. 2 (Tokyo: Bibliothek der Hitotsubashi University, 1955), which includes several portraits of Menger. In his two essays, "Menger and His Library", in the *Economic Review*, Hitotsubashi University, vol. 10, 1959, and "Aus Mengers nachgelassenen Papieren", in *Weltwirtschaftliches Archiv*, vol. 89, 1962, Professor Emil Kauder has discussed handwritten remarks in some of the books in Menger's library which throw a certain light on the develop-

It was not given to Menger to realise the ambition of his later years and to finish the great treatise which, he hoped, would be the crowning achievement of his work. But he had the satisfaction of seeing his great early work bearing the richest fruit, and to the end he retained an intense and never flagging enthusiasm for the chosen object of his study. The man who is able to say, as it is reported he once said, that if he had seven sons, they should all study economics, must have been extraordinarily happy in his work. That he had the gift to inspire a similar enthusiasm in his pupils is witnessed by the host of distinguished economists who were proud to call him their master.

Addendum: The Place of Menger's Grundsätze *in the History of Economic Thought*[107]

When the *Grundsätze* appeared in 1871, it was only ninety-five years since the *Wealth of Nations*, only fifty-four since Ricardo's *Principles*, and a mere twenty-three since the great restatement of classical economics by John

---

ment of his ideas. With his help the library of Hitotsubashi University has, in 1961 and 1963, mimeographed provisional editions of the remarks from two of these volumes under the following titles: "Carl Mengers Zusätze zu Grundsätze der Volkswirtschaftslehre" and "Carl Mengers erster Entwurf zu seinem Hauptwerk 'Grundsätze', geschrieben als Anmerkungen zu den 'Grundsätzen der Volkswirtschaftslehre' von Karl Heinrich Rau". [In his brief note on Menger in the *International Encyclopedia of the Social Sciences*, Hayek wrote of these annotations: "The recent [1963] publication of his annotations [1870] to Rau's *Grundsätze der Volkswirtschaftslehre* suggests that it was mainly his critical analysis of this textbook exposition of classical doctrine that led Menger, from 1867 on, to develop his own value theory. In his extensive reading, Menger must have found ample material in the early nineteenth-century German and French economic literature on which to build a fully developed utility analysis. (The utility tradition was not as strongly preserved in the English literature.) It now appears that the literature on which he was able to draw included also the work of an Austrian economist, Joseph Kudler (whose textbook, *Die Grundlehren der Volkswirtschaft* (Vienna: Braumüller & Seidel, 1846), he had probably used at the university), and one work by Cournot. Menger's sources, however, did not include the work of the author who had the most completely anticipated him, Gossen's *Entwicklung der Gesetze des menschlichen Verkehrs* (Braunschweig: Bieweg, 1854)". On Gossen see chapter 15 of F. A. Hayek, *The Trend of Economic Thinking*, op. cit. See also this chapter, note 14. -Ed.]

[107][Published in J. R. Hicks and W. Weber, eds., *Carl Menger and the Austrian School of Economics*, op. cit., pp. 1–14, and reprinted as chapter 17 of Hayek's *New Studies in Philosophy, Politics, Economics and the History of Ideas* (Chicago: University of Chicago Press; London: Routledge & Kegan Paul, 1978). Also published in abbreviated form in German as "Die Stellung von Menger's 'Grundsätzen' in der Geschichte der Volkswirtschaftslehre", *Zeitschrift für Nationalökonomie*, vol. 32, no. 2, 1972, pp. 3–9. -Ed.]

CARL MENGER (1840–1921)

Stuart Mill. It is well to begin by recalling these intervals, lest we should look for a mark on contemporary economics (100 years later) which should be greater than it in fact appears to be. There has of course occurred, in the latter part of this 100 years, another revolution—which shifted interest to aspects of economic analysis that were little cultivated in the earlier part of the century, the time when the impact of Menger's work was chiefly felt. Yet in a longer perspective the 'microeconomic' phase, which owed much of its character to Menger, had considerable duration. It lasted for more than a quarter of the nearly two centuries that have elapsed since Adam Smith.

It is also important, for proper appreciation of Menger, that we do not underestimate what had been achieved before. It is misleading to think of the preceding period, 1820–70, as simply dominated by Ricardian orthodoxy. At least in the first generation after Ricardo there had been plenty of new ideas. Both within the body of classical economics as finally expounded by John Stuart Mill and even more outside it there had been accumulated an array of tools of analysis from which later generations were able to build an elaborate and coherent structure of theory after the concept of marginal utility provided the basis of the unification. If there ever was a time in which a quasi-Ricardian orthodoxy was dominant, it was after John Stuart Mill had so persuasively restated it. Yet even his *Principles* contain very important developments which go far beyond Ricardo. And even before the publication of that work there had been most important contributions which Mill did not integrate in his synthesis. There had been not only Cournot, Thünen, and Longfield with their crucial work on the theory of price and on marginal productivity, but also a number of other important contributions to the analysis of demand and supply—not to speak of those anticipations of the marginal utility analysis that were overlooked at the time but later found to be contained in the works of Lloyd, Dupuit, and Gossen. Most of the material was thus available from which it was almost inevitable that somebody should sooner or later undertake a reconstruction of the whole body of economic theory—as Alfred Marshall ultimately did, and probably would have done in a not very different fashion [even] if the marginal[ist] revolution had not taken place before.

That the reaction against classical economics did take the particular form it did—that at almost the same time William Stanley Jevons in England, Carl Menger at Vienna, and Léon Walras at Lausanne made the subjective value of goods to individuals the starting point for their reconstruction—was probably as much as anything due to the fact that in his theory of value Mill had explicitly returned to Ricardo. In the work of Menger and Walras their theories of value do not indeed so directly spring from a reaction against Mill as is true in the case of Jevons. But what stood out so clearly in Mill, namely that he lacked a general theory of value which explained the determination of all prices by a uniform principle, was scarcely less true of the systems and textbooks of economic theory that were generally used on the continent. Though many of them contained much shrewd analysis of the factors that contributed to the determination of price in particular situations, they all lacked a general theory under which the particular

97

instances could be subsumed. It is true that even the demand and supply curves apparatus was beginning to be used; it perhaps deserves mention that the edition of the German textbook by Karl Heinrich Rau, which Menger carefully studied before he wrote the *Grundsätze*, contains at the end a diagram using such curves. But in general it remains true that the prevailing theories offered altogether different explanations of the determination of prices of augmentable and of non-augmentable goods; and in the case of the former they traced the prices of the products to their cost of production, that is to the prices of the factors used, which in turn were not adequately explained. This kind of theory could hardly satisfy. It is indeed quite difficult to understand how a scholar of the penetration and transparent intellectual honesty of John Stuart Mill could have singled out what was so soon felt to be the weakest part of his system for the confident assertion that "there is nothing in the laws of value which remains for the present or any future writer to clear up; the theory of the subject is complete".[108] That this foundation of the whole edifice of economic theory was inadequate was only too painfully evident to a number of critical thinkers of the time.

Yet it would probably not be just to suggest that the widespread disillusionment about the prevailing body of economic theory, which becomes noticeable soon after the great success of Mill's work, was due entirely or even chiefly to this fault. There were other circumstances that shook the confidence in the economic theory that had so triumphantly conquered public opinion during the preceding generation, such as in the case of Mill his abandonment of the wage-fund theory which had played so important a part in his work and for which he had nothing to substitute. There was further the growing influence of the historical school, which tended to question the value of all attempts at a general theory of economic phenomena. And the fact that the conclusions of the prevailing economic theory seemed to stand in the way of various new social aspirations produced a hostile attitude towards it which made the most of its undeniable defects.

But, though the contrary has been asserted, I can find no indication that Jevons, Menger, or Walras, in their efforts to rebuild economic theory, were moved by any desire to revindicate the practical conclusions that had been drawn from classical economists. Such indications as we have of their sympathies are on the side of the current movements for social reform. Their scientific work seems to me to have sprung entirely from their awareness of the inadequateness of the prevailing body of theory in explaining how the market order in fact operated. And the source of inspiration in all three cases seems to have been an intellectual tradition which, at least since Ferdinando Galiani in the eighteenth century, had run side by side with the labour and cost theories deriving from John Locke and Adam Smith. I cannot here spare the time to trace the now fairly well-explored history of this utility tradition in the theory of value. But while in the case of Jevons and Walras their indebtedness to particular earlier authors is fairly

---

[108]John Stuart Mill, *Principles of Political Economy*, op. cit., book 3, chapter 1, sec. 1.

clear, it is less easy in the case of Menger to discover to whom he owed the decisive suggestions. It is true that on the whole the German literature, on which he mainly drew in his early studies, had devoted more attention to the relation between value and utility than the English writers had done. Yet none of the works that he knew came very close to the solution of the problem at which he ultimately arrived; for it seems certain that he did not know, before he wrote the *Grundsätze*, the one German work in which he had been largely anticipated, that of Herman Heinrich Gossen.[109] Nor does it seem likely that the local environment in which he worked can have provided much stimulus to the pursuit of the problems with which he was concerned. He seems to have indeed worked in complete isolation, and in old age still regretfully told a young economist that in his youth he had had none of the opportunities for discussion that later generations enjoyed.[110] Indeed, Vienna could not have seemed at the time a likely place from which a major contribution to economic theory could be expected.

We know, however, very little about Menger's youth and education and I cannot help regretting that so little work has been done by Austrians to throw more light on it.[111] What little work has been done in modern times about the origin and history of his ideas has been done elsewhere and can scarcely replace what might be done from Austrian sources.[112] Even if the material for a proper biography of Menger does not exist, it should at least be possible to obtain a clearer picture than we have of the general intellectual background of his studies and early work. I must here confine myself to stating a few relevant facts, most of which I owe to the publications of Professor Emil Kauder.[113]

---

[109][But see now this chapter, note 14. -Ed.]

[110]Ludwig von Mises, *The Historical Setting of the Austrian School of Economics*, op. cit., p. 10.

[111]My own sketch [reprinted as this chapter] of Menger's life which I wrote in 1934 in London as an Introduction to his *Collected Works* can in no way fill this gap. It could in the circumstances be no more than a compilation from the available printed sources, supplemented only by information supplied by Menger's son and some of his pupils. [But see now note 96 above. -Ed.]

[112]See particularly George J. Stigler, "The development of utility theory", *Journal of Political Economy*, vol. 58, 1950, reprinted in his *Essays in the History of Economics* (Chicago: University of Chicago Press, 1965); Richard S. Howey, *The Rise of the Marginal Utility School 1870–1889* (Lawrence, Kans.: University of Kansas Press, 1960); Reginald Hansen, "Der Methodenstreit in den Socialwissenschaften zwischen Gustav Schmoller und Karl Menger: seine wissenschaftshistorische und wissenschaftstheoretische Bedeutung", in Alwin Diemer, ed., *Beiträge zur Entwicklung der Wissenschaftstheorie im 19. Jahrhundert* (Meisenheim am Glan: A. Hain, 1968); and the writings of Emil Kauder listed in the following note.

[113]Emil Kauder, "The retarded acceptance of marginal utility theory", *Quarterly Journal of Economics*, vol. 67, 1953, p. pp. 564–575; "Intellectual and political roots of the older Austrian school", *Zeitschrift für Nationalökonomie*, vol. 17, 1958, pp. 411–425; "Menger and his library", op. cit; "Aus Mengers nachgelassenen Papieren", op. cit.;

There had not been in Austria that great vogue of Smithian economics or that reception of English and French ideas in the field of economics that had swept most parts of Germany during the first half of the last century. Until as late as 1846 economics was in fact taught at the Austrian universities on the basis of the eighteenth-century cameralist textbook of Joseph von Sonnenfels.[114] In that year it was at last replaced by the work that Menger apparently used as a student, J. Kudler's *Grundlehren der Volkswirthschaft*.[115] In that work he would have found some discussion of the relation of value to utility and especially of the significance of the different urgency of the needs that the various commodities served. We have, however, no evidence that until some time after he left the university Menger began seriously to concern himself with these problems. He is reported to have himself said that his interest in them was aroused through having to write, as a young civil servant, reports on market conditions and through having become aware in doing this how little established theory did help to account for price changes. The earliest preserved notes in his copy of the textbook by Rau mentioned above suggest that by 1867, that is at the age of twenty-seven, he had started seriously to think about those questions and had already come fairly close to his ultimate solution. These extensive marginal annotations in his copy of the Rau volume, which with Menger's economic library is preserved at the Hitotsubashi University of Tokyo, have been edited by the Japanese, with the assistance of Professor Kauder, under the title of a "First Draft of the *Grundsätze*",[116] but they can hardly be called that. Though they show that he had already arrived at his conception of the value of a good to an individual as depending on the particular want for the satisfaction of which it is a condition; though they manifest the characteristic impatience with vague hints in this direction that is bound to be felt by one who had already arrived at a clearer view; they still (perhaps inevitably from their nature) fall far short of the methodical approach which distinguishes the *Grundsätze*. I conclude that the book was really worked out between 1867 and 1871, largely with reference to the extensive German discussions to which the footnotes refer.

What makes the exposition of the *Grundsätze* so effective is its persistent slow approach to its main object. We find Menger elaborating the properties, first of a useful object, then of a good, then of a scarce or economic good, from which he proceeds to the factors determining its value; then he passes [on] to define a marketable commodity (with various degrees of marketability) which takes him ultimately to money. And at every stage

and *A History of Marginal Utility Theory* (Princeton, N.J.: Princeton University Press, 1965).

[114][Joseph von Sonnenfels, *Grundsätze der Polizey, Handlung, und Finanz* (Vienna: Kirzbeck, 1765–7). -Ed.]

[115][Joseph Kudler, *Grundlagen der Volkswirtschaft*, op. cit. -Ed.]

[116]"Carl Mengers erster Entwurf zu seinem Hauptwerk 'Grundsätze' geschrieben als Ammerkungen zu den 'Grundsätzen Volkswirtschaftslehre' von Karl Heinrich Rau", op. cit., and cf. also "Carl Mengers Zusätze zu Grundsätze der Volkswirtschaftslehre", op. cit.

CARL MENGER (1840–1921)

Menger stresses (in a manner that to the modern reader, to whom these things have become commonplace, may well seem tedious) how these properties depend (1) on the wants of the person who is acting, and (2) upon his knowledge of the facts and circumstances that make the satisfaction of his need depend on that particular object. He continually emphasises that these attributes do not inhere in things (or services) as such; that they are not properties that can be discovered by studying the things in isolation. They are entirely a matter of relations between things and the persons who take action about them. It is the latter who, from their knowledge of their subjective wants, and of the objective conditions for satisfying those wants, are led to attribute to physical things a particular degree of importance.

The most obvious result of this analysis is of course the solution of the old paradox of value, through the distinction between the total and marginal utility of a good. Menger does not yet use the term 'marginal utility' which (or more precisely its German equivalent, *Grenznutzen*) was introduced only thirteen years later by Friedrich von Wieser.[117] But he makes the distinction fully clear by showing for the simplest possible case of a given quantity of a particular kind of consumers' good that can be used to satisfy different wants (each of which declines in urgency as it is more fully satisfied) that the importance of any one unit of it will depend on that of the last need for the satisfaction of which the available total quantity is still sufficient. But if he had stopped at this point he would neither have gone beyond what several predecessors, unknown to him, had already seen, nor would he in all probability have made a greater impact than they had made. What later were called (also by Wieser) the two laws of Gossen, namely the decreasing utility of the successive satisfaction of any want, and the equalisation of the utilities to which the satisfaction of the different wants that a given good served would be carried, were for Menger no more than the starting point for the application of the same basic ideas to much more complex relations.

What makes Menger's analysis so much more impressive than that of any of his predecessors is that he applied the basic idea systematically to situations in which the satisfaction of a want is only indirectly (or partially) dependent on a particular good. His painstaking description of the causal connexions between the goods and the satisfaction of the wants that they serve enables him to bring out such basic relations as those of complementarity, of consumers' goods as well as of factors of production, of the distinction between goods of a lower or higher order, of the variability of the proportions in which the factors of production can be used, and, finally and most importantly, of costs as determined by the utility that the goods used for a particular purpose might have had in alternative uses. It was this extension of the derivation of the value of a good from its utility, from the case of given quantities of consumers' goods to the general case of all

[117][In Wieser's *Ursprung und Hauptgesetze des wirtschaftlichen Wertes*, op. cit. -Ed.]

101

goods, including the factors of production, that was Menger's main achievement.

In thus providing, as a basis for his explanation of the value of goods, a sort of typology of the possible structures of the means-ends relationship Menger laid the foundation of what later has been called the pure logic of choice or the economic calculus. It contains at least the elements of the analysis of consumer behaviour and of producer behaviour; the two essential parts of modern microeconomic theory. It is true that his immediate followers developed mainly the former, and in particular did not take up the bare hint we find in Menger of a marginal productivity analysis which is essential for an adequate understanding of producer behaviour. The development of the essential complement, the theory of the firm, was largely left to Alfred Marshall and his school. Yet enough of it is suggested by Menger for it to be possible for him to claim that he has provided all the essential elements for the achievement of his ultimate aim, an explanation of prices which should be derived from an analysis of the conduct of the individual participants in the market process.

The consistent use of the intelligible conduct of individuals as the building stones from which to construct models of complex market structures is of course the essence of the method that Menger himself described as 'atomistic' (or occasionally, in manuscript notes, as 'compositive') and that later came to be known as methodological individualism. Its character is best expressed by his emphatic statement in the Preface to the *Grundsätze* in which he says that his aim is "to trace the complex phenomena of the social economy to their simplest elements which are still accessible to certain observation". But while he stresses that in doing this he is employing the empirical procedure common to all sciences, he implies at the same time that, unlike the physical sciences which analyse the directly observed phenomena into hypothetical elements, in the social sciences we start from our acquaintance with the elements and use them to build models of possible configurations of the complex structures into which they can combine and which are not in the same manner accessible to direct observation as are the elements.

This raises a number of important issues, on the most difficult of which I can touch only briefly. Menger believes that in observing the actions of other persons we are assisted by a capacity of *understanding* the meaning of such actions in a manner in which we cannot understand physical events. This is closely connected with one of the senses in which at least Menger's followers spoke of the 'subjective' character of their theories, by which they meant, among other things, that they were based on our capacity to comprehend the intended meaning of the observed actions. 'Observation', as Menger uses the term, has thus a meaning that modern behaviourists would not accept; and it implies a *Verstehen* ('understanding') in the sense in which Max Weber later developed the concept. It seems to me that there is still much that could be said in defence of the original position of Menger (and of the Austrians generally) on this issue. But since the later development of the indifference curve technique and particularly of the 'revealed preference' approach, which were designed to avoid the reliance on such introspective knowledge, have shown that at least in principle the hypothesis about individual behaviour that microeconomic theory requires can be stated independently of these 'psychological' assumptions, I will pass over this important point and will turn to another difficulty raised by the adherence to methodological individualism in all its forms.

The fact is, of course, that if we were to derive from our knowledge of individual behaviour specific predictions about changes of the complex structures into which the individual actions combine, we should need full information about the conduct of every single individual who takes part. Menger and his followers were certainly aware that we could never obtain all this information. But they evidently believed that common observation did supply us with a sufficiently complete catalogue of the various *types* of individual conduct that were likely to occur, and even with adequate knowledge of the probability that certain typical situations would occur. What they tried to show was that, starting from these known elements, it could be shown that they could be combined only into certain types of stable structures but not into others. In this sense such a theory would indeed lead to predictions of the kind of structures that would occur, that are capable of falsification. It is true, however, that these predictions would refer only to certain properties that those structures would possess, or indicate certain ranges within which these structures can vary, and rarely, if ever, to predictions of particular events or changes within these structures. To derive such predictions of specific events from this sort of micro-theory we should have to know not only the types of individual elements of which the complex structures were made up but the specific properties of every single element of which the particular structure was made up. Microeconomic theory, at least apart from such instances [in] which it could operate with a fairly plausible *ceteris paribus* assumption, remains thus confined to what I have called elsewhere 'pattern predictions'—predictions of the kinds of structures that could be formed from the available kinds of elements. This limitation of the powers of specific prediction, which I believe is true of all theories of phenomena characterised by what Warren Weaver has called 'organised complexity' (to distinguish them from the phenomena of unorganised complexity where we can replace the information about the individual elements by statistically ascertained probabilities about the occurrence of certain elements),[118] is certainly valid for large parts of microeconomic theory. The position that prevails here is well illustrated by an often-quoted statement by Vilfredo Pareto concerning the limited applicability of the systems of equations by which the Walrasian school describes the equilibrium position of a whole economic system. He explicitly stated that these systems of equations "had by no means the purpose to arrive at a numerical

---

[118]Warren Weaver, "Science and Complexity", *The Rockefeller Foundation Annual Report*, 1958. [Published previously in *American Scientist*, vol. 36, 1948, pp. 536–544. For further discussion of 'organised complexity' see Herbert A. Simon, "The Architecture of Complexity", *Proceedings of the American Philosophical Society*, vol. 106, December 1962, pp. 467–482. -Ed.]

calculation of prices" and that it would be "absurd" to assume that we could know all the particular facts on which these concrete magnitudes depended.[119]

It seems to me that Carl Menger was quite aware of this limitation of the predictive power of the theory he developed and was content with it because he felt that more could not be achieved in this field. There is to me even a certain refreshing realism about this modest aim which is content, for instance, to indicate only certain limits within which a price will settle down rather than a definite point. Even Menger's aversion against the use of mathematics seems to me directed against a pretence of greater precision than he thought could be achieved. Connected with this is also the absence in Menger's work of the conception of a general equilibrium. If he had continued his work it would probably have become even more apparent than it is in the introductory part (which is the *Grundsätze*) that what he was aiming at was rather to provide tools for what we now call process analysis than for a theory of static equilibrium. In this respect his work and that of the Austrians generally is, of course, very different from the grand view of a whole economic system that Walras gave us.

The limitation on the power of specific prediction to which I have referred seems to me to apply to the whole body of micro-theory which was gradually built up on the foundations of marginal utility analysis. It was ultimately the desire of achieving more than this modest aim that led to an increasing dissatisfaction with this sort of micro-theory and to attempts to replace it with a theory of a different type.

Before I turn to this reaction against the type of theory of which Menger's work is the prototype, I should say a few words about the curious manner in which his influence operated during the time when it was greatest. There have probably been few books that had an effect as great as the *Grundsätze* in spite of the fact that this work was read by no more than a comparatively small number of people. The effect of the book was chiefly indirect; it became significant only after a considerable interval. Though we commonly date the marginal[ist] revolution from the year in which the works of Menger and Jevons were published, the fact is that for the next ten years or so we shall seek in vain for signs in the literature that they had any effect. Of Menger's book we know that during that early period it had a few careful readers who included not only Eugen von Böhm-Bawerk and Friedrich von Wieser but also Alfred Marshall;[120] but it was only when the two former in the middle of the 1880s published works based on Menger's ideas that these began to be more widely discussed. It is only from this later date, so far as the general development of economic theory

---

[119]Vilfredo Pareto, *Manuel d'économie politique*, second edition (Paris: M. Giard, 1927), p. 223.

[120]Alfred Marshall's copy of the *Grundsätze*, preserved in the Marshall library at Cambridge, contains detailed marginal annotations summarising the main steps in the argument but without comment. They seem to me to be written in Marshall's handwriting of an early date.

is concerned, that we can speak of an effective marginal revolution. And the works that were widely read at that time were those of Böhm-Bawerk and Wieser rather than that of Menger. While the former were soon translated into English, Menger's book had to wait eighty years till it was made available in an English version.

The delay in the effect of Menger's work was probably also the reason why Menger himself, rather than continuing his theoretical work, turned to a defence of the theoretical method of the social sciences in general. By the time he started on his second book, the *Investigations into Method (Untersuchungen über die Methoden der Sozialwissenschaften)*, which appeared in 1883, he must indeed have been under the impression that his first book had had no effect whatever; not because it was thought wrong, but because the economists of the time, at least in the German-speaking world, regarded economic theory in general as irrelevant and uninteresting. It was natural, though perhaps regrettable, that in these circumstances it seemed more important to Menger to vindicate the importance of theoretical analysis than to complete the systematic exposition of his theory. But if in consequence the spreading and development of his theories were left almost wholly to the younger members of the Austrian school, there can be little doubt that during the fifty years from the mid-1880s to the mid-1930s they had, at least outside Britain where Alfred Marshall's ideas dominated, the greatest influence on the development of what, somewhat inappropriately, is now usually called neoclassical economics. For this we have the testimony of Knut Wicksell, who was probably the best-qualified judge because he was equally familiar with all the different strands of marginal theory, and who, in 1921 in an obituary of Carl Menger, could write that "no book since Ricardo's *Principles* has had such a great influence on the development of economics as Menger's *Grundsätze*".[121]

If fifty years later this statement could hardly be repeated, this is, of course, the consequence of the great shift of interest from micro- to macro-economics, due chiefly, though not entirely, to the work of Lord Keynes. Some tendency in this direction was already discernible before the appearance of the *General Theory*[122] and was due to an increasing dissatisfaction with those limitations of the predictive powers of micro-theory to which I have already referred. It was largely a growing demand for greater deliberate control of the economic process (which required more knowledge of the specific effects to be expected from particular measures) that led to the endeavour to use the obtainable statistical information as the foundation for such predictions. This desire was strongly supported by certain methodological beliefs, such as that in order to be truly scientific a theory must lead to specific predictions, that it must refer to measurable magnitudes, and that it must be possible to ascertain relationships between the quantitative changes

---

[121]Knut Wicksell, op. cit., p. 118.
[122][John Maynard Keynes, *The General Theory of Employment Interest and Money* (London: Macmillan, 1936). -Ed.]

in the relations between those aggregates that are statistically measurable. I have already suggested that it seems to me that a theory with much more modest aims may still be testable in the sense of being refutable by observation; and I will now add that it seems by no means certain that the more ambitious aims can be realised. It cannot, however, be denied that if it were possible to establish that some such relationships are in fact constant over reasonably long periods of time, this would greatly increase the predictive power and therefore the usefulness of economic theory. I am not sure that, in spite of all the efforts devoted to this task during the last twenty-five years, this aim has yet been achieved. My impression is that it will be found that in general such constancies are confined to states which must be defined in microeconomic terms, and that in consequence we shall have to rely on a diagnosis of the situation in microeconomic terms in order to decide whether such quantitative relationships between aggregates as were observed in the past can still be expected to prevail. I rather expect, therefore, that it will be the needs of macroeconomics that will in the future give a new stimulus to the further development of microeconomic theory.

Perhaps I should add that the marked lack of interest that so many of the younger economists have shown for micro-theory in the immediate past is a result of the particular form that macroeconomic theory took during that period. It had been developed by Keynes chiefly as a theory of employment which, at least as a first approach, proceeded on the assumption that there existed unused reserves of all the different factors of production. The deliberate disregard of the fact of scarcity that this involved led to the treatment of relative prices as historically determined and not requiring theoretical explanation. This sort of theory may, perhaps, have been relevant for the kind of general unemployment that prevailed during the Great Depression. But it is not of much help for the kind of unemployment with which we are faced now or that we are likely to experience in the future. The appearance and growth of unemployment in an inflationary period[123] shows only too clearly that employment is not simply a function of total demand but is determined by that structure of prices and production that only micro-theory can help us to understand.

It seems to me that signs can already be discerned of a revival of interest in the kind of theory that reached its first high point a generation ago—at the end of the period during which Menger's influence had been mainly felt. His ideas had by then, of course, ceased to be the property of a distinct Austrian school but had become merged in a common body of theory which was taught in most parts of the world. But though there is no longer a distinct Austrian school, I believe there is still a distinct Austrian tradition from which we may hope for many further contributions to the future development of economic theory. The fertility of its approach is by no means exhausted and there are still a number of tasks to which it can be profitably applied. But these tasks for the future will be the subject of

---

[123][That is, inflationary recession, what we now call 'stagflation'. -Ed.]

later papers. What I have tried to do is merely to sketch the general role that Menger's ideas have played during the hundred years that have passed since the appearance of his first and most important work. How much his influence is still a live influence I expect the following papers will show.[124]

[124][Hayek refers to the other papers in *Carl Menger and the Austrian School of Economics*, op. cit., a volume which in fact dates the approximate beginning (1973) of the 'Austrian revival' in economics. The following year brought the first major conference on Austrian economics outside of Austria, the Institute for Humane Studies conference at South Royalton, Vermont; and the award to Hayek of a Nobel prize. -Ed.]

FRIEDRICH VON WIESER (1851–1926)[1]

Friedrich von Wieser's unexpected death on July 23, 1926, came in
the aftermath of an insidious attack of pneumonia during his stay in
Brunnwinkel in the Salzkammergut. Less than two weeks earlier,
with a remarkable display of vigour, on his seventy-fifth birthday, he
seemed to have surmounted his serious illness. He had fallen ill
during his summer vacation, in the midst of vigorous scholarly
activities and projects, a few months after the publication of the
work that he considered his crowning achievement.[2] With his death,
modern theoretical economics has lost one of its greatest teachers
and economists worldwide have been deprived of one of the most
distinguished of their colleagues. Within the confines of his own
country, however, his death means far more than the loss of one of
the greatest scholars in his discipline. But neither the unrivalled
depth of his insight into social development, as finally revealed to a
wider audience by his last great work, nor even his contributions as
a statesman and patriot can adequately explain how great an inspiration this man was for those who knew him personally. It was his
singular human greatness and universality, which transpires from all
his works, that elicited the boundless respect and admiration of all
those who came into contact with this magnetic personality. To
those who never knew Wieser personally, however, his greatness can
be made comprehensible only by reviewing his entire life's work,
not merely his professional accomplishments. I would fall short of
the difficult task that I have assumed, namely, to portray my re-

[1][Published as "Friedrich Freiherr von Wieser" in the *Jahrbücher für Nationalökonomie und Statistik*, vol. 125, 1926, pp. 513–530, and republished, with minor alterations,
in Wieser's *Gesammelte Abhandlungen*, ed. F. A. Hayek (Tübingen: J. C. B. Mohr,
1929). The translation is by Dr. Grete Heinz. Professor Ralph Raico's assistance with
the translation and annotations is also gratefully acknowledged. An earlier translation
was published in abridged form in Spiegel, op. cit., pp. 554–567. The reader may
also wish to compare Hayek's essay on Wieser in the *International Encyclopedia of the
Social Sciences*, op. cit., vol. 16, pp. 549–550, and his article "Von gestern auf heute:
Professor Dr. Freidrich Wieser zu seinem 75. Geburtstag", in *Wiener Neueste Nachrich-
ten*, July 10, 1926. -Ed.]
[2][Friedrich von Wieser, *Das Gesetz der Macht* (Vienna: J. Springer, 1926). -Ed.]

vered teacher, and would be greatly remiss if I limited myself to an account of his scholarly career and to his contributions as an econo-mist. Although this is not customary in assessing a scholar's lifetime achievements, in Wieser's case a fuller account of his human quali-ties is indispensable.

Wieser was descended from a long line of Austrian civil servants. Like several of his ancestors, his father Leopold Wieser served in the military administration and earned a title for his valour in the Italian War of 1859. After being awarded the title of imperial privy councillor, division head and vice-president of the Joint Court of Accounts, he was raised to the baronetcy (*Freiherr*). Friedrich von Wieser was born in Vienna on July 10, as the fourth of nine chil-dren issued from Leopold's marriage to Mathilde Schulheim von Zandiel. Both parents—his father had originally hoped to become a painter—contributed to Wieser's strongly artistic temperament. Growing up in Vienna, Wieser attended the highly respected *Schot-tengymnasium* during his secondary school years. Its distinguished faculty included Ernst Hauswirth,[3] whose history classes left a lasting impression on him. He began his law studies at the University of Vienna at the precocious age of seventeen and completed his degree at twenty-one.

Wieser's academic career spans exactly half a century. It began in the spring of 1876 with a lecture in Knies's seminar, where he first presented some novel scientific ideas, and came to an end in June 1926 when he was completing his article on "Money" for the fourth edition of the *Handwörterbuch der Staatswissenschaften*.[4] During these fifty years, he steadily approached an objective that he had set himself early on. Although this objective is not clearly spelled out in his more familiar works, a key piece for understanding his specific approach is missing if one disregards this basic objective. His forma-tive school years are critical for a full grasp of his goals. He was then passionately interested in history. In a commemorative speech at the *Schottengymnasium*'s centennial anniversary celebration, Wieser recalls the lasting impressions of his school years and retraces his

---

[3][Ernst Hauswirth (1818–1901) was a professor of religion and history at the *Schottengymnasium* from 1848 to 1878. -Ed.]

[4][Friedrich von Wieser, "Geld", *Handwörterbuch der Staatswissenschaften*, fourth edition, vol. 4 (Jena: Gustav Fischer, 1926), pp. 681–717. The 1876 lecture, "Das Verhältnis der Kosten zum Werte", is discussed below. -Ed.]

shift from history to sociology to economics.[5] In this account, which has remained largely unfamiliar to a wider audience, but which contains the most significant autobiographical testimony about his intellectual development, Wieser describes how his above-mentioned teacher Hauswirth and later Macaulay's works incited him to study history, a field in which he competed with his classmate Heinrich Friedjung,[6] the later historian, to master the huge mass of historical facts presented to them. At the very time that he began his university studies, the newly promulgated Austrian constitution of 1867 was a matter of great concern in his social group and roused his own lively interest in the political and social movements and events of his time. It may well have been these impressions that impelled him to study law rather than history at the university. In his student days at the university, he paid scant attention to the discipline that was to become the focus of his work and was unimpressed by Lorenz von Stein's[7] economics lectures. Herbert Spencer's *The Study of Sociology*[8] in conjunction with Leo Tolstoy's *War and Peace* had such a strong impact on him, however, that he definitively abandoned his youthful preoccupation with history and became intensely involved with social phenomena. As he reports about this period, "Henceforth it became my dream to write anonymous history. This too, however, came to nothing. The most obvious social relationship manifests itself in the economy—that had to be clarified first before one could even consider fathoming more deeply concealed relations. But how could one explain the economy without having explained value? And so I started out by coming to grips with that and soon ventured forth on the almost boundless sea of social phenomena with nothing but the theory of value to keep me afloat".

The study of history left Wieser intellectually dissatisfied, because its methods did not lead to the discovery of the laws of social developments that he was seeking. His goal was to recognise the impact of vast impersonal forces in human society, to which each

---

[5]This speech was published under the title "Arma virumque cano" in the *Festschrift* for the centennial celebration of the *Schottengymnasium* (*Festschrift zum 100jährigen Jubiläum des Schottengymnasiums* (Vienna: Schottengymnasium, 1907)). A more condensed version of Wieser's own account of his intellectual development appears in the preface to his *Gesetz der Macht*, op. cit.; here several facts are added to those supplied in his speech and included above. [There is also a brief biographical sketch by Wesley Clair Mitchell in the Foreword to the English translation of *Theorie der gesellschaftlichen Wirtschaft*, namely *Social Economics*, op. cit., pp. ix–xii. -Ed.]

[6][Heinrich Friedjung (1851–1920). -Ed.]

[7][Lorenz von Stein (1815–1890). -Ed.]

[8][Herbert Spencer, *The Study of Sociology* (London: P. S. King, 1873). -Ed.]

individual is subjected against his own volition, forces that inevitably provoke events that were not wanted or even foreseen by anyone. He saw no way of attacking this problem until he came across a book that showed him the right approach for at least part of the problem. Just when he left the University of Vienna in 1872 with his fellow student and later brother-in-law Eugen von Böhm-Bawerk, he became acquainted with the *Grundsätze der Volkswirtschaftslehre* of Carl Menger, then an unknown young *Privatdozent* at the University of Vienna. Both Wieser and Böhm-Bawerk found in this work the groundwork for their subsequent research, which they carried on during their service with the finance administration of Lower Austria and then in 1875–76 and 1876–77 in Heidelberg, Leipzig, and Jena under Knies, Roscher, and Hildebrand, with the help of a travelling fellowship. Both young men apparently soon concentrated on the very problems that were to be their focus of interest from that time onward and in which they were to make their most important contributions. In the spring of 1876 they were both giving lectures in Knies's seminar, which already contained the seminal ideas of their later major economic works. Wieser reported on "Das Verhältnis der Kosten zum Werte" (The Relation of Costs to Value) and Böhm-Bawerk on the theory of capital.[9]

Wieser's first work is interesting in two respects. Not only does it show how early Wieser began to be concerned with the problems that were his primary focus at least during his first period of scholarly work, but it also settles beyond doubt who originated one of the most important principles of the modern school, the subjective theory of value.[10] Although Wieser is usually recognised as the originator of this theory, he is hardly ever given due credit for it, probably because it is difficult to establish the priority of his claim in the published literature. We must jump ahead to a later phase of Wieser's career to clarify this point. As is well known, his first

---

[9]A footnote in Böhm-Bawerk's *Positive Theorie des Kapitals*, third edition, second half-volume (Jena: Gustav Fischer, 1912), pp. 427ff. [in the English translation, *Capital and Interest*, op. cit., vol. 2, p. 439], mentions the fact that he had already set down the basic ideas of his theory of capital in 1876 in an early unpublished work. I was led a few years ago to check through the papers left in his widow's possession to locate this paper. I found an undated little notebook containing such an early work. When I reported this discovery to Wieser, he told me that he had mentioned in an introduction to the fourth edition of Böhm-Bawerk's book that both he and Böhm-Bawerk had given papers on the same subject in Knies's seminar. He recognised the little notebook as the work in question and lent me the text of his own seminar report. Copies of both these papers are in my possession.

[10][I.e., the principle of 'opportunity cost'. -Ed.]

published work, *Ursprung und Hauptgesetze des wirtschaftlichen Wertes* appeared only in 1884, three years after Böhm-Bawerk's first publication.[11] The book's main topic covers the same ground as his earliest work. His inquiry into the relationship between costs and value in the light of the subjective theory of value leads him to envisage costs as indirect utility (opportunity costs), on the basis of a detailed presentation of the averaging of utility in production. Ever since Pantaleoni, this modernised form of the law of costs has been rightly known as Wieser's law.[12] It is nevertheless true that Böhm-Bawerk developed the law of costs with utmost lucidity three years before Wieser, albeit in off-hand fashion and in an obscure part of his book.[13] It is also true, furthermore, that Böhm-Bawerk in one of his later works gave the most complete version of the new doctrine, including the law of costs, the form in which the doctrine was popularised. Böhm-Bawerk's brilliant exposition[14] is actually a review of Menger's and Wieser's doctrines, insofar as it deals with the theory of subjective value and not with price theory. As a result, this highly important complement to Menger's value theory came to be predominantly or exclusively attributed to Böhm-Bawerk. The truth of the matter is that Böhm-Bawerk was eager to incorporate Wieser's ideas, which the latter had communicated to him in their student days in Germany, but only insofar as they clarified the exposition of his own ideas. As Wieser had published nothing up to that point, Böhm-Bawerk could not cite him as a source.

Although this early work by Wieser lacks the precision of expression and the clear structure of his later works, it resembles them closely in its approach to the problem of the value of goods. In line with the solution proposed by Menger, most of his epigones have tried to explain special problems of value determination, such as the determination of the value of production goods, by simply applying

---

[11][Friedrich von Wieser, *Über den Ursprung und die Hauptgesetze des wirtschaftlichen Wertes*, op. cit.; Eugen von Böhm-Bawerk, *Rechte und Verhältnisse vom Standpunkt der wirtschaftlichen Güterlehre*, op. cit. -Ed.]

[12]Maffeo Pantaleoni, *Principii di economia pura*, op. cit. In addition to this proposition, which is generally recognised as Wieser's law in the economic literature, L. V. Birck (*The Theory of Marginal Value* (London: G. Routledge & Sons, 1922), pp. 320f.) also refers to Wieser's rules about value imputation as Wieser's law. Joseph Schumpeter (*Theorie der wirtschaftlichen Entwicklung* (Leipzig: Duncker & Humblot, 1912), p. 9) speaks furthermore of "Wieser's continuity principle".

[13]In a footnote on pp. 105–106 of his *Rechte und Verhältnisse vom Standpunkte der volkswirtschaftlichen Güterlehre*, op. cit.

[14]Eugen von Böhm-Bawerk, "Grundzüge der Theorie des wirtschaftlichen Güterwerts", *Jahrbücher für Nationalökonomie und Statistik*, 1886, pp. 1–82 and 477–541.

Menger's explanation for fixed quantities of consumption goods; to wit, their utility determines their value. Wieser felt that the simple application of this formula was not adequate. It had been revealed by Menger's investigations that the value of goods is determined by the need to choose a particular use among the many possible uses for a limited quantity of available goods; hence human behaviour, with respect to the problem of utilisation of available amounts of goods, determines their value. Wieser therefore took human behaviour for the starting point of his explanation of value in explaining more complex situations, particularly in the area of production. These investigations about economically motivated behaviour in the face of certain situations leads directly to Wieser's explanations about the reciprocal relationship between the value of products and the value of production goods.

It is not possible to give a detailed account of the genesis of Wieser's ideas. Let me quote a single passage here to demonstrate that his famous law of costs is already contained in this early work. Recapitulating the relationship between the value of products and that of the production goods, he states: "The value of products is therefore determined in every case by wants that are dependent on them, and in every case these wants are contingent on available supplies and demand. Instead of comparing quantity and demand for each kind of good (i.e., each kind of product), one has to compare the overall demand for products made from a higher-level product and the overall supply of this product. The value of the last unit of any kind of good yet to be produced determines the value of the production good, which is in turn reflected in all other kinds of goods (products). The want that is decisive for the value of a product may therefore be quite unconnected with the particular product and related to it only through the intervention of the production good, which is connected with the totality of products".[15]

It is not surprising that Wieser encountered little sympathy for his work among his colleagues in Heidelberg and in the seminar of one of the founders of the historical school.[16] What is more difficult to understand is that even Carl Menger showed little interest in this work, which constituted an extension of his theory, when Wieser showed it to him after his return from his first year in Germany. Menger at least helped to get Wieser's and Böhm-Bawerk's fellow-

[15][Friedrich von Wieser, *Über den Ursprung und die Hauptgesetze des wirtschaftlichen Wertes*, op. cit. -Ed.]
[16][Karl Knies. -Ed.]

ships extended for a second year on the strength of the work shown to him. Wieser refused to be discouraged by Menger's lack of interest and diligently continued his research during the next seven years, which he spent at the Finance Administration of Lower Austria, where he had been employed previously. On the strength of a draft of part of his book *Ursprung und Hauptgesetze des wirtschaftlichen Wertes*, which was published that same year, he was able to obtain his habilitation at the University of Vienna in 1884. Despite his initially negative response, Menger gave a highly laudatory review of the book and recommended Wieser's immediate appointment to the University of Prague, where he received an untenured professorship in political economy that same year.

Wieser's first book, which has been out of print for many years and is difficult to obtain, has been eclipsed by his later work and is therefore not at all well known. Menger's theory of the subjective value of goods had had a very limited range of application in its original form. It had not been applied to the laws governing the structure of production nor was its extension to the most important economic problem, the laws of income distribution, ever undertaken. It was not Menger's failure to provide the instrinsic elements for such an application, but his failure to work out the application appropriately and, despite his precise formulation, to present individual aspects of the theory more graphically that accounted for its remaining inaccessible to a wider audience. This all changed with the introduction of the concept of marginal utility, its application to production goods, costs as indirect utility,[17] and imputation of value,[18] all concepts that first appeared in Wieser's book and that now belong to the core of economic theory. Wieser's graphic formulation of these major constructs of the subjective theory of value was a precondition for their far-reaching influence. Other nearly equally important parts of the book are nearly forgotten today, notably Wieser's very characteristic introductory passage on the scientific relevance of terminology, and his conclusion, which explores the difference between value assessment of goods by marginal and by total utility.

Wieser himself regarded this fine and completely self-contained work as nothing more than an interim publication, which had been forced upon him by the demands of his academic career, and he therefore continued to work on these problems during his first five

---

[17][Opportunity costs. -Ed.]
[18][On imputation, see this volume, chapter 2. -Ed.]

years at the University of Prague. He remained his own severest critic, never entirely satisfied with the formulation of his theoretical insights. Force of circumstances finally compelled him to submit a summary version of his findings to a broader audience. The 1889 publication of Wieser's next book, *Der Natürliche Wert*,[19] among the most brilliantly written and organised books on economic theory, was a side product of his efforts to obtain a full professorship at the University of Prague, which he was in fact awarded that same year. For thirteen years prior to the publication of this analysis he had worked unremittingly on problems of economic value. This book became the definitive expression of his views for the next twenty-five years and is likely to remain one of the classic works on the subject. *Der natürliche Wert* is a high point for Wieser's expository skill, and it is one that he hardly ever attained again in his economic writings. The difference between this work and his first work on the theory of value lies less in an expansion of his original ideas, though it is considerable, than in methodological innovations, which Wieser subsequently extended to his analysis of economic theory as a whole.

Wieser never paid great heed to methodology as a separate discipline and hardly ever concerned himself with the literature on the subject. He always regretted the fact that Carl Menger devoted such a large part of his energy to methodological refinements.[20] He did not believe that methodological speculations divorced from the treatment of concrete problems could advance science and was convinced that theoretical analysis of a specific topic would yield an appropriate method for the particular task. This did not prevent him from giving a rigorous account of his own procedure. He expressed his views on this point at great length in his *Theorie der gesellschaftlichen Wirtschaft*[21] and in his review of Schumpeter's first book.[22] His above-mentioned comments on the importance of scientific terminology and his description of how he used reductive and idealising assumptions and decreasing levels of abstractness have

[19][Friedrich von Wieser, *Der natürliche Wert* (*Natural Value*), op. cit. -Ed.]

[20][On Menger and the *Methodenstreit* with Schmoller, see this volume, chapter 2. -Ed.]

[21][Friedrich von Wieser, *Theorie der gesellschaftlichen Wirtschaft* (*Social Economics*), op. cit. -Ed.]

[22]Friedrich von Wieser, "Das Wesen unter der Hauptinhalt der theoretischen Nationalökonomie: Kritische Glossen zu Schumpeters gleichnamigem Werk," Schmoller's *Jahrbuch für Gesetzgebung, Verwaltung und Volkswirtschaft im Deutschen Reich*, vol. 35, no. 2, 1911. [An excerpt from Schumpeter's book is discussed by Hayek in this volume, chapter 5. -Ed.]

been recognised as exemplary and trendsetting social science methodology.

Wieser made extensive use of the method of reductive and idealising assumptions in his work on natural value and thereby laid the groundwork for his treatment of a complete theory of the economy. He uses the term "natural value" in this context to designate value as it would manifest itself in a communal economy, i.e., in an economy without exchange. With the operation of the whole economy in the hands of a single central authority, value would emerge as the consequence of the social relationship between the quantity of goods and their utility. This assumption was formulated clearly and incontrovertibly in Wieser's later work, *Theorie der gesellschaftlichen Wirtschaft*, in which he designates the hypothetical situation with which the analysis begins as that of a "simple economy". The usefulness of this assumption is already apparent in *Der natürliche Wert*. With its help he manages in this book to derive the facts of subjective valuation that are most relevant for the phenomena of social exchanges not only under the simplified situation of a Robinson Crusoe but also with respect to all the more complicated situations in a society's economy. And in so doing he avoids falling into the dangerous trap of using the phenomena of an exchange economy as the basis of its explanation. Since the object of investigation, as Wieser was later to state in his major economic work, "is not to be envisaged as a scantily supplied and isolated household but . . . the visible phenomena of an economy disposing of all the resources of wealth and technology, it is the essential problems of such a society that we are challenged to solve by the economic calculus."[23] Wieser can therefore deal fully with the relevance of the value calculus for production in an advanced technology and the rules that govern the valuation of individual factors of production. It is in this work that he first examines the characteristics of the individual production factors from the point of view of value theory and makes extensive additions to the law of costs developed earlier. He also perfects his imputation theory in a way that assures natural value an indisputed place in this question. He makes a decisive contribution to the elementary theory of value in *Der Natürliche Wert* with respect to its psychological underpinnings—which he refers to

---

[23][Friedrich von Wieser, *Social Economics*, op. cit. -Ed.]

here as Gossen's law of the satiation of wants.[24] In a second part, entitled "Value in the Economy of the State", Wieser offers some interesting suggestions for applying the new value theory to the administration of state finances, suggestions that have been largely overlooked until now.

Der natürliche Wert brought the first phase of Wieser's work in economic theory more or less to a close. There followed only two articles in English and American journals acquainting the Anglo-Saxon world with the Austrian value theory and defending its tenets.[25] Fifteen years of the most intensive labour devoted to the most difficult theoretical problems had finally taken its toll and produced a mental fatigue which incapacitated Wieser for many years in the field of theory. While the consequences of overwork forced him to relinquish the pursuit of his main interests for a considerable span of time, this did not mean that an energetic man like Wieser had to give up all scholarly and literary activity. He turned to work on problems of economic policy and finances during the 1890s, a shift which, as he frequently mentioned, allowed him to recuperate from the strains of the heavy theoretical labour of the previous years. At the same time he became involved in many aspects of public life in Prague, where, characteristically, he soon acquired a leading role in German circles. After his marriage to Marianne Wolf in 1886, his house became a center of Bohemia's cultural life. His large range of interests brought him into close contact with many scholars and personalities in public life, but at the same time his own strong artistic temperament also attracted him to local artistic circles. He put his organisational talents at the disposal of German cultural interests in Bohemia and contributed greatly to the German educational system in Prague. He was very active as president of the Society for the Advancement of German Science, Art, and Literature in Bohemia, and among his contributions was the establishment of various institutions to promote the welfare of the students at the German University of Prague. Despite the fact that he sympathised greatly with the position of Germans in Bohemia and defended their interests on many occasions out of

[24][On Gossen, the largely unnoticed German theorist who anticipated the later discoveries of the marginal utility theorists, see chapter 15 of F. A. Hayek, *The Trend of Economic Thinking*, op. cit. -Ed.]

[25]Friedrich von Wieser, "The Austrian School and the Theory of Value", *Economic Journal*, vol. 1, 1891, pp. 108–121; "The Theory of Value (A Reply to Professor Macvane)", *Annals of the American Academy of Political and Social Science*, vol. 2, March 1892, pp. 600–628.

national feeling and a strong sense of justice, and despite his lively interest in all public affairs, he could never make up his mind to participate in political life. He held strongly liberal views, but his stance towards all political doctrines was far too critical to allow his affiliation with any political party. Even so, several of his studies dating from these years acquired great significance for the nationality conflict in Bohemia,[26] inasmuch as he extended his research on financial problems to statistical investigations on income and taxation in Bohemia and its nationalities. These studies, which showed his masterly statistical methods, were received with considerable attention at the time. During his Prague residence he also resumed his studies on social theory, whose first findings he incorporated in his famous rectoral address at the University of Prague, "Uber die gesellschaftlichen Gewalten" (On Social Authorities).[27]

After Carl Menger's retirement from his professorship at the University of Vienna, Wieser was appointed to fill his chair in the winter semester of 1903. At the time of his transfer to Vienna, Wieser was in the midst of the most varied activities: Sociological, political, and financial investigations were among the problems that occupied him simultaneously. He had also become interested in monetary theory. Wieser's inaugural lecture at the University of Vienna,[28] which focused on the value of money and its fluctuations throughout history, called attention to one of his most significant contributions to a second field of economic theory, which stimulated a number of important studies. By applying the basic ideas of the subjective value theory to the problem of monetary value, he was able to find the key to its solution, which was subsequently successfully expanded by Wieser's [followers] (Ludwig von Mises and F. X. Weiss).[29] As a result of the convergence of this approach with a

---

[26]Friedrich von Wieser, "Nationale Einkommensverhältnisse in Böhmen", *Deutsche Arbeit, Monatsschrift für das geistige Leben der Deutschen in Böhmen*, vol. 1, 1901; "Die Deutsche Steuerleistung und der öffentliche Haushalt in Böhmen," *Deutsche Arbeit, Monatsschrift für das geistige Leben der Deutschen in Böhmen*, 1903, and in book form, Leipzig: Duncker & Humblot, 1904.

[27]Published in the Report of Charles Ferdinand University [now Charles University], Prague, 1902.

[28]["Der Geldwert und seine geschichtlichen Veränderungen", inaugural lecture, University of Vienna, October 26, 1903, published in *Zeitschrift für Volkswirtschaft, Sozialpolitik und Verwaltung*, vol. 13, 1904, pp. 43–64. -Ed.]

[29][In Mises's *Theorie des Geldes und der Umlaufsmittel*, op. cit., and Weiß's "Die moderne Tendenz in der Lehre vom Geldwert", *Zeitschrift für Volkswirtschaft, Sozialpolitik, und Verwaltung*, vol. 19, 1910, pp. 502–560. Both Mises and Weiß were actually the direct students of Böhm-Bawerk, Wieser's later colleague at Vienna. -Ed.]

related one taken up somewhat later in the Anglo-Saxon countries, this now seems to have become the conventional view of the matter. Wieser's widely applauded talk at the 1909 meeting of the *Verein für Sozialpolitik* (Association for Social Policy) in Vienna focused once more on the problem of fluctuating monetary value, including the question of its statistical documentation.[30]

The works on monetary theory published during Wieser's first six years in Vienna are among the fruits of his earlier efforts to construct a unified system of economic theory, which he had developed in the course of his teaching and was continuing to refine in this period. It is doubtful, however, that he would have made up his mind to turn this material into a publication had not a particularly felicitous occasion for doing so intervened. He had actually reached the point where, on the strength of his inner mastery of economic questions, he felt ready to apply this knowledge to the investigation of more general social laws and had for some time been devoting himself primarily to sociological questions. Initial results of this research were presented in 1909 in his lectures at the University of Salzburg and published in the form of his widely read book, *Recht und Macht*.[31] It was at this juncture that he was persuaded by Max Weber to compose the theoretical, introductory volume to a new basic work on socioeconomic questions.[32] For several years he concentrated once more on economic theory. Though he had originally allotted two years to this task, it took him far longer to complete the work on his major book in the field of economics, and even then he was reluctant to turn over the manuscript for publication because he deemed it incomplete. And yet Wieser's *Theorie der gesellschaftlichen Wirtschaft* offers not only the sole consistent treatment of economic theory produced by the modern subjectivist school,[33] but it also constitutes, above all, what may well be the greatest synthesis achieved by economic theory in our time. Very few works indeed since the days of the classical school have succeeded in dealing with all relevant problems within a comprehensive

---

[30]Friedrich von Wieser, "Der Geldwert und seine Veränderungen," *Schriften des Vereins für Sozialpolitik*, vol. 132, 1909; "Über die Messung der Veränderung des Geldwertes," a talk delivered before the Vienna meeting of the *Verein für Sozialpolitik*.

[31]Friedrich von Wieser, *Recht und Macht: Sechs vorträge*, six lectures delivered at the Salzburger Hochschulkursen in September 1909 (Leipzig: Duncker & Humblot, 1910).

[32][The *Grundriß der Sozialökonomik*, vol. 1 of which was Wieser's *Theorie der gesellschaftlichen Wirtschaft*, op. cit. -Ed.]

[33][What we would now call the older Austrian school, i.e., the generations preceding that of Mises and Schumpeter. Recall that Hayek is writing in 1926. -Ed.]

system and at the same time offering so many profound new insights into the world of economic phenomena. It is not feasible to review here in detail the theoretical analyses contained in this work, but only to trace Wieser's development up to this major work, whose contents are undoubtedly familiar to all economists. A few remarks follow on the overall significance of the book and the extent to which it exemplifies Wieser's intellectual and methodological approach.

Joseph Schumpeter's newspaper article on the occasion of Wieser's seventieth birthday[34] has characterised the special nature of Wieser's work in so few sentences, yet so discerningly, that I will simply quote him here: "Any professional colleague who penetrates Wieser's intellectual universe is at once aware of a new atmosphere. It is as though one had stepped into a house that bears no resemblance to other houses one knows, whose organisation and furnishings are alien to our era and at first disconcerting; and indeed, many of Wieser's colleagues were bewildered for years by his work. Rarely has an author owed as little to other authors as Wieser.[35] At bottom his only indebtedness is to Menger, and all that he owes Menger is the initial impetus. His construction material consists entirely of his own intellectual property, even when stating something that has already been stated previously. His mind has no room for the prefabricated, each sentence and each phrase is the product of a precious insight. With sovereign calm he waves aside what other specialists have written when he creates his own work, and the rest of us have come to accept this as his due. He reads neither rapidly nor extensively and rarely seeks to grasp the finer points of other people's intellectual systems. Polemics either on a professional or on a personal level are alien to him." Wieser's characteristic scholarly stance could not have been described more aptly. He never concerned himself with established scientific knowledge, or the reconciliation of existing principles with one another, or deducing new conclusions from the existing stock of knowledge by mere logical manipulation. Wieser was anything but the prototypical theoretician. Few men could rival his ability to see things sharply and to focus on reality in all its profusion in the midst of theoretical disquisitions.

[34]*Neues Wiener Tagblatt*, July 10, 1921.

[35][This is reminiscent of Schumpeter's earlier statement that "[a]s if out of another world—unexplainable and uncaused—Menger, Böhm-Bawerk and Wieser surfaced in the social economics of that day". *Neue Freie Presse*, February 23, 1915, quoted in Erich Streissler, "The Influence of German Economics on the Work of Menger and Marshall", op. cit., p. 31. -Ed.]

Few men shared his determination to apply his own and other people's abstract constructs only as instruments for the most accurate description of observed reality. Wieser was so deeply immersed in observation that he had no time left to explore or criticise the intellectual systems of others. He found that other people's constructs distracted him from grasping reality with his own eyes, a fact that made him shy away even from oral discussions, unless they contributed to a clearer expression of his own ideas.[36] He never gave in to the temptation to do violence to the facts for the sake of logical elegance. At times he even sacrificed consistency and intellectual completeness by introducing incompletely assimilated ideas of others into his system, if he could thus render reality more faithfully. His last great economic work is a very good example of this tendency. In terms of intellectual consistency and elegance, it is undoubtedly inferior to Böhm-Bawerk's work in economic analysis,[37] but the fault lies with the incomparably greater number of phenomena taken into account by Wieser. The greater approximation to the multifacetedness of reality makes it unavoidable that many things are only suggested and not completely worked through, that many points seem to be irreconcilable. For anyone who gives primacy to a complete logical consistency, Böhm-Bawerk's self-contained system will certainly seem more impressive. Wieser's work offers incomparably more as a point of departure for further elaboration, perhaps because of the very parts that have been criticised as inconsistent.

There are numerous problems in his *Theorie der gesellschaftlichen Wirtschaft* that are treated there in a completely novel way, problems that Wieser had left aside in his earlier writings, and parts of his analysis that are decisively improved. For the problems presented in the first part, which deals with the theory of simple economies, a topic on which he had concentrated in his earlier work, the major improvement consists of preceding it with an extensive section that does not deal at all with the theory of value. In this introductory section, he covers the structure of production in great detail and analyses the behaviour elicited by any given economic situation so thoroughly that in the subsequent section difficult problems of valuation fall into place. The most important findings from this investigation of the structure of production are Wieser's capital

---

[36]Apparently he even refrained from discussing economic problems with his brother-in-law Böhm-Bawerk, with whom he admittedly differed on various points. The latter even complained on occasion that Wieser did not pay due attention to his writings.

[37][Eugen Böhm-Bawerk, *Kapital und Kapitalzins* (*Capital and Interest*), op. cit. -Ed.]

theory and his distinction between "cost productive means" and "specific productive means",[38] which in value theory serves as the basis for the highly important distinction between various marginal utilities, a distinction that Wieser never developed fully, however, and that is therefore poorly understood.

The section on exchange economies is preceded by a short statement of Wieser's social theory, which is inseparable from the contents of that section. The most important and completely novel contribution of the book, however, is Wieser's price theory, which he applies to all phenomena of the advanced market economy far more completely than he had done in any previous work. Among the most significant and fruitful concepts introduced here are the following: stratification of prices, market indices, and monopoloid institutions. Wieser's masterly power of observation and presentation of relationships enabled him to bring treasures to light that will provide generations of economists with ample material for work. The sections on money and credit, which are closely connected with price theory and far transcend his earlier presentations, are nearly as suggestive for future research and equally full of new insights. They lead us to expect that Wieser's final work, his article on money in the fourth edition of the *Handwörterbuch für Staatswissenschaften*,[39] will be of equally high caliber. As Wieser moves closer to the description of the manifold phenomena of the present-day economy in the later sections of the book, it becomes clearer and clearer what a perfect instrument for explaining them he has created in the first parts of his book.

After the completion of his great work on the principles of social economics, Wieser concluded his economic research—and not only because he had done his utmost in that field. The book had been published a few weeks before the outbreak of the [First] World War—which explains in part why the book was so slow to have an impact—and the overwhelming events of the next few years ineluctably and irreversibly shifted Wieser's interests to what had been his ultimate objective, understanding the great forces behind all social developments. Here was a man who had at an early stage learned to envisage all events from a world historical perspective, who as an Austrian had been deeply and continuously preoccupied in the previous years with the evolution and disintegration of the monarchy, and whose deeply-rooted affirmative spirit had been most

[38][Cf. *Social Economics*, op. cit., pp. 119–127. -Ed.]
[39][I.e., "Geld", op. cit. -Ed.]

severely tested.[40] It was natural that for him involvement in his country's experiences helped bring to maturity ideas that had been of deep concern to him lifelong. He had been disinclined up to that time to take a leading role in public affairs, but now he felt the constant pressure of the sighted among the blind, the urge to offer his contemporaries guidance in the turmoil of events by showing them the broad connexions that made these happenings meaningful. Several of the essays in the first years of the war were an outgrowth of this urge and demonstrate both his insight into the difficult problems faced by his country and his faith in the mission of old Austria. His appointment to the Upper House of the Austrian parliament in 1917 gave him the opportunity to make his influence felt in public life along these lines.

His literary and scholarly activity was interrupted during the last two years of the war as a result of his appointment as minister of commerce in August 1917, a capacity in which he served during Seidler's and Lammasch's terms as prime minister,[41] the last governments under the monarchy. He was in charge of negotiations about a customs union with Germany and had brought them to the point of an agreement in principle. His other main tasks were the preparations for the transition to a peacetime economy and demobilisation, commercial agreements with Bulgaria and Turkey, and the peace treaty of Bucharest.

No sooner had he been relieved of his official duties by the collapse of old Austria than he immediately resumed his sociological research. One of his most brilliant pieces of writing, the brochure on *Österreichs Ende* (*Austria's End*)[42] was set down under the fresh impression of the great historical events that he had shared. Despite his intense involvement in these experiences, he succeeded in viewing events with full lucidity and due historical perspective. To a certain extent it fulfilled his youthful dream of writing anonymous history. By the summer of 1919 he resumed his professorship at the University of Vienna, where he was in charge of the main lecture sequence in economics until 1922. He also gave a seminar on monetary theory in the summer semester of 1920.

---

[40][The Hapsburg dynasty began to fall apart in late 1918 with the impending defeat of Austria-Hungary in the First World War. -Ed.]

[41][Ernest Seidler von Feuchtenegg (1862–1931) was prime minister from June 1917 to June 1918; Heinrich Lammasch (1853–1920) held that office in October and November 1918. -Ed.]

[42][*Österreichs Ende* (Berlin: Ullstein, 1919). The pamphlet was published anonymously. -Ed.]

Even in his seminars he tended to avoid real discussions and preferred to develop his own theory in conjunction with seminar papers and the comments elicited by them, rather than engaging in criticisms of other people's views. Yet all those present remember the seminars as brilliant examples of the most fruitful academic instruction. His lectures were flawless in presentation. For the students who attended them, the lectures left an indelible memory of the imposing presence of the tall and distinguished personage, whose exposition of the most difficult economic problems was so simple, so impeccable, and so clear that it was a pleasure just to follow the masterly organisation of his lectures. Outside his lectures and seminars, Wieser had little contact with students, because his dignified reserve tended to keep them at a distance. But a question that showed genuine interest could lead to a lasting relationship. As a result, Wieser's contacts were limited to a very small circle of economists. Since he also refrained from influencing any work in progress, he had very few students working directly under him. However, even without keeping close track of individual students' academic progress, he was a sufficiently good judge of people to be able to spot talented theorists. Once Wieser's interest in a young theorist was aroused, he proved to be a tireless friend and guide in practical matters.

Wieser retired in 1922, after completing his year as honourary professor. Hans Mayer, whose approach was very much in tune with Wieser's, was appointed to his chair.[43] Wieser kept up a high level of literary activity, both as co-editor of the fourth edition of the *Handwörterbuch für Staatswissenschaften* and as head of the Austrian section of the Carnegie Foundation, which was working on the economic and social history of the [First] World War. Despite this multitude of interests, he reserved the bulk of his energies for the book that was to be the culmination of his life's work, the product of his lifelong sociological research. It was published under the title *Gesetz der Macht*[44] a few months prior to his death. Almost all of the numerous articles that he published in his last years were actually preliminary studies for this book, into whose completion he poured all his vigour. All the lectures delivered between 1922 and 1925, after his official retirement, focused on problems related to the book in progress. Since Wieser's major sociological work has been reviewed in full by a highly qualified specialist in the preceding issue

[43][On Mayer see the text and references in this volume, chapter 1. -Ed.]
[44][Friedrich von Wieser, *Das Gesetz der Macht*, op. cit. -Ed.]

of this journal,[45] its contents need not be described here. To judge by its initial reception, it seems that the great man's favourite child will be regarded equally highly by his contemporaries and may well be considered his crowning achievement by persons who are not trained economists. The quality of its exposition secures it a place far above that of a specialised treatise. It is convincing evidence that a work inspired by a lofty idea almost inevitably turns into a work of true artistic merit. Given his undisputed mastery of scientific knowledge, Wieser was singularly unencumbered by laboured technical information even in his previous writings and could thus demonstrate the affinity between scholarship and artistic creation. Little as he had been constrained by them previously, in this last work Wieser liberated himself completely from the shackles of iron-clad disciplinary and methodological compartmentalisation and revealed his unusual personality in all its greatness. It will be obvious to the reader of this book why Wieser's friends and students were prompted to compare him to Goethe. Wide-ranging interests encompassing all fields of culture and art, worldly wisdom and the worldly tact of the minister of old Austria combined with an aloofness from daily trivia and a comprehensive human sympathy are as much elements of this similarity as is the absence of nationalist narrowmindedness. He was wholeheartedly a German and perhaps even more wholeheartedly an Austrian of the best sort, which found in him its most perfect expression.

[45][I.e., Eduard Spranger, in the *Jahrbücher für Nationalökonomie und Statistik*, third series, vol. 70, 1926, pp. 578–584. -Ed.]

FOUR

LUDWIG VON MISES (1881–1973)[1]

Ludwig von Mises: an Overview[2]

The foundations of the great system of social thought that we now know as the work of Ludwig von Mises were laid half a century ago when he was a busy administrator for whom research and teaching could be only spare-time occupations. So long as he lived in his native Vienna, that is, far into his fifties, most of his time was devoted to his work as financial consultant to the most important semi-official organisation of Austrian enterprise, the Vienna Chamber of Commerce, and he could do only a little teaching at the University [of Vienna] on the side. Even this was interrupted by long service as an artillery officer during the First World War. Yet shortly before and after that, he published the two works which contain the outline of most of the ideas that he later developed into his comprehensive system.

---

[1][This chapter contains a number of short essays written by Hayek at various times concerning Ludwig von Mises. The arrangement of the selections is as follows: After two introductory sections, the essays are ordered by the original publication date of the work by Mises under discussion; the source of each section is indicated at the beginning thereof. Three other Hayek essays relating to Mises are not reprinted here but may be of some interest. They are "Die Überlieferung der Ideale der Wirtschaftsfreiheit", *Schweizer Monatshefte*, vol. 31, September 1951, published in English as "The Ideals of Economic Freedom: A Liberal Inheritance", in *The Owl* (London), 1951, pp. 7–12, and republished as "A Rebirth of Liberalism" in *The Freeman*, July 1952, pp. 729–731, and as "The Transmission of the Ideals of Economic Freedom" in *Studies in Philosophy, Politics and Economics* (London: Routledge & Kegan Paul; Chicago: University of Chicago Press; Toronto: University of Toronto Press, 1967); "In Memoriam Ludwig von Mises 1881–1973", *Zeitschrift für Nationalökonomie*, vol. 33, 1973; and "Coping with Ignorance", *Imprimis*, vol. 7, no. 7, July 1978, pp. 1–6, reprinted in *Champions of Freedom* (Hillsdale, Mich.: Hillsdale College Press, 1979). -Ed.]

[2][Published as "Tribute to von Mises, Vienna Years", *National Review*, November 9, 1973, pp. 1244–1246 and p. 1260. -Ed.]

In 1912 his *Theory of Money*[3] appeared, for many years the most profound and satisfying work on the subject available. That it did not have the immediate effect it deserved—which might have saved the world many of the monetary troubles of the postwar period—was due mainly to the fact that he had found it necessary to go deeply into the problems of the general theory of value. This deterred many who might have profited from his elucidation of questions of more immediate practical value. After the war, in 1922, there followed his great work *Socialism*,[4] which established his fame. Its central thesis was not, as it is sometimes misleadingly put, that socialism is impossible, but that it cannot achieve an efficient utilisation of resources.[5] That can be achieved only on the basis of a calculation in terms of value or price, which in turn can be ascertained only if there is a competitive market. It was this thesis which attracted the widest attention and led to discussions extending over many years in which Mises certainly was victorious, at least in the sense that the defenders of socialism were driven to far-reaching changes in their doctrines.

The book on socialism was particularly important in that it marked Mises as the leading interpreter and defender of the free enterprise system. Though he had been taught as a very young man the mild 'Fabian' socialism then prevalent among the Viennese intelligentsia, he soon reacted against it, thereby isolating himself from most of his contemporaries. He probably owed this conversion to Eugen von Böhm-Bawerk, the teacher at the University who had the greatest influence on him. Böhm-Bawerk, before his premature death, had begun to work on the lines which Mises later developed. By the time he published *Socialism*, Mises had become so strongly convinced that socialist aspirations were based on an intellectual confusion and a failure to comprehend the task which the economic system had to perform that his later attempts to develop social theory and his defense of a libertarian political order often became inextricably intertwined. His tendency, particularly in his younger years, to defend his position with stubbornness and intransigence made him many enemies. This was largely the reason he never obtained a regular university position in Vienna and why many academicians treated even his purely theoretical works as ideological-

---

[3][Ludwig von Mises, *Theorie des Geldes und der Umlaufsmittel*, op. cit. -Ed.]
[4][Ludwig von Mises, *Die Gemeinwirtschaft: Untersuchungen über den Sozialismus*, op. cit. -Ed.]
[5][On this point see this volume, Introduction. -Ed.]

ly suspect for so long.[6] He continued to teach occasional courses at the university, but for many years it was through an informal discussion circle, his *Privatseminar*, as it came to be known in Vienna, which ranged widely over problems of social theory and philosophy, that he extended his personal influence. Among the best-known members of this circle are not only the economists Gottfried Haberler and Fritz Machlup,[7] but also sociologists like the late Alfred Schutz and philosophers like the late Felix Kaufmann.[8]

During these years, the 1920s and early 1930s, Mises was extraordinarily fertile, and in a long series of monographs on economic, sociological, and philosophical problems built up the comprehensive philosophy of society that he first expounded in a German work[9] and then summed up in the *magnum opus* by which he is mainly known to American readers, *Human Action*.[10] This was written in New York. Mises had left Vienna for a professorship at Geneva shortly before Hitler occupied Austria, and in 1940, about as late as was still possible, he moved from Geneva to the United States. The years in America were happy. Newly married, in the care of a congenial companion, for the first time in his life he was able to devote himself entirely to writing and teaching. But not even a brief sketch of his life can conclude without a mention of three character-

---

[6][Anti-Semitism may have also figured in Mises's inability to get a university appointment. In his unfinished essay on the Austrian school for the *New Palgrave* dictionary (see this volume, chapter 1, note 1), however, Hayek adds the following to his description of the University of Vienna just after the First World War: "Mises, who had served in the army throughout the war, had resumed teaching as a *Privatdozent*, and would have seemed an obvious choice for a professorship. That he did not succeed is usually explained by anti-Semitism, but has more complex causes which deserve to be explained. The Faculty of Law, at which economics was taught, had a considerable number of highly respected Jewish professors, and others, such as Hans Kelsen, were still being appointed at the time. But to make such an appointment, it was necessary that the candidate have the approval of the Jewish community, which was predominantly inclined to the Left. By that time, however, Mises by his criticism of the socialist programme had made himself highly unpopular with the majority of the group. It was chiefly this which prevented his appointment to a full professorship." See also this volume, pp. 157–158, and Earlene Craver, "The Emigration of the Austrian Economists", op. cit., p. 5. -Ed.]

[7][Haberler and Machlup are among the group of Mises's students who later became prominent in the United States. Both were presidents of the American Economic Association. -Ed.]

[8][Hayek himself was of course also a member of this circle. See the discussion in this volume, Prologue to Part I. -Ed.]

[9][Ludwig von Mises, *Nationalökonomie: Theorie des Handelns und Wirtschaftens* (Geneva: Editions Union, 1940). Hayek's review is reprinted in this chapter. -Ed.]

[10][Ludwig von Mises, *Human Action: A Treatise on Economics* (New Haven, Conn.: Yale University Press, 1949; third revised edition, Chicago: Henry Regnery, 1966). -Ed.]

istics of his work as a scholar: the rare lucidity of his exposition, his astounding historical erudition, and his deep pessimism about the future of our civilisation—a pessimism which led him often to predictions that did not come true as soon as he had expected but that were usually confirmed in the end. I believe the world would be a better place if Ludwig von Mises had more often been listened to.

In Honour of Professor Mises[11]

There has not been, and I do not expect that there ever will be, in my life, another occasion when I have felt so honoured and pleased to be allowed to stand up and to express on behalf of all those here assembled, and of hundreds of others, the profound admiration and gratitude we feel for a great scholar and a great man. It is an honour which I no doubt owe to the fact that among those available I am probably the oldest of his pupils and that, in consequence, I may be able to tell you some personal recollections about certain phases of the work of the man we honour today. Before addressing Professor Mises directly, I trust he will therefore permit me to talk to you about him. But, although my recollections cover nearly forty of the fifty years which have passed since the event whose anniversary we celebrate, I cannot speak from my own knowledge about the earlier part of this period. When I first sat at the feet of Professor Mises, immediately after the [F]irst [World] [W]ar, he was already a well-known figure with the first of his great works firmly established as the outstanding book on the theory of money.[12] That work had appeared in 1912 and yet was by no means his first. Indeed, his first book on economics[13] had appeared fully ten years earlier, four years before Professor Mises even got his doctorate. How he ever did it I have never quite understood. I believe it was

---

[11][Address delivered by Hayek at the dinner given by the Foundation for Economic Education on the occasion of the presentation to Ludwig von Mises of the volume *On Freedom and Free Enterprise*, op. cit., prepared to honour the fiftieth anniversary of his doctorate, at the University Club, New York, March 7, 1956. The address was previously published in Margit von Mises, *My Years with Ludwig von Mises* (second enlarged edition, Cedar Falls, Iowa: Center for Futures Education, 1984), pp. 217–223. -Ed.]

[12][Ludwig von Mises, *Theorie des Geldes und der Umlaufsmittel*, op. cit. -Ed.]

[13][Ludwig von Mises, *Die Entwicklung des gutsherrlichbäuerlichen Verhältnisses in Galizien, 1772–1848* (Vienna and Leipzig: Franz Deuticke, 1902), in volume 6 of the series *Wiener Staatswissenschaftliche Studien*. -Ed.]

written before he came into contact with the one man of the older generation who can claim to have exercised an important influence on his scientific thinking, Eugen von Böhm-Bawerk. It was in Böhm-Bawerk's seminar that a brilliant group was then emerging who were to become the third generation of the Austrian school founded by Carl Menger. Among them it must soon have been evident that Mises was the most independent minded.

Before I leave the student period which led up to the degree conferred fifty years ago, I will interrupt this account for an announcement. We are by no means the only ones who have thought of making this anniversary the occasion for honouring Professor Mises. I fear it will not be news to him, much as I should like to be the first bringer of this news, that the University of Vienna has also wished to celebrate the occasion. As I have learned only a few days ago, the Faculty of Law of that university had resolved some time ago formally to renew the degree it granted so long ago. If the new diploma has not yet reached Professor Mises, it should do so any day. In the meantime, I can read to you the citation which the Dean let me have by airmail: The Faculty of Law of the University of Vienna resolved at its meeting of December 3, 1955, to renew the doctor's diploma conferred on February 20, 1906, on Ludwig von Mises, "who has earned the greatest distinction by his contributions to the economic theory of the Austrian school, has greatly added to the reputation of Austrian science abroad, and who has also done most beneficial work as director of the Vienna Chamber of Commerce and to whose initiative the foundation of the Austrian Institute of Economics[14] is due".

But I must return to his first outstanding contribution to economics.[15] To me that first decade of our century when it was written may seem a far-away period of peace; and even in Central Europe the majority of people deluded themselves about the stability of their civilisation. But it was as it appeared to an acute observer endowed with the foresight of Professor Mises. I even believe that first book was written in the constant feeling of impending doom and under all the difficulties and disturbances to which a young officer in the reserve is exposed at the time of constant alarms of war. I mention this because I believe it is true of all of Professor Mises's works that they were written in constant doubt whether the

[14][I.e., the *Österreichische Konjunkturforschungsinstitut* or Austrian Institute for Business-Cycle Research. On the Institute see this volume, Prologue to Part I. -Ed.]
[15][I.e., *Theorie des Geldes und der Umlaufsmittel*, op. cit. -Ed.]

civilisation which made them possible would last long enough to allow their appearance. Yet, in spite of this sense of urgency in which they were written, they have a classic perfection, a rounded comprehensiveness in scope and form which might suggest a leisurely composition.

The *Theory of Money* is much more than merely a theory of money. Although its main aim was to fill what was then the most glaring gap in the body of accepted economic theory, it also made its contribution to the basic problems of value and price. If its effect had been more rapid, it might have prevented great suffering and destruction. But the state of monetary understanding was just then so low that it would have been too much to expect that so sophisticated a work should have a rapid effect. It was soon appreciated by a few of the best minds of the time, but its general appreciation came too late to save his country and most of Europe the experience of a devastating inflation. I cannot resist the temptation to mention briefly one curious review which the book received. Among the reviewers was a slightly younger man by the name of John Maynard Keynes, who could not suppress a somewhat envious expression of admiration for the erudition and philosophical breadth of the work, but who unfortunately, because, as he later explained, he could understand in German only what he knew already, did not learn anything from it.[16] The world might have been saved much if Lord Keynes's German had been a little better.

It was not long after publication of the book and the appointment to a position at the university to which it led that Professor Mises's scientific work was definitely interrupted by the outbreak of the first great war and his being called to active service. After some years in the artillery, I believe in the end commanding a battery, he found himself at the conclusion of the war in the economics section of the War Ministry where he evidently was again thinking actively on wider economic problems. At any rate, almost as soon as the war was over he was ready with a new book, a little-known and now

---

[16][Keynes reviewed the book in the *Economic Journal*, vol. 24, September 1914, pp. 417–419, where he says "Dr. von Mises's treatise is the work of an acute and cultivated mind. But it is critical rather than constructive, dialectical and not original. . . . Dr. Mises strikes an outside reader as being the very highly educated pupil of a school, once of great eminence, but now losing its vitality." Sixteen years later, however, in the *Treatise on Money*, Keynes reveals that "[in] German I can only clearly understand what I know already!—so that *new* ideas are apt to be veiled from me by the difficulties of language." See *The Collected Writings of John Maynard Keynes*, op. cit., vol. 5, p. 178, note 2. -Ed.]

rare work called *Nation, Staat und Wirtschaft*[17] of which I particularly treasure my copy because it contains so many germs of later developments.

I suppose the idea of his second *magnum opus* must already have been forming in his mind since the crucial chapter of it appeared less than two years later as a famous article on the problem of economic calculation in a socialist community.[18] Professor Mises had then returned to his position as Legal Advisor and Financial Expert of the Vienna Chamber of Commerce. Chambers of Commerce, I should explain, are official institutions whose main task is to advise the government on legislation. At that same time Professor Mises was combining this position with that of one of the heads of the special office connected with carrying out certain clauses of the peace treaty. It was in that capacity that I first came to know him well. I had, of course, been a member of his class at the university.[19] But since, as I must mention in my own excuse, I was rushing through an abridged post-war course in law and did not spend *all* my spare time on economics, I have not profited from that opportunity as much as I might have. But then it so happened that my first job was as Professor Mises's subordinate in that temporary government office; there I came to know him mainly as a tremendously efficient executive, the kind of man who, as was said of John Stuart Mill, because he does a normal day's work in two hours, has always a clear desk and time to talk about anything. I came to know him as one of the best-educated and -informed men I had ever known, and, what was most important at the time of great inflation, as the only man who really understood what was happening. There was a time then when we thought he would soon be called to take charge of the finances of the country. He was so clearly the only man capable of stopping inflation and much damage

---

[17][Ludwig von Mises, *Nation, Staat und Wirtschaft: Beiträge zur Politik und Geschichte der Zeit*, op. cit. -Ed.]

[18][The article, "Die Wirtschaftsrechnung im sozialistischen Gemeinwesen", appeared in the *Archiv für Sozialwissenschaften*, vol. 47, 1920, pp. 86–121. An English translation by S. Adler was published as "Economic Calculation in the Socialist Commonwealth" in F. A. Hayek, ed., *Collectivist Economic Planning* (London: Routledge; reprinted, Clifton, N.J.: Augustus M. Kelley, 1975), pp. 87–130, and republished in pamphlet form, with a Postscript by Joseph T. Salerno (Auburn, Ala.: Ludwig von Mises Institute, 1990). -Ed.]

[19][Hayek means that he was a student at the University of Vienna when Mises lectured there as an unpaid *Privatdozent*; he was also a member of Mises's private seminar group. Hayek was actually the direct student of Friedrich von Wieser, the chairholder in economics at Vienna. -Ed.]

might have been prevented if he had been put in charge. It was not to be.

Of what I had not the least idea at that time, however, in spite of daily contacts, was that Professor Mises was also writing the book which would make the most profound impression on my generation. *Die Gemeinwirtschaft*, later translated as *Socialism*, appeared in 1922. Much as we had come to admire Mises's achievements in economic theory, this was something of much broader scope and significance. It was a work on political economy in the tradition of the great moral philosophers, a Montesquieu or Adam Smith, containing both acute knowledge and profound wisdom. I have little doubt that it will retain the position it has achieved in the history of political ideas. But there can be no doubt whatever about the effect on us who have been in their most impressionable age. To none of us young men who read the book when it appeared the world was ever the same again. If Röpke[20] stood here, or Robbins,[21] or Ohlin[22] (to mention only those of exactly the same age as myself) they would tell you the same story. Not that we at once swallowed it all. For that it was much too strong a medicine and too bitter a pill. But to arouse contradiction, to force others to think out for themselves the ideas which have led him, is the main function of the innovator. And though we might try to resist, even strive hard to get the disquieting considerations out of our system, we did not succeed. The logic of the argument was inexorable.

It was not easy. Professor Mises's teaching seemed directed against all we had been brought up to believe. It was a time when all the fashionable intellectual arguments seemed to point to socialism and when nearly all 'good men' among the intellectuals were socialists. Though the *immediate* influence of the book may not have been as great as one might have wished, it is in some ways surprising that it had as great an influence as it did. Because for the young idealist

---

[20][Wilhelm Röpke (1899–1966) taught in the 1920s at the Universities of Jena, Graz, and Marburg. After exile in 1933 he went to the University of Istanbul and the Graduate Institute of International Studies in Geneva, serving as an adviser to Minister Ludwig Erhard after the Second World War. See Hayek's discussion of Röpke in this volume, Prologue to Part II. -Ed.]

[21][Lionel Robbins (1898–1984), later Lord Robbins of Clare Market, was Professor of Economics at the London School of Economics and for many years one of Hayek's closest friends and colleagues. -Ed.]

[22][Bertil Gotthard Ohlin (1899–1979) was Professor at the Stockholm School of Business Administration, a member of the Swedish Parliament from 1938 to 1970, and leader of the Liberal Party in Sweden. He received the 1977 Nobel prize for his work in international trade theory. -Ed.]

of the time it meant the dashing of all his hopes; and since it was clear that the world was bent on the course whose destructive nature the work pointed out, it left us little but black despair. And to those of us who knew Professor Mises personally, it became, of course, soon clear that his own view about the future of Europe and the world was one of deep pessimism. How justified a pessimism we were soon to learn.

Young people do not readily take to an argument which makes a pessimistic view of the future inevitable. But when the force of Professor Mises's logic did not suffice, another factor soon reinforced it—Professor Mises's exasperating tendency of proving to have been right. Perhaps the dire consequences of the stupidity which he chastised did not always manifest themselves as soon as he predicted. But come they inevitably did, sooner or later.

Let me here insert a comment. I cannot help smiling when I hear Professor Mises described as a conservative. Indeed, in this country and at this time, his views may appeal to people of conversative minds. But when he began advocating them, there was no conservative group which he could support. There could not have been anything more revolutionary, more radical than his appeal for reliance on freedom. To me Professor Mises is and remains, above all, a great radical, an intelligent and rational radical but, nonetheless, a radical on the right lines.[23]

I have now spoken about *Socialism* at length because for our generation it must remain the most memorable and decisive production of Professor Mises's career. We did, of course, continue to learn and profit from the series of books and papers in which during the next fifteen years he elaborated and strengthened his position. I cannot mention them here individually, though each and every one of them would deserve detailed discussion. I must turn to his third *magnum opus*, which first appeared in Switzerland in a German edition in 1940[24] and nine years later in a rewritten English edition under the title *Human Action*. It covers a wider field than even political economy and it is still too early definitely to evaluate its significance. We shall not know its full effects until the men whom it struck in the same decisive phase of their intellectual evolution have in turn reached their productive stage. I, for myself, have no

[23][The reader may wish to compare this passage with Hayek's essay "Why I Am Not a Conservative", in *The Constitution of Liberty* (London: Routledge & Kegan Paul, and Chicago: University of Chicago Press, 1960), where Hayek describes himself in a similar way. -Ed.]
[24][I.e., *Nationalökonomie: Theorie des Handelns und Wirtschaftens*, op. cit. -Ed.]

doubt that in the long run it will prove at least as important as *Socialism* has been.

Even before the first version of this work had appeared, great changes had occurred in Professor Mises's life which I must now briefly mention. Good fortune had it that he was a visiting professor at Geneva[25] when Hitler marched into Austria. We know that the momentous events which followed soon afterwards gave him to this country and this city which has since been his home. But there occurred at the time another event about which we must equally rejoice. We, his old pupils of the Vienna days, used to regard him as a most brilliant but somewhat severe bachelor, who had organised his life in a most efficient routine, but who in the intensity of intellectual efforts was clearly burning the candle at both ends. If today we can congratulate a Professor Mises who not only seems to me as young as he was twenty years ago, but genial and kind even to adversaries as we hardly expected the fierce fighter of yore ever to be, we owe it to the gracious lady which at that critical juncture joined her life to his and who now adorns his house and tonight our table.[26]

I need not speak to you at length about Professor Mises's activities since he has resided among you. Many of you have, during these last fifteen years, had more opportunity to know him and to benefit by his counsel than is true of most of his old pupils. Rather than telling you more about him I will now turn to him to express in a few words the grounds on which we admire and revere him.

Professor Mises, it would be an impertinence to enlarge further on your learning and scholarship, on your wisdom and penetration, which have given you world renown. But you have shown other qualities which not all great thinkers possess. You have shown an undaunted courage even when you stood alone. You have shown a relentless consistency and persistence in your thought even when it led to unpopularity and isolation. You have for long not found the recognition from the official organisation of science which was your due. You have seen your pupils reap some of the rewards which were due to you but which envy and prejudice have long withheld. But you have been more fortunate than most other sponsors of unpopular causes. You knew before today that the ideas for which

---

[25][I.e., at the *Institut Universitaire des Hautes Etudes Internationales* (Graduate Institute of International Studies). -Ed.]

[26][Margit von Mises. Her brief memoir has been published as *My Years with Ludwig von Mises*, op. cit. -Ed.]

THE FORTUNES OF LIBERALISM

you had so long fought alone or with little support would be victorious. You have seen an ever-growing group of pupils and admirers gather round you and, while you continue to push further, endeavour to follow up and elaborate your ideas. The torch which you have lighted has become the guide of a new movement for freedom which is gathering strength every day. The token of admiration and gratitude which we have been privileged today to present to you on behalf of all your disciples is but a modest expression of what we feel. I wish I could claim a little of the credit of having organised this; but it was in fact entirely the younger generation of your pupils who took the initiative of actually doing what many of us older ones had long wished should be done. It is to the editor[27] of the volume and to the Foundation for Economic Education[28] that the credit belongs of having provided this opportunity for the expression of our wishes.

Socialism[29]

When *Socialism* first appeared in 1922, its impact was profound. It gradually but fundamentally altered the outlook of many of the young idealists returning to their university studies after [the First] World War. I know, for I was one of them.

We felt that the civilisation in which we had grown up had collapsed. We were determined to build a better world, and it was this desire to reconstruct society that led many of us to the study of economics. Socialism promised to fulfil our hopes for a more rational, more just world. And then came this book. Our hopes were dashed. *Socialism* told us that we had been looking for improvement in the wrong direction.

A number of my contemporaries, who later became well known but who were then unknown to each other, went through the same experience: Wilhelm Röpke in Germany and Lionel Robbins in England are but two examples. None of us had initially been Mises's pupils. I had come to know him while working for a temporary Austrian government office which was entrusted with the implemen-

---

[27][Mary Sennholz (1913–). -Ed.]

[28][On the Foundation for Economic Education see Hayek's tribute to Leonard Read, reprinted in this volume, chapter 14. -Ed.]

[29][Written in 1978 and published as the Foreword to Ludwig von Mises, *Socialism: An Economic and Sociological Analysis* (Indianapolis, Ind.: Liberty*Classics*, 1981), pp. xix–xxiv. -Ed.]

tation of certain clauses of the Treaty of Versailles. He was my superior, the director of the department.

Mises was then best known as a fighter against inflation. He had gained the ear of the government and, from another position as financial adviser to the Vienna Chamber of Commerce, was immensely busy urging the government to take the only path by which a complete collapse of the currency could still be prevented. (During the first eight months I served under him, my nominal salary rose to 200 times the initial amount.)

As students during the early 1920s, many of us were aware of Mises as the somewhat reclusive university lecturer who, a decade or so earlier, had published a book[30] known for its successful application of the Austrian marginal-utility analysis theory of money—a book Max Weber described as the most acceptable work on the subject.[31] Perhaps we ought to have known that in 1919 he had also published a thoughtful and farseeing study on the wider aspects of social philosophy, concerning the nation, the state, and the economy.[32] It never became widely known, however, and I discovered it only when I was his subordinate at the government office in Vienna. At any rate, it was a great surprise to me when *Socialism* was first published. For all I knew, he could hardly have had much free time for academic pursuits during the preceding (and extremely busy) ten years. Yet this was a major treatise on social philosophy, giving every evidence of independent thought and reflecting, through Mises's criticism, an acquaintance with most of the literature on the subject.

For the first twelve years of this century, until he entered military service, Mises studied economic and social problems. He was, as was my generation nearly twenty years later, led to these topics by the fashionable concern with *Sozialpolitik*, similar in outlook to the 'Fabian' socialism of England.[33] His first book,[34] published while he

---

[30]Ludwig von Mises, *Theorie des Geldes und der Umlaufsmittel*, op. cit.

[31][Max Weber, *Wirtschaft und Gesellschaft* (Tübingen: J. C. B. Mohr (Paul Siebeck), 1922; fifth revised edition, with subtitle *Grundriß der verstehenden Soziologie*, Tübingen: J. C. B. Mohr (Paul Siebeck), 1976), p. 40. -Ed.]

[32][Ludwig von Mises, *Nation, Staat und Wirtschaft: Beiträge zur Politik und Geschichte der Zeit*, op. cit. -Ed.]

[33][The German *Sozialpolitik* movement for social reform opposed the 'Manchester Liberalism' of British classical political economy. Inspired by the German *Kathedersozialisten* (Socialists of the Chair), these reformers advocated state intervention to improve working-class conditions, which in their view had deteriorated due to the 'excesses' of liberal economic policies. Schumpeter tells us that "[m]ost German economists were pillars of *Sozialpolitik* and thoroughly averse to 'Smithianism' or

was still a young law student at the University of Vienna, was in the spirit of the predominant German historical school of economists who devoted themselves mainly to problems of 'social policy'. He later even joined one of those organisations[35] which prompted a German satirical weekly to define economists as persons who went around measuring workingmen's dwellings and saying they were too small. But in the course of this process, when he was taught political economy as part of his law studies, Mises discovered economic theory in the shape of the *Grundsätze der Volkswirtschaftslehre* of Carl Menger, then about to retire as a professor at the university. As Mises says in his fragment of an autobiography,[36] this book made him an economist. Having gone through the same experience, I know what he means.

Mises's initial interests had been primarily historical, and to the end he retained a breadth of historical knowledge rare among theoreticians. But, finally, his dissatisfaction with the manner in which historians and particularly economic historians interpreted their material led him to economic theory. His chief inspiration came from Eugen von Böhm-Bawerk, who had returned to a professorship at the University of Vienna after serving as Austrian minister of finance. During the decade before the war, Böhm-Bawerk's seminar became the great center for the discussion of economic theory. Its participants included Mises, Joseph Schumpeter,[37] and the outstanding theoretician of Austrian Marxism, Otto Bauer,[38] whose defense of Marxism long dominated the discussion. Böhm-Bawerk's ideas on socialism during this period appear to have

---

'Manchesterism'". *History of Economic Analysis*, op. cit., p. 765. See also Karl Erich Born, *Staat und Sozialpolitik seit Bismarcks Sturz* (Weisbaden: F. Steiner, 1957). -Ed.]

[34]Ludwig von Mises, *Die Entwicklung des gutsherrlichbäuerlichen Verhältnisses in Galizien, 1772–1848*, op. cit.

[35][The *Sozialwissenschaftlicher Bildungsverein* (Association for Education in the Social Sciences). -Ed.]

[36]Ludwig von Mises, *Notes and Recollections*, op. cit., p. 33.

[37][On Schumpeter see this volume, chapter 5. -Ed.]

[38][Otto Bauer published two influential works on Marxism during this period: "Marx's Theorie der Wirtschaftskrisen", *Die Neue Zeit*, vol. 23, 1904, an analysis of the Marxian theory of economic fluctuations, and *Die Nationalitätenfrage und die Sozialdemokratie* (Vienna: Wiener Volksbuchhandlung, 1907) still the standard Marxian work on nationalism. Bauer later led the Austrian socialist party (SPO). Mises calls him the "only [Marxian theorist] who surpassed modest mediocrity" of all those he met in Western and Central Europe. Mises, *Notes and Recollections*, op. cit., p. 16. For a sample of Bauer's work see the translation by J. E. King of Bauer's 1913 article on capital accumulation in *History of Political Economy*, vol. 18, no. 1, 1986, pp. 87–110. –Ed.]

developed a good deal beyond what is shown by the few essays he published before his early death.[39] There is no doubt that the foundations of Mises's characteristic ideas on socialism were laid then, though almost as soon as he had published his first major work, *The Theory of Money and Credit*, the opportunity for further systematic pursuit of this interest vanished with Mises's entry into service for the duration of [the First] World War.

Most of Mises's military service was spent as an artillery officer on the Russian front, but during the last few months he served in the economic section of the Ministry of War. It must be assumed that he started on *Socialism* only after his release from military duty. He probably wrote most of it between 1919 and 1921—the crucial section on economic calculation under socialism was in fact provoked by a book by Otto Neurath published in 1919, from which Mises quotes.[40] That under the prevailing conditions he found time to concentrate and to pursue a comprehensive theoretical and philosophical work has remained a wonder to one who at least during the last months of this period saw him almost daily at his official work.

As I suggested before, *Socialism* shocked our generation, and only slowly and painfully did we become persuaded of its central thesis. Mises continued, of course, thinking about the same range of problems, and many of his further ideas were developed in the 'private seminar' which began about the time *Socialism* was published. I joined the seminar two years later, upon my return from a year of postgraduate study in the United States.[41] Although there were few unquestioning followers at first, he gained interest and admiration among a younger generation and attracted those who were concerned with problems of the borderline of social theory and philosophy. Reception of the book by the profession was mostly either indifferent or hostile. I remember but one review that showed any recognition of *Socialism*'s importance and that was by a surviving liberal statesman of the preceding century. The tactics of

[39][Several of these essays have been collected by Hans Sennholz and translated as *Shorter Classics of Böhm-Bawerk* (South Holland, Ill.: Libertarian Press, 1962). A bibliography of Böhm-Bawerk's major works appears on pp. xii–xiii of that volume. -Ed.]

[40][Otto Neurath, *Durch die Kriegswirtschaft zur Naturalwirtschaft* (Munich: G. D. W. Callwey, 1919). -Ed.]

[41][On Hayek's experiences in the United States in 1923–24 see this volume, Prologue to Part I. -Ed.]

his opponents were generally to represent him as an extremist whose views no one else shared.

Mises's ideas ripened during the next two decades, culminating in the first (1940) German version of what became famous as *Human Action*.[42] But to those of us who experienced its first impact, *Socialism* will always be his decisive contribution. It challenged the outlook of a generation and altered, if only slowly, the thinking of many. The members of Mises's Vienna group were not disciples. Most of them came to him as students who had completed their basic training in economics, and only gradually were they converted to his unconventional views. Perhaps they were influenced as much by his disconcerting habit of rightly predicting the ill consequences of current economic policy as by the cogency of his arguments. Mises hardly expected them to accept all his opinions, and the discussions gained much from the fact that the participants were often only gradually weaned from their different views. It was only later, after he had developed a complete system of social thought, that a 'Mises school' developed. The very openness of his system enriched his ideas and enabled some of his followers to develop them in somewhat different directions.[43]

Mises's arguments were not easily apprehended. Sometimes personal contact and discussion were required to understand them fully. Though written in a pellucid and deceptively simple prose, they tacitly presuppose an understanding of economic processes—an understanding not shared by all his readers. We see this most clearly in his crucial argument on the impossibility of an economic calculation under socialism. When one reads Mises's opponents,[44] one gains the impression that they did not really see why such calculation was necessary. They treat the problem of economic

---

[42]Ludwig von Mises, *Nationalökonomie: Theorie des Handelns und Wirtschaftens*, op. cit.

[43][For more on the *Privatseminar* and its members see this volume, Prologue to Part I, and the last section of this chapter. See also Craver, op. cit., pp. 1–32, esp. pp. 14–17. -Ed.]

[44][Most notably Oskar Lange "On the Economic Theory of Socialism", *Review of Economic Studies*, vol. 4, no. 1, 1936, and vol. 4, no. 2, 1937; Fred M. Taylor, "The Guidance of Production in a Socialist State", *American Economic Review*, vol. 19, 1929 (Taylor reprinted and Lange revised and republished in Lange and Taylor, *On the Economic Theory of Socialism*, ed. Benjamin E. Lippincott (Minneapolis, Minn.: University of Minnesota Press, 1938; reprinted, New York: McGraw-Hill, 1964)), and a series of articles by Abba P. Lerner, summarised in his *The Economics of Control: Principles of Welfare Economics* (New York: Macmillan, 1944). See also this volume, Introduction. -Ed.]

calculation as if it were merely a technique to make the managers of socialist plants accountable for the resources entrusted to them and wholly unconnected with the problem of what they should produce and how. Any set of magic figures appeared to them sufficient to control the honesty of those still-indispensable survivors of a capitalist age. They never seemed to comprehend that it was not a question of playing with some set of figures, but one of establishing the only indicators those managers could have for deciding the role of their activities in the whole structure of mutually adjusted activities. As a result, Mises became increasingly aware that what separated him from his critics was his wholly different intellectual approach to social and economic problems, rather than mere differences of interpretation of particular facts. To convince them, he would have to impress on them the necessity of an altogether different methodology. This of course became his central concern.

Publication in 1936 of the English translation was largely the result of the efforts of Professor Lionel C. Robbins (later Lord Robbins). He found a highly qualified translator in a former fellow student at the London School of Economics, Jacques Kahane,[45] who had remained an active member of a circle of academic economists of that generation, although he himself had not remained in the profession. After many years of service with one of the great firms of grain dealers in London, Kahane concluded his career with the United Nations Food and Agricultural Office at Rome and the World Bank at Washington. The typescript of Kahane's translation was the last form in which I had read the entire text of *Socialism*, before doing so again in preparation for writing this essay.

This experience necessarily makes one reflect on the significance of some of Mises's arguments after so long a period. Much of the work now[46] inevitably sounds much less original or revolutionary than it did in its early years. It has in many ways become one of those 'classics' which one too often takes for granted and from which one expects to learn but little that is new. I must admit, however, that I was surprised at not only how much of it is still highly relevant to current disputes, but how many of its arguments, which I initially had only half accepted or regarded as exaggerated and one-sided, have since proved remarkably true. I still do not agree with all of it, nor do I believe that Mises would. He certainly was not one to expect that his followers receive his conclusions

[45][Jacques Kahane (1900–1969). -Ed.]
[46][I.e., in 1978. -Ed.]

uncritically and not progress beyond them. In all, though, I find that I differ rather less than I expected.

One of my differences is over a statement of Mises on basic philosophy over which I always felt a little uneasy. But only now can I articulate why I was uncomfortable with it. Mises asserts in this passage that liberalism "regards all social cooperation as an emanation of rationally recognised utility, in which all power is based on public opinion, and can undertake no course of action that would hinder the free decision of thinking men".[47] It is the first part of this statement only which I now think is wrong. The extreme rationalism of this passage, which as a child of his time he could not escape from, and which he perhaps never fully abandoned, now seems to me factually mistaken. It certainly was not rational insight into its general benefits that led to the spreading of the market economy. It seems to me that the thrust of Mises's teaching is to show that we have *not* adopted freedom because we understood what benefits it would bring: that we have *not* designed, and certainly were not intelligent enough to design, the order which we now have learned partly to understand long after we had plenty of opportunity to see how it worked. Man has *chosen* it only in the sense that he has learned to prefer something that already operated, and through greater understanding has been able to improve the conditions for its operation.[48]

It is greatly to Mises's credit that he largely emancipated himself from that rationalist-constructivist starting point, but that task is still to be completed. Mises as much as anybody has helped us to understand something which we have not designed.

There is another point about which the present-day reader should be cautioned. It is that half a century ago Mises could still speak of liberalism in a sense which is more or less the opposite of what the term means today in the United States, and increasingly elsewhere. He regarded himself as a liberal in the classical, nineteenth-century meaning of the term. But almost forty years have now elapsed since Joseph Schumpeter was constrained to say that in the United States

---

[47]Ludwig von Mises, *Socialism*, 1981 edition, op. cit., p. 418.

[48][This passage is a reference to Hayek's theory of spontaneous order. On this idea see Hayek's essay "The Results of Human Action but not of Human Design", in *Studies in Philosophy, Politics and Economics*, op. cit., pp. 96–105. -Ed.]

the enemies of liberty, "as a supreme, if unintended, compliment . . . have thought it wise to appropriate this label".[49]

In the epilogue,[50] which was written in the United States twenty-five years after the original work, Mises reveals his awareness of this and comments on the misleading use of the term "liberalism". An additional thirty years have only confirmed these comments, as they have confirmed the last part of the original text, "Destructionism". That shocked me for its inordinate pessimism when first I read it. Yet, on rereading it, I am awed rather by its foresight than by its pessimism. In fact, most readers today will find that *Socialism* has more immediate application to contemporary events than it had when it first appeared in its English version just over forty years ago.

Interventionism[51]

After the two great works with which Ludwig von Mises established his position as a leading thinker in the field of economic theory, *The Theory of Money and Credit* and *Socialism*, he concerned himself for a number of years predominantly with the problems of those intermediate forms between a pure market economy and a socialist order which were apparently in the process of being formed. In his main occupation as financial consultant (and chief scientific advisor) to the Vienna Chamber of Commerce, in addition to which he could devote only a little time to his teaching activity as *Privatdozent* in the University of Vienna, he had constantly to come to terms with the interventionism taught by the sociological-historical school of German economics, and had, in occupying himself with its literature,

---

[49][Joseph Schumpeter, *History of Economic Analysis*, op. cit., p. 394. Note that the quotation was actually published in 1954. Hayek may have seen the quotation earlier, or he may have misremembered the date. -Ed.]

[50][Mises's pamphlet *Planned Chaos* (Irvington, N.Y.: Foundation for Economic Education, 1947) was included as an Epilogue to the 1951 English edition of *Socialism* (New Haven, Conn.: Yale University Press) and reprinted in the 1981 edition for which Hayek wrote the present Foreword. -Ed.]

[51][Published as the Foreword to the 1976 edition of Ludwig von Mises, *Kritik des Interventionismus: Untersuchungen zur Wirtschaftspolitik und Wirtschaftsideologie der Gegenwart* and *Verstaatlichung des Kredits?* (Darmstadt: Wissenschaftliche Buchgesellschaft, 1976). Translated by W. W. Bartley, III. Mises's *Kritik des Interventionismus* was first published in 1929 (Jena: Gustav Fischer) and later translated by Hans Sennholz as *A Critique of Interventionism* (New Rochelle, N.Y.: Arlington House, 1977). -Ed.]

taken up an increasingly critical attitude toward the academic economics of the German-speaking area.[52] Among his German professional colleagues he really only became friendly with Max Weber,[53] with whom, during his Vienna summer semester of 1918, he entered into close association; apart from this, he esteemed only a very few, such as Heinrich Dietzel,[54] Passow,[55] Pohle,[56] Andreas Voigt,[57] Adolf Weber,[58] and Leopold von Wiese,[59] because of their courageous opposition to the dominant views, without however being able to learn much from them (although he valued very highly representatives of the previous generation who were at that time hardly appreciated, such as Thünen, Hermann, and Mangoldt[60]). He himself had, like most economists of recent generations, been led to his studies by the aspirations of *Sozialpolitik* and of the Fabians—as the views which still came to expression in his earliest works verify—but had then experienced a radical conversion to classical liberalism, chiefly in Böhm-Bawerk's seminar (in which he sat together with Schumpeter and the other leading members of the

[52][Of these German professors Mises says "[t]hey did not know the economic literature, had no conception of economic problems, and suspected every economist as an enemy of the state, as non-German, and as protagonists of business interests and of free trade. . . . They were dilettantes in everything they undertook." Ludwig von Mises, *Notes and Recollections*, op. cit., p. 102. -Ed.]

[53][Max Weber taught at the Universities of Freiburg, Heidelberg, and Munich and edited the leading academic journal in the social sciences, the *Archiv für Sozialwissenschaft und Sozialpolitik*. His *Protestant Ethic and the Spirit of Capitalism*, op. cit., first published in German in 1904–5, is of course one of the classics of sociology. Of him Mises states: "The early death of this genius was a serious blow for Germany. If Weber had lived longer, the German nation could today [1940] point to the example of this 'Aryan' whom Nazism could not bend." *Notes and Recollections*, op. cit., p. 104. -Ed.]

[54][Heinrich Dietzel (1857–1935) taught economics and philosophy at several German universities. His *Theoretische Sozialökonomie* (Leipzig: Winter, 1895), a theoretical comparison of capitalism and socialism, inspired the work of Walter Eucken (1891–1950) and the liberal Freiburg school. See Hayek's discussion of Eucken in this volume, Prologue to Part II. -Ed.]

[55][Richard Passow (1880–?) was Professor of Economics at the University of Göttingen in Prussia. -Ed.]

[56][Ludwig Pohle (1869–1926) taught at the Universities of Frankfurt and Leipzig and was editor of the *Zeitschrift für Sozialwissenschaft*. -Ed.]

[57][Andreas Heinrich Voigt (1860–?). -Ed.]

[58][Adolf Weber (1876–1963) was Professor at the University of Frankfurt. -Ed.]

[59][Leopold von Wiese (1876–1969) taught sociology at the Cologne University of Commerce and Business Administration, where he edited several journals and reestablished the German Sociological Association after the Second World War. -Ed.]

[60][Hans Karl Emil von Mangoldt (1824–1868) taught at the Universities of Göttingen and Freiburg. He is best known for his *Grundriß der Volkswirtschaftslehre* (Stuttgart: J. Maier, 1863). -Ed.]

third generation of the Austrian school), a classical liberalism to which from then on his work on economic policy was devoted. This is expressed occasionally already in his *Theory of Money and Credit*; it was then further developed in 1919 in his rich book on *Nation, State and Economy*,[61] a book which, however, due to the circumstances of the time, was almost completely overlooked. His position finds its first great development in 1922, in his *Socialism*. (The short, indeed rather hastily written, book *Liberalism*[62] was less successful.)

His *Critique of Interventionism* led to a controversy with his German professional colleagues, and the sharpness with which he turned against leading figures such as Werner Sombart,[63] Gustav Schmoller, Lujo Brentano,[64] and Heinrich Herkner,[65] and which aroused great offence at the time, can be reckoned today only as a great service on his part. I know that Mises had planned to include in the volume his essay on "Verstaatlichung des Kredits", which had also appeared in 1929 in volume 1 of the new *Zeitschrift für National-ökonomie*. This was prevented in that the editor of this journal had misplaced the manuscript and did not find it again until it was too late—as was usual at that time, and with Mises's clear handwriting quite possible, a real manuscript and hence the only copy.[66]

Mises ranks not only as an extremely sharp critic, but rather also as a pessimist who was, unfortunately, all too often right. Other contemporaries besides myself will also remember that occasion when, in September 1932, during a committee meeting of the *Verein für Sozialpolitik* in Bad Kissingen, a rather large group of

---

[61][Ludwig von Mises, *Nation, Staat und Wirtschaft: Beiträge zur Politik und Geschichte der Zeit*, op. cit. -Ed.]

[62][Ludwig von Mises, *Liberalismus* (Jena: Gustav Fischer, 1927), translated by Ralph Raico as *The Free and Prosperous Commonwealth: An Exposition of the Ideas of Classical Liberalism* (Princeton, N.J.: D. Van Nostrand, 1962). Later English editions were entitled *Liberalism: A Socio-Economic Exposition* (Kansas City, Mo.: Sheed Andrews and McMeel, 1978) and *Liberalism: In the Classical Tradition* (Irvington, N.Y.: Foundation for Economic Education, and San Francisco: Cobden Press, 1985). -Ed.]

[63][Werner Sombart (1863–1941) taught at the Universities of Breslau and Berlin. As a member of the younger historical school he is said to have "out-Schmollered Schmoller" in his attempts to combine economic and historical analysis (Joseph Schumpeter, *History of Economic Analysis*, op. cit., p. 817). -Ed.]

[64][Lujo Brentano (1844–1931) was Professor at several universities in Germany and Austria and a founder of the *Verein für Sozialpolitik*. His brother was the influential philosopher Franz Brentano. -Ed.]

[65][Heinrich Herkner (1863–1932) was a student of Brentano and a Professor at the Universities of Zurich and Berlin. -Ed.]

[66][This article by Mises was included in the book for which Hayek wrote the present essay. Mises's article was also translated by Louise Sommer and included in *Essays in European Economic Thought* (Princeton, N.J.: D. Van Nostrand, 1960). -Ed.]

professional colleagues was sitting together at tea in a garden, and Mises suddenly asked whether we were aware that we were sitting together for the last time. The remark at first aroused only astonishment and later laughter, when Mises explained that after twelve months Hitler would be in power. That appeared to the other members too improbable, but more than anything they asked why the *Verein für Sozialpolitik* should not meet again after Hitler had come to power. Of course it did not meet again until after the end of the Second World War![67]

Mises remained in Vienna until after Hitler's seizure of power in Germany and began during these years to occupy himself more and more with the philosophical and methodological foundations of the social sciences. He could however devote himself completely to scientific work for the first time only after 1934, when, at the age of fifty-three, he went to the Graduate Institute of International Studies in Geneva. In 1933 he was still able to publish in Germany a volume of essays entitled *Grundprobleme der Nationalökonomie*,[68] important essays on the "Procedures, Tasks, and Content of Economic and Social Theory". This was followed in 1940 by his last great book in German, *Nationalökonomie: Theorie des Handelns und Wirtschaftens* (later published in a revised edition in English as *Human Action*), which appeared in Geneva, but which at that time in Germany remained, unavoidably, practically unknown.

In 1940, Mises was, together with his wife, able to reach the United States by way of southern France, Spain, and Portugal. There, in New York, for more than thirty years, he engaged in extremely fruitful teaching and research. In addition to a completely revised English edition of *Nationalökonomie*, which appeared in 1949

---

[67][Of the *Verein für Sozialpolitik* (Association for Social Policy) Mises recalls that "[a]s an Austrian, as a *Privatdozent* without a chair, as a 'theorist', I always was an outsider in the Association. I was treated with the utmost courtesy, but the other members always looked upon me as an alien". *Notes and Recollections*, op. cit., p. 104. For a history of that organisation see Franz Boese, op. cit. -Ed.]

[68][Ludwig von Mises, *Grundprobleme der Nationalökonomie: Untersuchungen über Verfahren, Aufgaben und Inhalt der Wirtschafts- und Gesellschaftslehre* (Jena: Gustav Fischer, 1933), translated by George Reisman as *Epistemological Problems of Economics* (Princeton, N.J.: D. Van Nostrand, 1960; reprinted, New York and London: New York University Press, 1981). Hayek's review of the English edition is reprinted in this chapter, section following. -Ed.]

under the title *Human Action*, his book *Theory and History: An Interpretation of Social and Economic Evolution*,[69] is especially to be mentioned.

Epistemological Problems of Economics[70]

Though the work of a living and active author, this publication must be regarded as the belated issue of an English version of a classic. The book marks a decisive stage in the development of a system of ideas which has since become well known in the English-speaking world through its exposition in a comprehensive treatise. If Professor Mises's *Human Action* (published in English in 1949 and preceded by a German version of 1940) must be regarded as the definitive statement of his views, the distinctive features of his notions of the nature of social science have found their freshest expression in the present series of essays, dating from 1928 to 1933 and first issued together in German in the latter year—which also marked the end of his opportunity to publish in Germany. These statements show more clearly than the later exposition the immediate occasion which led to the particular form in which the author's views were formulated. But if his arguments are directed chiefly against conceptions then defended mainly by German writers, the reader should not be misled into believing that the argument applies only to them. Indeed, the sort of uncritical empiricism against which this book is mainly directed is today probably found more frequently and in a more naive form among American social scientists than anywhere else.

When these essays were first published they marked the transition of the author then mainly known for his theory of money and credit and his critical analysis of socialism from an economist in the narrow sense of the term to a general theorist and philosopher of society. Though he had not yet introduced the term "praxeology" (which he has since used in preference to "sociology") for the general theory of human action, all the chief elements of his later system are already present. With the exception of a brief last essay

[69][Ludwig von Mises, *Theory and History: An Interpretation of Social and Economic Evolution* (New Haven, Conn.: Yale University Press, 1957; reprinted, New Rochelle, N.Y.: Arlington House, 1969, and Auburn, Ala.: Ludwig von Mises Institute, 1985). -Ed.]

[70][Review of Mises's *Epistemological Problems of Economics* [1933], op. cit. Hayek published the review in the *Teachers College Record*, March 1964, pp. 556–557. -Ed.]

on a special problem in economic theory,[71] economics serves in this volume mainly as an illustration of the problems raised by any theoretical science of society. His critical efforts are directed against the view that theory can, as it were, be distilled from historical experience, and his main contention, now more familiar than when he first advanced it, is that logically the statements of theories are independent of any particular experience. He would presumably not deny that the applicability of a theory to particular circumstances depends on the presence or absence of facts which can be ascertained only by experience. If his emphasis on the a priori character of theory sometimes gives the impression of a more extreme position than the author in fact holds, it should be remembered that in a certain sense the abstract descriptions of a kind of pattern, as it is provided by logic and mathematics, is always deductive and analytical; only the assertion that this or that pattern will be found in certain circumstances can be tested empirically. Thus, on examination, the difference between the views which Professor Mises has long held and the modern 'hypothetico-deductive' interpretation of theoretical science (e.g., as stated by Karl Popper in 1935[72]) is comparatively small, while both are separated by a wide gulf from the naive empiricism which has long been predominant.[73]

It is true that with respect to social theory Professor Mises goes further in one point. But that we must know more about people with whom we communicate before we can do so than we need to know about any other objects about which we can communicate seems also fairly obvious and is bound to affect the nature of the data we can use for explanation in the two fields. Our capacity for 'comprehending' human action undoubtedly adds information which we can use in explaining it, data of a kind which we lack when dealing with inanimate objects; and in the third essay in the volume Professor Mises contributes much to distinguish this kind of compre-

[71][This is an essay on the problem of "Inconvertible (i.e., non-redeployable) Capital", written for a *Festschrift* for the Dutch economist C. A. Verrijn Stuart. -Ed.]

[72][Karl Popper, *Logik der Forschung, zur Erkenntnistheorie der modernen Naturwissenschaft* (Vienna: J. Springer, 1935), translated as *The Logic of Scientific Discovery* (London: Hutchinson, 1959; revised editions, 1968 and 1972). -Ed.]

[73][Mises himself would probably not agree with this statement. He wrote in 1962 that Popper's views, while appropriate for the natural sciences, "cannot refer in any way to the problems of the sciences of human action". For Mises on Popper see Mises's *The Ultimate Foundation of Economic Science* (Princeton, N.J.: D. Van Nostrand, 1962; reprinted, Kansas City, Mo.: Sheed Andrews and McMeel, 1978), pp. 69–70 and 119–120. -Ed.]

hension which can furnish the basis of a theory from the empathic 'understanding' sometimes claimed as the basis of explanation.

The translation, made less difficult by Professor Mises's limpid German than is often the case with works in this field, still deserves praise for its faithfulness and fluency. Since for the reviewer the appearance of the translation has been the occasion for re-reading the work after nearly thirty years, he may perhaps add that it has stood the test of time remarkably well.

Nationalökonomie[74]

It is always a matter of great interest, though sometimes a source of disappointment, when a scholar who in the course of many years has enriched many special parts of a science achieves a comprehensive survey of the whole field. Such an achievement must command even greater attention when a man whose interests have ranged so widely and whose views have been the cause of so much controversy as have those of Professor Mises presents a systematic exposition of his conclusions. Still more so if, as the title of the present work only partly indicates, it ranges from the most general philosophical problems raised by all scientific study of human action to the major problems of economic policy of our own day.

The reader who knows Professor Mises's earlier works on money, socialism, and the methods of the social sciences will find much that is already familiar if not accepted doctrine, particularly in the central part of the work, which deals with the problems of economic theory in the narrower sense. Yet even here there are major sections dealing with problems, as particularly the theory of interest, which Mises has never before explicitly discussed in his published

---

[74][Review of Mises's *Nationalökonomie: Theorie des Handelns und des Wirtschaftens* (Geneva: Editions Union, 1940), published in *The Economic Journal*, vol. 51, April 1941, pp. 124–127. Mises's *Human Action* (first published in 1949), a book more familiar to English-speaking readers, is a revised and expanded version of *Nationalökonomie*. Margit von Mises reports that upon Mises's arrival in the United States in 1940 "he was determined to revise *Nationalökonomie*, which was written for European conditions. He now wanted to write an enlarged new version in English for a wider audience and, hopefully, a wiser world. Therefore *Human Action* is not an English translation of *Nationalökonomie*, as many people think. Although it springs from the same basic philosophy my husband was always true to, it applies his principles to a wider field and his logic to all of life." Margit von Mises, Preface to limited 1985 reprint of the third revised edition of *Human Action* (Chicago: Henry Regnery, 1966). -Ed.]

work. It would be inappropriate in a brief review of a treatise which ranges over so wide a field to go into detail on a particular point. Only this much may be said, that on a first reading his development of the psychological element in the Böhm-Bawerkian theory, although highly illuminating in some respects, seems to the reviewer as a whole less convincing than most parts of the work.

On most of the other theoretical problems the exposition is largely a restatement, often more precise and more carefully phrased, of views expounded in the earlier works. Much of it sounds now far less revolutionary than it did twenty or thirty years ago—indeed, nothing is more instructive than a glance at the reviews which the earlier works of the author received (in this journal as well as elsewhere[75]) or proves better how much of his views which then were hotly attacked or even ridiculed have since become common property. In their new systematic setting his views assume in many ways new significance and certainly gain in impressiveness by their thorough consistency. Nor are the signs of a gradual but continuous and continuing evolution of the ideas of the author lacking. But it must be admitted that he seems to have been little affected by the general evolution of our subject during the period over which his work extends. What growth there is appears to be decidedly autonomous, and one even feels that the author, having been so often attacked for what later proved to be correct views, has developed a certain contempt for contemporary economics which has prevented him from deriving much advantage from it. This seems to be particularly true with regard to the more recent developments of the theory of competition—a field in which a more sympathetic treatment of other views might have made easier the understanding of the author's position.

To give in a review an adequate idea of the positive contributions in this theoretical part is difficult because they consist so largely in the consistent application of a single philosophy and the general perspective which this conveys. But as an instance of the happy generalisations to which this often leads we may quote the interesting treatment of the law of comparative costs, not in its special application to the theory of international trade, but in its most general form as the basis of the formation of societies. The *Ricar-*

---

[75][For example, the review of *Theorie des Geldes und der Umlaufsmittel* by John Maynard Keynes in the *Economic Journal*, vol. 24, September 1914, pp. 417–419 (see note 16 above); and E. Schwiedland's review of *Die Gemeinwirtschaft* in the *Economic Journal*, vol. 33, September 1923, pp. 406–408. -Ed.]

do'sche Vergesellschaftungsgesetz, as Professor Mises christens it in this most general form (a phrase which, I fear, is almost untranslatable), is thus given a well-deserved place at the head of the whole discussion of an exchange society, the very existence of which is based on it.[76]

The main interest of the book to most readers will, however, not lie in what—in accordance with the arrangement of the subject matter—we have called its central part,[77] but in the sections at the beginning and the end where Professor Mises deals with the most general methodological and philosophical problems of any science of society and with the applications to the problems of policy in our time. To the latter also applies to some extent what has been said about the central part. Much of it will be familiar to the readers of Professor Mises's earlier work, and the gain is largely one of systematic and condensed treatment of what before has been available only in a number of separate books and essays. Yet there were perhaps even greater opportunities for the author to fill in gaps, and the result is a really imposing unified system of a liberal social philosophy. It is here also, more than elsewhere, that the author's astounding knowledge of history as well as of the contemporary world helps most to illustrate his argument. And although the only *Weltanschauung* to which the author's views bear any resemblance is that of mid-nineteenth century liberalism, the reader must not be misled to believe that it is just a restatement of the *laissez-faire* views of that period. Similar as the conclusions may be in many points, the philosophy on which it is all based has moved as far as that of most other people, though in a very different direction.

The most original and at the same time probably the most controversial developments in Professor Mises's views will, however, be found in the opening parts of the book, in which he gives the outlines of a general theory of human action of which economic theory is a special part. In several of his earlier works he had

---

[76][In *Human Action* Mises renames the *Ricardo'sche Vergesellschaftungsgesetz* as "The Ricardian Law of Association", which he calls "a particular instance of the more universal law of association", the general principle showing how "the division of labour brings advantages to all who take part in it", even when one participant has fewer skills or resources than the others. (This principle, now called 'comparative advantage', is usually illustrated with the special case of international trade; Mises, by contrast, uses the example of a surgeon hiring a less-skilled assistant to clean his instruments.) The discussion is on pp. 127–133 of the German version; pp. 159–164 of the third (1966) edition of the English version. -Ed.]

[77][Pp. 188–628 of the German edition; pp. 200–688 of the 1966 English edition. -Ed.].

already consistently defended what he described as the a priori character of economic reasoning, and had criticised the importation of alien and inappropriate methods from the natural sciences. In the new volume he now proceeds to vindicate the autonomous character of the method of the social sciences by systematically building up a general theory of human action, or, as he now calls it (reviving an older French term), the science of "praxeology". Although I fear that even in its new form his argument will scarcely assuage the prejudices which any such attempt today arouses, it is certainly the most impressive and consistent argument in favour of this view yet put forward and, if it receives the attention it deserves, should form the starting point of much fruitful discussion. Although the reviewer would put many things differently, he must confess, at the risk of being condemned with Professor Mises as holding views conflicting with the whole trend of modern scientific development, that on the main point Professor Mises's lone voice seems to him considerably nearer the truth than the commonly accepted views.

A real discussion of any of the numerous interesting points raised by this work would require a long article rather than a brief review. Yet we cannot leave it without saying that, at least to the reviewer, there appears to be a width of view and an intellectual spaciousness about the whole book which are much more like that of an eighteenth-century philosopher than that of a modern specialist. And yet, or perhaps because of this, one feels throughout much nearer reality, and is constantly recalled from the discussion of technicalities to the consideration of the great problems of our time. Professor Mises accepts none of the ruling dogmas without close scrutiny, and perhaps sometimes even brushes away too lightly refinements which to him seem not to affect the much wider issues of his social philosophy. To the many who will disagree with most of it, this will no doubt prove a profoundly irritating book, but not one which they can afford to disregard, however much they may feel that parts of it are not *au courant* with the latest refinements of mathematical analysis in which they are wont to wallow.

LUDWIG VON MISES (1881–1973)

Notes and Recollections[78]

Although without a doubt one of the most important economists of his generation, in a certain sense Ludwig Mises remained an outsider in the academic world until the end of his unusually long scholarly career—certainly within the German-speaking world, but also during the last third of his life, when in the United States he raised a larger circle of students. Before this his strong immediate influence had essentially been restricted to his Viennese *Privatseminar*, whose members for the most part only became attracted to him once they had completed their original studies.

If it would not have unduly delayed the publication of these memoirs found among his papers, I would have welcomed the opportunity to analyse the reasons for this curious neglect of one of the most original thinkers of our time in the field of economics and social philosophy. But in part the fragmentary autobiography he left provides itself the answer. The reasons why he never acquired a chair at a German-speaking university during the 1920s or before 1933, while numerous and often indisputably highly unimportant persons did, were certainly personal. His appointment would have been beneficial for every university. Yet the instinctive feeling of the professors that he would not quite fit into their circle was not entirely wrong. Even though his knowledge of the subject surpassed that of most occupants of professorial chairs, he was nonetheless never a real specialist. When in the realm of the social sciences I look for similar figures in the history of thought, I do not find them among the professors, not even in Adam Smith; instead, he must be compared to thinkers like Voltaire or Montesquieu, Tocqueville and John Stuart Mill. This is an impression that has by no means been reached only in retrospect. But when more than fifty years ago I tried to explain Mises's position in pretty much the same words to Wesley Clair Mitchell in New York, I only encountered—perhaps understandably—a politely ironic scepticism.

Essential to his work is a global interpretation of social development, and in contrast to the few comparable contemporaries such as

[78][This essay was written by Hayek in 1977 and published as the introduction to Ludwig von Mises, *Erinnerungen von Ludwig von Mises* (Stuttgart and New York: Gustav Fischer, 1978), pp. xi–xvi. The present translation is a slightly altered version of one prepared by Hans-Hermann Hoppe and was published in the *Austrian Economics Newsletter*, vol. 10, no. 1, Fall 1988, pp. 1–3. *Erinnerungen* was originally published posthumously in an English translation by Hans F. Sennholz as *Ludwig von Mises, Notes and Recollections*, op. cit. -Ed.]

Max Weber, with whom he was connected by a rare mutual respect, in this Mises had the advantage of a genuine knowledge of economic theory.

The following memoirs[79] say much more about his development, position, and views than I know or could tell. I can only attempt here to supplement or confirm information regarding the ten years of his time in Vienna during which I was closely associated with him. I came to him rather characteristically not as a student, but as a fresh Doctor of Law and a civil servant, subordinate to him, at one of those temporary special institutions that had been created to execute the provisions of the peace treaty of St. Germain. The letter of recommendation by my university teacher Friedrich von Wieser,[80] who described me as a highly promising young economist, was met by Mises with a smile and the remark that he had never seen me in his lectures. However, when he found my interest confirmed and my knowledge satisfactory, he helped me in every regard and contributed much to make my lengthier visit to the United States possible (before the time of the Rockefeller fellowship), to which I owe a great deal.[81] But although I saw him during the first years daily in an official capacity, I had no idea that he was preparing his great book on *Socialism*, which upon its publication in 1922 influenced me decisively.

Only after I returned from America in the summer of 1924 was I admitted to that circle which already existed for some time and through which Mises's scholarly work in Vienna mainly exerted its influence. This 'Mises seminar', as we all called the biweekly nightly discussions in his office, is described in his memoirs in detail, even though Mises does not mention the hardly less important regular continuations of the discussions of the official part, until late at night, in a Viennese coffeehouse. As he correctly describes, these were not instructional meetings, but discussions presided over by an older friend whose views were by no means shared by all members. Strictly speaking, only Fritz Machlup was originally Mises's student. As regards the others, of the regular members only Richard Strigl,[82] Gottfried Haberler, Oskar Morgenstern, Helene Lieser,[83] and Martha

---

[79][I.e., the text of *Erinnerungen von Ludwig von Mises*, op. cit. -Ed.]

[80][On Wieser see this volume, chapter 3. -Ed.]

[81][This is Hayek's visit to the United States in 1923–24, described in more detail in this volume, Prologue to Part I. -Ed.]

[82][On Strigl see this volume, chapter 6. -Ed.]

[83][Helene Lieser was later secretary of the International Economic Association in Paris. -Ed.]

Stefanie Braun[84] were specialists in economics. Ewald Schams[85] and Leo Schönfeld, who belonged to the same highly gifted but early deceased intermediate generation as Richard Strigl, were, to my knowledge, never regular participants in the Mises Seminar. But sociologists like Alfred Schutz, philosophers like Felix Kaufmann and historians like Friedrich Engel-Jánosi[86] were equally active in the discussions, which frequently dealt with the problems of the methods of the social sciences, but rarely with special problems of economic theory (except those of the subjective theory of value). Questions of economic policy, however, were discussed often, and always from the angle of the influence of different social philosophies upon it.[87]

All this seemed to be the rare mental distraction of a man, who, during the day, was fully occupied with urgent political and economic problems, and who was better informed about daily politics, modern history, and general ideological developments than most others. What he was working on even I who officially saw him almost daily during those years did not know; he never spoke about it. We could even less imagine when he would actually write his works. I only knew from his secretary that from time to time he had a text written in his distinctively clear handwriting typed. But many of his works existed only in such handwritings until publication, and an important article was considered lost for a long time, until it finally resurfaced among the papers of a journal editor. No one knew anything regarding his private work methods until his marriage. He did not speak about his literary activity until he had completed a work. Though he knew that I was most willing on occasion to help him, he only asked me once, when I mentioned that I wanted to consult a work on the canonists in the library, to look up a quote in this work. He never had, at least in Vienna, a scholarly assistant.

The problems with which he concerned himself were mostly problems regarding which he considered the prevailing opinion false. The reader of the following book[88] might gain the impression that he was prejudiced against the German social sciences as such.

---

[84][Martha Stephanie Braun, later Browne, taught at Brooklyn College and New York University. -Ed.]

[85][On Schams see this volume, chapter 6. -Ed.]

[86][Friedrich Engel-Jánosi (1893–1978). -Ed.]

[87][Some of the participants in the Mises seminar share their recollections in the *Wirtschaftspolitische Blätter*, vol. 4, April 1981. -Ed.]

[88][I.e., Mises's *Erinnerungen*. -Ed.]

This was definitely not the case, even though in the course of time he developed a certain understandable irritation. But he valued the great early German theoreticians like Thünen, Hermann, Mangoldt, or Gossen more highly than most of his colleagues, and knew them better. Also, among his contemporaries he valued a few similarly isolated figures such as Dietzel, Pohle, Adolf Weber, and Passow, as well as the sociologist Leopold von Wiese and, above all, Max Weber, with whom a close scholarly relationship had been formed during Weber's short teaching activity in Vienna in the spring of 1918 which could have meant a great deal if Weber had not died so soon. But in general there can be no doubt that he had nothing but contempt for the majority of the professors who, occupying the chairs of the German universities, pretended to teach theoretical economics. Mises does not exaggerate in his description of the teachings of economics as espoused by the historical school. Just how far the level of theoretical thinking in Germany had sunk is indicated by the fact that it needed the simplifications and coarseness of the—herein certainly meritorious—Swede Gustav Cassel in order to again find an audience for theory in Germany. Notwithstanding his exquisite politeness in society and his generally great self-control (he could also occasionally explode), Mises was not the man to successfully hide his contempt.

This drove him to increased isolation among professional economists generally as well as among those Viennese circles with which he had scholarly and professional contacts. He became estranged from his cohorts and fellow students when he turned away from the advancing ideas of social policy. Twenty-five years later I could still feel the sensation and anger his seemingly sudden break with the dominating ideals of the academic youth of the first few years of the century had caused, when his fellow student F. X. Weiss (the editor of the shorter writings of Böhm-Bawerk) told me about the event with unconcealed indignation, obviously in order to prevent me from a similar betrayal of 'social' values and an all-too-great sympathy for an 'outlived' liberalism.

If Carl Menger had not aged relatively early and Böhm-Bawerk had not died so young, Mises probably would have found support among them. But the only survivor of the older Austrian school, my revered teacher Friedrich von Wieser, was himself more of a Fabian; proud, as he believed, to have provided a scientific justification for progressive income taxation with his development of the theory of marginal utility.

Mises's return to classical liberalism was not only a reaction to a dominating trend. He completely lacked the adaptability of his brilliant seminar fellow Joseph Schumpeter,[89] who always quickly accommodated current intellectual fashions, as well as Schumpeter's joy in *épater le bourgeois*. In fact, it appeared to me as if these two most important representatives of the third generation of leading Austrian economists (one can hardly consider Schumpeter a member of the Austrian school in the narrower sense), despite all mutual intellectual respect, both got on each other's nerves.

In today's world Mises and his students are regarded as the representatives of the Austrian school, and justifiably so, although he represents only one of the branches into which Menger's theories had already been divided by his students, the close personal friends Eugen von Böhm-Bawerk and Friedrich von Wieser. I only admit this with some hesitation, because I had expected much of the Wieser tradition that Wieser's successor Hans Mayer attempted to advance. These expectations have not yet been fulfilled, even though that tradition may yet prove more fruitful than it has been so far. Today's active Austrian school, almost exclusively in the United States, is really the followers of Mises, based on the tradition of Böhm-Bawerk, while the man in whom Wieser had set such great hopes and who had succeeded him in his chair[90] has never really fulfilled his promise.[91]

Because he never occupied a regular chair in his field in the German-speaking world and had to devote most of his time to other than scholarly activities until his late fifties, Mises remained an outsider in academia. Other reasons contributed to isolating him in his position in public life and as a representative of a great social-philosophical project. A Jewish intellectual who advocated socialist ideas had his respected place in the Vienna of the first third of this century, a place that was accorded to him as a matter of course. Likewise, the Jewish banker or businessman who (bad enough!) defended capitalism had his natural rights. But a Jewish intellectual who justified capitalism appeared to most as some sort of monstrosity, something unnatural, which could not be categorised and with which one did not know how to deal. His undisputed knowledge of the subject was impressive, and one could not avoid consulting him in critical economic situations, but rarely was his advice understood and followed. Mostly he was regarded as somewhat of an eccentric

---

[89][On Schumpeter see this volume, chapter 5. -Ed.]

[90][I.e., Hans Mayer. -Ed.]

[91][Yet Hayek underestimates here his own influence on the modern Austrian school, an influence not entirely congruent with that of Mises. On this point see the Introduction to this volume. -Ed.]

whose 'old-fashioned' ideas were impracticable 'today'. That he himself had constructed, in long years of hard work, his own social philosophy was only understood by a very few and perhaps could not be understood by distant observers until 1940, when in his *Nationalökonomie* he presented his system of ideas in its entirety for the first time, but could no longer reach readers in Germany and Austria.[92] Apart from the small circle of young theoreticians who met at his office and some highly gifted friends in the business world who were similarly concerned about the future and who are mentioned in [his memoirs], he only encountered genuine understanding among occasional foreign visitors like the Frankfurt banker Albert Hahn, whose work in monetary theory he smiled at, however, as an excess of youth.

Yet he did not always make it easy for them. The arguments by which he supported his unpopular views were not always completely conclusive, even though some reflection could have shown that he was right. But when he was convinced of his conclusions and had presented them in clear and plain language—a gift that he possessed to a high degree—he believed that this would also have to convince others and only prejudice and stubbornness prevented understanding. For too long he had lacked the opportunity to discuss problems with intellectual equals who shared his basic moral convictions, to see how even small differences in one's implicit assumptions can lead to different results. This manifested itself in a certain impatience that easily suspected an unwillingness to understand, whereas an honest misunderstanding of his arguments was the case.

I must admit that often I myself did not initially think his arguments were completely convincing and only slowly learned that he was mostly right and that, after some reflection, a justification could be found that he had not made explicit. And today, considering the kind of battle that he had to lead, I also understand that he was driven to certain exaggerations, like that of the a priori character of economic theory, where I could not follow him.

For Mises's friends of his later years, after his marriage and the success of his American activity had softened him, the sharp outbursts in [his] memoirs, written at the time of his greatest bitterness and hopelessness, might come as a shock.[93] But the Mises who

[92][Mises was then Visiting Professor of International Economic Relations at the Graduate Institute of International Studies in Geneva. -Ed.]

[93][Mises's *Erinnerungen* was written in late 1940, shortly after his arrival in the United States after fleeing Europe. -Ed.]

speaks from the following pages is without question the Mises we knew from the Vienna of the 1920s, of course without the tactful reservation that he invariably displayed in oral expression, but the honest and open expression of what he felt and thought. To a certain extent this may explain his neglect, even though it does not excuse it. We, who knew him better, were at times outraged, of course, that he did not get a chair, yet we were not really surprised. He had too much to criticise about the representatives of the profession into which he was seeking entrance to appear acceptable to them. And he fought against an intellectual wave which is now subsiding, not least because of his efforts, but which was much too powerful then for one individual to successfully resist.

That they had one of the great thinkers of our time in their midst, the Viennese have never understood.[94]

[94][For complete bibliographies of Mises's writings, see *Erinnerungen von Ludwig von Mises*, op. cit., pp. 92–109; David Gordon, *Ludwig von Mises: An Annotated Bibliography* (Auburn, Ala.: Ludwig von Mises Institute, 1988); and Bettina Bien Greaves, "The Contributions of Ludwig von Mises in the Fields of Money, Credit and Banking", in Mises's *On the Manipulation of Money and Credit*, ed. Percy L. Greaves, Jr. (Dobbs Ferry, N.Y.: Free Market Books, 1978), pp. 281–288, a translation of *Geldwertstabilisierung und Konjunkturpolitik* and two other essays. -Ed.]

FIVE

JOSEPH SCHUMPETER
(1883–1950)

Methodological Individualism[1]

In 1908, when Joseph Schumpeter at the age of twenty-five published his *Wesen und Hauptinhalt der theoretischen Nationalökonomie*, it attracted much attention by the brilliance of its exposition. Moreover, though he had been trained at the University of Vienna and had been a leading member of the famous seminar of Eugen von Böhm-Bawerk, he had also absorbed the teaching of Léon Walras, who had received little notice by the Austrians and had adopted the positivist approach to science expounded by the Austrian physicist Ernst Mach.[2] In the course of time he moved further away from the characteristic tenets of the Austrian school so that it became increasingly doubtful later whether he could still be counted as a member of that group.

Schumpeter was very much a 'master of his subject', in contrast to the 'puzzlers' or 'muddlers' who follow their own distinct ideas;[3] he also showed a strong receptivity to the dominant opinions in his environment and the prevailing fashion of his generation. Nowhere does this show more clearly than in the still entirely Mengerian chapter of his early book, now translated into English for the first time and regarded as the classic exposition of a view which he later abandoned. Many of his students will be surprised to learn that the enthusiast for macroeconomics and co-founder of the econometrics movement had once given one of the most explicit expositions of the Austrian school's 'methodological individualism'. He even

---

[1][Published as the Preface to Joseph Schumpeter, *Methodological Individualism* (Brussels: Institutum Europaeum, 1980), an English translation of an excerpt from Schumpeter's *Das Wesen und der Hauptinhalt der theoretischen Nationalökonomie* (Leipzig: Duncker & Humblot, 1908). -Ed.]

[2][See Hayek's discussion of Mach's influence in this volume, chapter 7. -Ed.]

[3][On 'masters of their subjects' and 'puzzlers' see Hayek's essay "Two Types of Mind", in *The Trend of Economic Thinking*, being vol. 3 of *The Collected Works of F. A. Hayek*. -Ed.]

appears to have named the principle and condemned the use of statistical aggregates as not belonging to economic theory.

That this first book of his was never translated is, I believe, due to his understandable reluctance to see a work distributed which, in part, expounded views in which he no longer believed. His reluctance to keep his brilliant first book in print, much less having it translated, can probably be explained by his awareness that his own distinct opinions emerged only in his second book on the *Theorie der wirtschaftlichen Entwicklung*,[4] which came out four years after the first. Though the author may later no longer have been prepared to defend the ideas of his first work, they are certainly essential enough to the understanding of the development of economic theory. Indeed Schumpeter made a contribution to the tradition of the Austrian school which is sufficiently original to be made available to a wider public.

History of Economic Analysis[5]

Although there is no lack of histories of economics, there are few good ones, and most of the latter are no more than sketches. It is therefore a real tragedy that it was not given to the late Professor Schumpeter to complete an achievement for which he had almost

[4][Joseph Schumpeter, *Theorie der wirtschaftlichen Entwicklung* (*Theory of Economic Development*), op. cit. -Ed.]

[5][Published as "Schumpeter on the History of Economics", a review of Schumpeter, *History of Economic Analysis*, op. cit., in *Studies in Philosophy, Politics and Economics*, op. cit., pp. 339–341. An abridged version was published in *The Freeman*, November 1954, p. 60. Thirty-five years after its publication the *History of Economic Analysis* is still the standard work on its subject. Schumpeter's volume is additionally important and of special interest to Austrians, however, for its role in bringing about a shift of emphasis in the historiography of economic thought. The older history, which placed the beginnings of economics with Adam Smith and the classical school, was challenged in the mid-1950s by three sources: Schumpeter's book; Raymond de Roover's "Scholastic Economics: Survival and Influence from the Sixteenth Century to Adam Smith", *Quarterly Journal of Economics*, vol. 69, May 1955, pp. 161–190, reprinted in his *Business, Banking, and Economic Thought*, op. cit., pp. 306–335; and Emil Kauder's "Genesis of the Marginal Utility Theory from the End of the Eighteenth Century", *Economic Journal*, vol. 63, September 1953, pp. 638–650. These works stimulated a revival of interest in scholastic economic thought, a tradition ignored by the British classical political economists but one in which the early Austrians were deeply steeped. See also the references in Murray N. Rothbard, "New Light on the Prehistory of the Austrian School", in Edwin G. Dolan, ed., *The Foundations of Modern Austrian Economics* (Kansas City, Mo.: Sheed & Ward, 1976), pp. 52–74. -Ed.]

unique qualifications. Forty years ago, after he had already established a reputation as an original theorist, he had published a brilliant outline of the development of economic theory[6] which many regarded as the best available, but with which he himself was so little satisfied that he would not permit the issue of an English translation of the original German version. Some nine or ten years before his death in 1950 he had started on a revision of this early work which gradually grew into a monumental achievement of scholarship which has no equal in its field and on which he was still engaged at the time of his death. He had then covered almost the entire field he had intended to treat and there are few important gaps in the version now published. But much was still in the form of first drafts and all would probably have undergone very careful revision. The whole is evidently based on a systematic examination of a range of original literature which is truly amazing in its extent; and it shows an encyclopaedic knowledge far beyond the confines of economics which is hardly less impressive. If, as no doubt the author had intended, in the course of the revision the secondary literature had been as fully worked in as the originals had already been, we would have got such a handbook of the history of economics as one would not expect from a single man but only from a committee of specialists. As it was, the author's widow, herself a distinguished economist in her own right,[7] undertook to get the manuscript ready for publication, intent to preserve it as closely as possible as her husband had left it. But Mrs. Schumpeter too died before the task was completed and various friends and pupils of the author appear to have prepared the volume for the press.

There are inevitably many details on which other students will disagree with the author, but as one reads on, all such occasional misgivings pale into insignificance against the impressive nature of the general picture which emerges. In a short review, at any rate, it would not be appropriate to say more about any minor faults one could find and most of which the author himself would have

---

[6][Joseph Schumpeter, *Epochen der Dogmen- und Methodengeschichte* (Tübingen: J. C. B. Mohr (Paul Siebeck), 1914), published as part of Max Weber's *Grundriß der Sozialökonomik*. English translation by R. Aris, *Economic Doctrine and Method* (New York: Oxford University Press, 1954). -Ed.]

[7][Elizabeth Boody Schumpeter published *English Overseas Trade Statistics, 1697–1808* (Oxford: Clarendon Press, 1960) and edited *The Industrialisation of Japan and Manchuko, 1930–1940* (New York: Macmillan, 1940). -Ed.]

remedied if he had lived. We shall attempt no more than to indicate what he aimed at and has so largely achieved.

The book is designed as a history of the science of economics in the strict sense, not of the wider field of political economy.[8] But as, more than perhaps in the case of any other science, the development of economics is hardly intelligible without the political, sociological and intellectual currents which determined the direction of interests at different times, we are throughout given masterly sketches of this background which make the book much more than a history of merely one branch of knowledge. And although Schumpeter was a man of strong and highly individual and sometimes unpopular views, the manner in which he succeeds on the whole to keep his personal prejudices out is wholly admirable. Indeed, his endeavour to do justice to any genuine effort which in the past had not been given sufficient credit, and to find justification even for the less plausible arguments in the circumstances of the time, goes surprisingly far. To those who know his general theoretical views it will be no surprise to find that Quesnay, Cournot, and Walras ("so far as pure theory is concerned . . . the greatest of all economists") are his heroes, and that he rates Adam Smith, Ricardo, and even Marshall decidedly lower than is usual.[9] Most of this is just and all of it can be defended with good argument. A great merit is the proper recognition of the great role played by men like Cantillon,[10] Senior,[11] and Böhm-Bawerk, and

[8][Hayek is presumably following the nomenclature of Lionel Robbins here. In his famous *Essay on the Nature and Significance of Economic Science* (second edition, London: Macmillan, 1935) Robbins defines economics as "the science which studies human behaviour as a relationship between ends and scarce means which have alternative uses" (p. 16), reserving the older term 'political economy' for the applied topics covered in his later work *The Economic Basis of Class Conflict and Other Essays in Political Economy* (London: Macmillan, 1939): monopoly, protectionism, planning, government fiscal policy, and the like. Schumpeter himself includes economic history, statistics, and 'theory' as parts of "Economic Analysis", excluding applied fields and what he calls "Economic Sociology" (*History of Economic Analysis*, op. cit., chapter 2). -Ed.]

[9][François Quesnay (1694–1774) was a French lawyer and physician and author of the *Tableau Économique* [1758], which compared the flow of wealth through a nation to the circulation of blood within the body. Indeed, Schumpeter's *Theory of Economic Development*, op. cit., begins with "The Circular Flow of Economic Life". David Ricardo (1772–1823) was a financier and protegé of James Mill, and author of *On the Principles of Political Economy and Taxation* [1817], reprinted as vol. 1 of *The Works and Correspondence of David Ricardo* (Cambridge: Cambridge University Press, for the Royal Economic Society, 1951–55). -Ed.]

[10][Richard Cantillon (c. 1680–1734) was an Irish Banker whose *Essai sur la nature du commerce en général* appeared only posthumously in 1755. See Hayek's essay on Cantillon in *The Trend of Economic Thinking*, op. cit. On Cantillon as a 'proto-Austrian'

compared with this the occasional cavalier treatment of some secondary yet still not unimportant figures like Robert Torrens[12] is a minor matter. Even the great attention given to Karl Marx is probably justified, if not by any important contribution he made to economic theory, yet by the influence he has exercised and by his early efforts to work sociological considerations into economic analysis—which is evidently the aspect of his work which appealed to Schumpeter. Indeed the fact that Schumpeter himself was at times almost as much interested in sociology as in pure economics has contributed a good deal to the character of this last work, some parts of which are fascinating essays in the sociology of science. They are stimulating even where one cannot entirely agree. Readers of this journal will probably be irritated by the unnecessary if not contemptuous manner in which Schumpeter usually refers to nineteenth-century liberalism, individualism, and *laissez faire*. But they should remember that it comes from an author who knew as well as anybody that capitalist evolution "tends to peter out because the modern state may crush or paralyse its motive forces", yet who also seems to have had an irrepressible urge to *épater les bourgeois*.

With its over 1,200 closely printed pages this is not likely to be a popular book, though it is so well written that it should give pleasure not only to the specialists. This is not to say that it is an easy book, or suitable for the kindergarten atmosphere in which so much college education proceeds. Nor is it in every respect a 'safe' book: The orthodox of any description must be prepared for constant shocks, and the literal-minded will miss much that is said only between the lines. But for the mature and thoughtful reader, whether he be an economic theorist or merely generally interested in the growth of ideas on human affairs, it should be an invaluable source of instruction. And nobody should profit more from it than the economists of the younger generation: as in other subjects the increasing technicality of the theory carries with it the danger of a

see Robert F. Hébert, "Was Richard Cantillon an Austrian Economist?", *Journal of Libertarian Studies*, vol. 7, no. 2, Fall 1985, and the other essays in that number of that journal. -Ed.]

[11][Nassau William Senior (1790–1864) was Professor of Political Economy at Oxford University. His views on economic method are quite similar to those later developed by Mises; on this see Murray N. Rothbard, "In Defense of 'Extreme Apriorism'", *Southern Economic Journal*, vol. 23, January 1957, pp. 314–320, esp. note 2 and the references cited therein. -Ed.]

[12][Robert Torrens (1780–1864) was a leader of the English currency school. See Hayek's essay "The Dispute Beteween the Currency School and the Banking School, 1821–1848", chapter 12 of *The Trend of Economic Thinking*, op. cit. -Ed.]

narrow specialism which is peculiarly harmful in this field. I know of no better antidote than this book to the belief, which seems to dominate some of the younger men, that nothing that happened before 1936[13] can be of importance to them, and no work better suited to show what they ought to know if they are to be not merely economists but cultivated persons competent to use their technical knowledge in a complex world. And they will also find in the later part of the book an—alas incomplete—survey of the contemporary state of economics which, at least to one reader, seems much more stimulating and satisfactory than the various collective efforts which have in recent years been directed to the same end.

[13][I.e., the publication of John Maynard Keynes's *General Theory of Employment, Interest and Money*, op. cit. -Ed.]

SIX

EWALD SCHAMS (1899–1955)
AND RICHARD VON STRIGL (1891–1942)

Ewald Schams[1]

Ewald Schams was one of the three members of an intermediate generation of Viennese economists, of whom only Richard Strigl was an academic by profession, but who all exerted a substantial influence within the Viennese circle during the 1920s and 1930s. While the third of these men, Leo Schönfeld (later Leo Illy) hardly had any personal contact with the other members of this circle, Ewald Schams was an active and highly respected participant in the discussions, in which he intervened with the full weight to which his obvious familiarity with all problems of economic theory entitled him. The three men were midway in age between the third generation of the Austrian school, namely Mises, Schumpeter, Hans Mayer, F. X. WeSS, and several others (coming after Carl Menger as the founder of the Austrian school and Eugen von Böhm-Bawerk and Friedrich von Wieser and their contemporaries as the second generation) and the generation that we were inclined to designate as the fourth, in which I was slightly older than my colleagues Gottfried Haberler, Fritz Machlup, Oskar Morgenstern, and Paul Rosenstein-Rodan. Schams differed from his contemporaries especially in that he had received his education at the University of Graz under Schumpeter and was thus in fact Schumpeter's only Austrian disciple; he had therefore been introduced from the very beginning to the ideas of both the Lausanne and the Austrian school. As a professional civil servant, he had no contact with academic life and only came to lectures and organised discussions in our circle. He was a man of great discipline and few words, whose erect, military bearing and elegance set him somewhat apart from the livelier younger members, as did his other interests and background, about

---

[1][Written in 1980 in German as the preface to Ewald Schams, *Gesammelte Aufsätze* (Munich: Philosophia Verlag, forthcoming). Translated by Dr. Grete Heinz. -Ed.]

which we knew very little. He was a remarkable figure, who was greatly respected in the Economic Society[2] and, if I remember rightly, in the seminar of Professor Mises, as well for his unusual knowledge not only of economic theory but also of philosophy and history.

To the best of my knowledge he never undertook a major scholarly work. His essays are small, finely polished jewels that were the product of extremely conscientious work, concerned at first mainly with contemporary writings.[3] When a Rockefeller fellowship later gave him the opportunity to work for a longer period in Paris and perhaps also in Italy, he became a passionate and very selective book collector and grew increasingly interested in the history of economic theory. It so happened that at the beginning of his stay in Paris I was in a position to introduce him to antiquarian specialists in this field with whom I had become acquainted. It was only after his death that I found out how effectively he had utilised this opportunity. I was able to acquire his small but exquisite special collection of French eighteenth-century economic works from his widow, and this collection has now been taken over by the University of Salzburg's School of Jurisprudence and Political Science as part of my own library.

Schams's growing interest in the history of economic theory was primarily an outgrowth of his interest in economic methodology.[4] His strength in this area was less in philosophical questions than in his familiarity with the different theoretical schools, particularly of German- and French-language authors. He was of course familiar with English writings, but on the whole he devoted himself to continental developments. After the emigration of most of his colleagues[5] he seems to have been quite isolated. There is a large hiatus between his articles from the late 1920s and early 1930s and

[2][I.e., the *Nationalökonomische Gesellschaft.* -Ed.]

[3][For example, his essay on Gustav Cassel, "Die Casselschen Gleichungen und die mathematische Wirtschaftstheorie", *Jahrbücher für Nationalökonomie und Statistik,* third series, vol. 72, 1927, and his work in the historiography of economic thought, "Die Anfänge lehrgeschichtlicher Betrachtungsweise in der Nationalökonomie", *Zeitschrift für Nationalökonomie,* vol. 3, 1931, and "Eine Bibliographie der allgemeinen Lehrgeschichten der Nationalökonomie", *ibid.,* vol. 5, 1933, the latter co-authored with Oskar Morgenstern. -Ed.]

[4][See Schams's "Die zweite Nationalökonomie", *Archiv für Sozialpolitik,* vol. 64, 1930, and his "Wirtschaftslogik", Schmoller's *Jahrbuch für Gesetzgebung, Verwaltung und Volkswirtschaft im Deutschen Reich,* vol. 58, 1934. -Ed.]

[5][On this emigration see Earlene Craver, "The Emigration of the Austrian Economists", op. cit., pp. 1–32, and this volume, Prologue to Part I. -Ed.]

his major 1950 essay, which was probably written much earlier. We have no way of knowing for how many years he was actively concerned with economic theory. His widow informs me that no additional manuscripts have turned up in his literary estate. Those of us who left Vienna did not meet him again after the war. But a new look into his old writings convinced me that there is still a great deal that we can learn from him.

Richard von Strigl[6]

The death is reported from Vienna of Professor Richard von Strigl, the last member of the group of younger Austrian economists who had remained at the original home of the school. Still in his early fifties at the time of his death, he was probably the youngest of the men who had still belonged to Eugen von Böhm-Bawerk's famous seminar; and to his immediate juniors who came to the university after the last war[7] he represented the closest link with that influential tradition. Though for many years an eminently successful teacher, his academic work, as was true of so many of his colleagues, was done in the time he could spare from his main occupation as an official of the Unemployment Insurance Board of Vienna, in which he rose to a high position. Most of the young economists who graduated in Vienna in the years immediately preceding the present war owed more to him than to any other teacher; and it was because he gave more of his time to the *Hochschule für Welthandel* than to the university that during those years the former tended to become the more important center for the teaching of economics.

Of his works, the first book which he published in 1923, *Die ökonomischen Kategorien und die Organisation der Wirtschaft*,[8] is a subtle methodological study which exercised considerable influence and gained its author at once a wide reputation. It was followed by a less-known but in its kind equally valuable volume on *Angewandte*

---

[6][Published as "Richard von Strigl" in *The Economic Journal*, vol. 54, June–September 1944, pp. 284–286. -Ed.]

[7][I.e., the First World War. -Ed.]

[8]Richard von Strigl, *Die ökonomischen Kategorien und die Organisation der Wirtschaft* (Jena: Gustav Fischer, 1923).

Lohntheorie,[9] which broke new ground in a different direction. A series of theoretical articles published over a period of years prepared the volume on *Kapital und Produktion*,[10] notable mainly for the simplicity and clarity of exposition of a notoriously difficult subject. It was followed by *Einführung in die Grundlagen der Nationalökonomie*,[11] which, though Strigl denied himself the use of some of the more recently introduced theoretical tools, was probably the best modern introduction to economic theory available in German. So far as we know, it was his last book.

To those who last saw Strigl before the present war and had not heard of him since, the news of his death comes as a shock. It is a great loss to his friends and colleagues, among whom he was appreciated as much for his intellectual gifts as for his character; and who hoped that his best work was yet to come when he should at last be relieved from his official duties. But it is his students who will most feel the loss. One of them, Dr. J. Steindl, now of the Oxford Institute of Statistics, writes: "Bred in the tradition of liberal thought, which permeated his teaching, he was, in the midst of the reactionary influence of Austrian academic life, an attraction to those who were repelled by the mystic and hysterical nationalism rampant in those years. Even those whom his teaching could not always convince could not fail to recognise the immense superiority of the tradition which he represented over the ideologies which now bedevil 'Greater Germany'. His personality contributed to this: Humane and cultured, a good pedagogue and a great friend to his pupils, he had the mark of a great teacher who is able to transmit permanent values which stretch beyond the errors of his time. There are few of his pupils or of the foreign economists who would visit Vienna and sojourn in his circle of those days who did not very much like him. Since the invasion of Austria he has been silent; we have not heard of any further publication of his. This is not surprising to those who knew him, and it is probably not only due to an illness which befell him in 1939. The spectacle of the

---

[9]Richard von Strigl, *Angewandte Lohntheorie: Untersuchungen über die wirtschaftlichen Grundlagen der Sozialpolitik*, in vol. 9 of the *Wiener Staatswissenschaftliche Studien* (Leipzig and Vienna: Franz Deuticke, 1926). [See this chapter, Addendum. -Ed.]

[10]Richard von Strigl, *Kapital und Produktion* (Vienna: Julius Springer, 1934). [Reprinted by Philosophia Verlag (Munich, 1982). An English translation, *Capital and Production*, has been prepared in manuscript form by Margaret Rudelich Hoppe and Hans-Hermann Hoppe and is in the possession of the Ludwig von Mises Institute, Auburn University. -Ed.]

[11]Richard von Strigl, *Einführung in die Grundlagen der Nationalökonomie* (Vienna: J. Springer, 1937).

conversion overnight of so many to a new creed was not congenial to him who had so conspicuously lacked the talents of a careerist in all his professional life."

Public recognition of his services Strigl indeed had little. The admission as *Privatdozent* in the University of Vienna about 1923 was soon followed by the conferment of the title of Professor. In 1936 the University of Utrecht conferred on him an honourary doctorate, which he greatly prized. But, an essentially modest and quiet man, he remained almost unknown beyond the circles with whom he had professional contact. Yet with his death disappears the figure on whom one's hope for a preservation of the tradition of Vienna as a centre of economic teaching and of a future revivial of the Austrian school had largely rested.

Addendum: Strigl's Theory of Wages[12]

Strigl's book is the kind of study one would like to encounter more frequently. Here a researcher well versed in all the finer aspects of theory sets out to demonstrate the value of simple, fundamental economic propositions. Dismissing polemical arguments, he utilises theoretical findings to explain a multifaceted empirical subject, which he knows well from extensive professional experience. In an earlier book,[13] Strigl had focused on the logical foundations of economic theory. Here he draws on his role as secretary to the Vienna Industrial District Commission, which allowed him to act as a neutral observer in wage negotiations for nearly all branches of the economy, to validate and broaden theoretical insights into the determination of wages. This role enabled him to shift his perspective more easily from abstract theory to real-life phenomena in all their variety, something that theorists generally find hard to do. He is therefore in a good position to counter effectively the objections practical men are inclined to raise against such theoretical analyses. This work on wage theory should thus provide much useful knowledge to men involved in the practical end, employers and trade union leaders alike. The author has rendered a great service by extending theoretical analysis of the determinants of wages to the individual phenomena that it can best explain. As a result, even persons who are not

[12][Review of Strigl's *Angewandte Lohntheorie: Untersuchungen über die wirtschaftlichen Grundlagen der Sozialpolitik*, op. cit. Hayek published the review in *Zeitschrift für Nationalökonomie*, vol. 1, no. 1, May 1929, pp. 175–177. The translation for this volume is by Dr. Grete Heinz. Professor Ralph Raico's assistance with the translation is gratefully acknowledged. -Ed.]

[13][Richard von Strigl, *Die ökonomischen Kategorien und die Organisation der Wirtschaft*, op. cit. -Ed.]

highly trained in economics stand to benefit from applying the propositions presented here to concrete phenomena.

The special merit of Strigl's book does not in the least consist in its popularisation of theory but in its extending the assumptions underlying the general wage theory to phenomena hitherto excluded from fundamental principles because of the overly general character of the assumptions. Strigl's distinction between a strictly defined monopoly position and that of trade union and employer associations in wage negotiations is of particular interest. Negotiators for such associations are in a fundamentally different situation from monopolists, inasmuch as they are not representatives of a homogeneous economic entity and the impact of changes in prices and in amounts sold affects several persons. This is bound to be of decisive importance for the position of the labour representatives, who can never envisage the additional wages going to some workers as a compensation for loss of work affecting other workers. After this criticism of the application of monopoly pricing theory to wage determination in collective bargaining, Strigl continues with a detailed examination of the decisive factors determining supply and demand for both parties to the contract. Here he clearly identifies the economic significance of circumstances usually characterised as 'power relations'. We cannot discuss here all the possible effects produced by a deviation of contractual wages from 'natural' wages that Strigl examines. Strigl makes an interesting attempt to prove that production can cope with an artificial wage increase without permanent damage and that lasting unemployment need not result from wage increases, if the production apparatus can adjust to the new wage level. Here he fails to demonstrate his point, because he ends with the conclusion that this is possible only when an increase in the capital equipment of the particular industry raises the marginal productivity of labour at a later point to the level of the artificially high wages attained previously.

The fruitfulness of Strigl's research is based largely on its dealing with friction phenomena neglected by the basic theoretical propositions and the resulting deviations from the regularities expected from purely theoretical assumptions, precisely what any applied theory ought to do. A particularly interesting example of a phenomenon due to frictional resistance is the calculation of a traditional entrepreneurial profit as a 'fictitious' cost factor, whose existence may be threatened by increased wage demands by the workers, without giving rise necessarily to any changes in the economy as a consequence. Here even under static conditions the wage level may be the outcome of power relationships, a situation that undoubtedly arises occasionally in current economic life. . . .

Let us just mention the particularly good sections on unemployment and social costs. These are exemplary in their application of theoretical insights to current phenomena and are a model for research into social policies. Economic theory has no surer way of acquiring new supporters than when it permits successful applications to practical questions, as exemplified at its best in this work.

SEVEN

ERNST MACH (1838–1916)
AND THE SOCIAL SCIENCES IN VIENNA[1]

My task is limited to testifying briefly about the pervasiveness of
Ernst Mach's influence in Vienna even before the 'Vienna circle'
around Moritz Schlick[2] was formed in 1922. It so happens that in
the three years between 1918 and 1921 I was studying at the
university in my native Vienna and that during this time Mach's
ideas were the main focus of philosophical discussions. Vienna as a
whole was already exceptionally favourable towards a natural sci-
ence-oriented philosophy; aside from Heinrich Gomperz,[3] Adolf
Stöhr[4]—whose thinking was along the same lines—was teaching in
Vienna, as was Robert Reininger,[5] who was at least in sympathy
with such an interpretation of philosophy. I no longer remember
exactly how I happened to come across Mach almost immediately
on my return from the battle lines in November 1918; my reading
list unfortunately begins only in the spring of 1919 and there soon
appears in it the observation: "Now also *Erkenntnis und Irrtum*",[6]
which indicates that I had already become acquainted with other
philosophical works by Mach during the four months that I had
been studying. I know that I had been very engrossed in Mach's
Populär-wissenschaftliche Vorlesungen, Die Mechanik in ihrer Entwicklung,

[1][Published as "Diskussionsbemerkungen über Ernst Mach und das sozialwissen-
schaftliche Denken in Wien", in *Symposium aus Anlaß des 50. Todestages von Ernst Mach*
(Freiburg: Ernst Mach Institut, 1967). The translation for this volume is by Dr. Grete
Heinz. -Ed.]

[2][Moritz Schlick (1882–1936) was Professor of Philosophy at the University of
Vienna and leader of the 'logical positivists', notably Otto Neurath, Rudolph Carnap,
Friedrich Waismann, Hans Kahn, Kurt Gödel, and Herbert Feigl. -Ed.]

[3][Heinrich Gomperz (1873–1942). -Ed.]

[4][Adolf Stöhr (1855–1921). -Ed.]

[5][Robert Reininger (1869–1955). -Ed.]

[6][Ernst Mach, *Erkenntnis und Irrtum: Skizzen zur Psychologie der Forschung* (Leipzig:
J. A. Barth, 1905). -Ed.]

and particularly his *Analyse der Empfindungen*.[7] The upshot of it was that during the three years that I was officially enrolled as a law student, I divided my time about equally between economics and psychology, while my law studies were merely a sideline.

It is hard to say what was the direct cause of our preoccupation with Mach's philosophy. Things probably were similar even in the years immediately prior to the war. In this respect it is characteristic that Schumpeter was so obviously influenced by Mach's ideas when he wrote his first work in 1908[8] that Friedrich von Wieser devoted almost his entire book review[9] to the question of the applicability of Mach's thinking to the social sciences. And I also know that a contemporary, the philosopher Ludwig Wittgenstein,[10] a distant cousin of mine, was coming to grips with Mach during those same years.

Right after the [First World] War, when I came to the university, there was a special reason for the social sciences to be interested in Mach. Lenin had attacked Mach's philosophy, and Friedrich Adler, then one of the most prominent political figures in Austria, had, as I recall, written a book in Mach's defense while he was in prison for shooting to death Minister Stürgkh.[11] As a result, a lively discussion about these problems took place within the socialist left, between the real Communists and the leftist socialists. But this carried over to us non-socialists as well, and the topic became particularly relevant when Othmar Spann, a metaphysically-oriented economist, was appointed as Wieser's successor in Vienna.[12] At that point we were looking for anti-metaphysical arguments, which we found in Mach, although it was not so easy for us to swallow Mach's positiv-

[7][Ernst Mach, *Populär-wissenschaftliche Vorlesungen* (Leipzig: Barth, 1896), translated as *Popular Scientific Lectures* (Chicago: Open Court, 1985); *Die Mechanik in ihrer Entwicklung* (Leipzig: F. A. Brockhaus, 1883); and *Die Analyse der Empfindungen und das Verhältnis des Physischen zum Psychischen* (Jena: Gustav Fischer). -Ed.]

[8][I.e., Schumpeter, *Das Wesen und der Hauptinhalt der theoretischen Nationalökonomie* (Duncker & Humblot, 1908). -Ed.]

[9][In Schmoller's *Jahrbuch für Gesetzgebung, Verwaltung und Volkswirtschaft im Deutschen Reich*, vol. 35, no. 2, 1911. -Ed.]

[10][On Wittgenstein (1889–1951), see this volume, chapter following. -Ed.]

[11][Friedrich Adler, *Ernst Machs Überwindung des mechanischen Materialismus* (Vienna: Wiener Volksbuchhandlung, 1918). Friedrich Adler (1879–?) was the son of Victor Adler, leader of the Austrian Social-Democratic Party; Stürgkh headed the Austrian war government, considered absolutist by the Social Democrats. Adler's sentence was commuted in 1917, less than a year after the assassination, and he was released from prison the following year. On this episode see Mark E. Blum, *The Austrian Marxists*, op. cit., pp. 203–204. -Ed.]

[12][On Spann see this volume, Prologue to Part I. Spann was actually Wieser's colleague; Wieser's chair went to Hans Mayer. -Ed.]

ism whole. Another stumbling block was that he was being exploited too explicitly to support a socialist approach that was not congenial to us, particularly by Otto Neurath, one of the founders of the later Vienna circle.[13] Neurath hoped to convert Mach's positivism—by a very rough approximation—into a physicalism or, as he called it at times, a scientism. On the other hand Mach was practically the only source of arguments against a metaphysical and nebulous attitude, and so we endeavoured all these years to take positivism, which obviously contained much that was true, and pick out those parts that were to some extent applicable to the social sciences and the humanities and which clearly held a large kernel of truth.

From a personal point of view, I was stimulated by Mach's work to study psychology and the physiology of the senses—I even wrote a study at that time about these questions, which finally, thirty years later, resulted in a book.[14] What actually stimulated me to write this study was my scepticism about Mach's concept of phenomenalism, in which pure, simple sensations are the elements of our entire sensory perceptions. A revelation came to me similar to one that Mach describes from his own experience, when he suddenly recognised that the concept of "things in themselves" in Kant's philosophy served no purpose, that it could be omitted. I had the revelation that Mach's concept of "simple and pure sensations" in his sensory psychology was actually meaningless. Since Mach had qualified so many of the connexions between sensations as "relations", I was finally forced to conclude that the whole structure of the sensory world was derived from "relations" and that one might therefore throw out altogether the concept of pure and simple sensations, which plays such a large role in Mach. But this is just an example of the important role Mach played in our thinking during those years.

One might say that for a young man interested in philosophical questions who came to the University in Vienna right after the war, that is in the year 1918–19, and for whom orthodox philosophy was not appealing, Mach offered the only viable alternative. We did try to look into Avenarius,[15] but we soon gave up the attempt, I do not

[13][Neurath is discussed in this volume, Prologue to Part I. -Ed.]

[14][F. A. Hayek, *The Sensory Order: An Inquiry into the Foundations of Theoretical Psychology* (London: Routledge & Kegan Paul, and Chicago: University of Chicago Press, 1952). -Ed.]

[15][Richard Avenarius (1843–1896) was Professor at the University of Zurich from 1877 to 1896. Avenarius gained notoriety from the attacks on him by Husserl and Lenin. -Ed.]

know why; in any case, we found Avenarius quite incomprehensible. From Mach the road was more likely to lead to Helmholtz,[16] to Poincaré,[17] and thinkers along these lines, and for those who went about it systematically, like my friend Karl Popper, it led of course to all the contemporary natural scientists and philosophers.

That more or less exhausts what I wished to say. I only wanted to suggest that Ernst Mach played an especially large role not only in the narrower realm of the natural sciences but specifically in disciplines where the methodological or scientific character of their theory was even far shakier than in the natural sciences and where there was an even greater compulsion to clarify what science really was. That had little connexion with the fact that Mach became to some extent a political symbol; I should say that purely accidental circumstances led to the fact that at a later date, when I was about to leave Vienna, the 'Ernst Mach society' which . . . was already founded in 1929, acquired a certain political colouration. It admittedly consisted predominantly of socialists, but that does not imply that it was politically active, though this served as a pretext for its suppression under Dollfuss.[18]

[16][Hermann Ludwig Ferdinand von Helmholtz (1821–1894) is the German physicist and physiologist who enunciated the principle of the conservation of energy. -Ed.]
[17][Henri Poincaré (1854–1912) was a French mathematician and philosopher of science. -Ed.]
[18][Englebert Dollfuss (1892–1934) was Chancellor of Austria, 1932–34. -Ed.]

REMEMBERING MY COUSIN LUDWIG
WITTGENSTEIN (1889–1951)[1]

Between the rails and the building of the railway station of Bad Ischl there used to be ample space where, sixty years ago, in the season, a regular promenade used to develop before the departure of the night train to Vienna.

I believe it was on the last day of August 1918 that here, among a boisterous crowd of young officers returning to the front after visiting their families on furlough in the Salzkammergut district, two artillery ensigns became vaguely aware that they ought to know one another. I am not sure whether it was a resemblance to other members of our families or because we had actually met before[2] that led each of us to ask the other, "Aren't you a Wittgenstein?" (or, perhaps, "Aren't you a Hayek?"). At any rate it led to our travelling together through the night to Vienna, and even though most of the time we naturally tried to sleep we did manage to converse a little.

Some parts of this conversation made a strong impression on me. He was not only much irritated by the high spirits of the noisy and probably half-drunk party of fellow officers with which we shared the carriage without the least concealing his contempt for mankind in general, but he also took it for granted that any relation of his no matter how distantly connected must have the same standards as himself. He was not so very wrong! I was then very young and inexperienced, barely nineteen and the product of what would now be called a puritanical education: the kind in which the ice-cold bath my father took every morning was the much admired (though

---

[1][Published in *Encounter*, August 1977, pp. 20–22. -Ed.]

[2][In a later recollection, Hayek believed that he had in fact seen Wittgenstein much earlier. "Very likely Wittgenstein had been one of the handsome and elegant young men whom I remembered around 1910, when my grandparents rented for the spring and autumn a Swiss cottage on a property adjoining the park of the Wittgensteins in the suburb of Neuwaldegg, having frequently called from their much more grandiose villa for the much younger sisters of my mother to take them to tennis, so that it would probably have been I who recognised him [in 1918] and not he me." From an interview with W. W. Bartley III. -Ed.]

rarely imitated) standard of discipline for body and mind. And Ludwig Wittgenstein was just ten years my senior.

What struck me most in this conversation was a radical passion for truthfulness in everything (which I came to know as a character- istic vogue among the young Viennese intellectuals of the generation immediately preceding mine only in the following university years). This truthfulness became almost a fashion in that border group between the purely Jewish and the purely Gentile parts of the intelligentsia in which I came so much to move. It meant much more than truth in speech. One had to 'live' truth and not tolerate any pretence in oneself or others. It sometimes produced outright rudeness and, certainly, unpleasantness. Every convention was dissected and every conventional form exposed as fraud. Wittgen- stein merely carried this further in applying it to himself. I some- times felt that he took a perverse pleasure in discovering falsehood in his own feelings and that he was constantly trying to purge himself of all fraud.

That he was very highly strung even at that time cannot be doubted. Among the remoter relatives he was thought of (though hardly known by them) as the maddest member of a rather extraor- dinary family, all of whom were exceptionally gifted and both ready and in a position to live for what they most cared for. Before 1914 I had heard much of (though being too young to attend) their famous musical soirées at the 'Palais Wittgenstein', which ceased to be a social centre after 1914. For many years the name meant to me chiefly the kind old lady who, when I was six years old, had taken me for my first car ride—in an open electromobile round the Ringstrasse.

Apart from an even earlier memory of being taken to the luxuri- ous apartment of an extremely old lady and being made to under- stand that she was the sister of my maternal great-grandfather—and, as I now know, Ludwig Wittgenstein's maternal grandmother—I have no direct knowledge of the Wittgenstein family at the height of their social position at Vienna. The tragedy of the three elder sons apparently all ending their lives by suicide had attenuated it even more than the death of the great industrialist at its head would otherwise have done. I am afraid that my earliest recollection of the name of Wittgenstein is connected with the shocked account of one of my Styrian maiden great-aunts, surely inspired by envy rather than malice, that their grandfather "sold his daughter to a rich Jewish banker. . . ." This is the kind old lady I still remem- ber—just.

I did not meet Ludwig Wittgenstein again for ten years; but I heard from him from time to time through his eldest sister who was a second cousin, an exact contemporary, and a close friend of my mother. The regular visiting had made 'Aunt Minning' a familiar figure to me (actually, she spelt her name, which is an abbreviation of Hermine, with a single 'n', but this would sound odd to English ears), and she remained a frequent visitor. Her youngest brother's problems evidently occupied her much, and though she deprecated all talk about the 'Sonderling' (the crank) and strongly defended him when occasional and undoubtedly often much-distorted accounts of his doings circulated, we did soon learn of them. The public eye did not take notice of him, while his brother Paul Wittgenstein, a one-armed pianist, became a well-known figure.[3]

But I did, through these connexions, become probably one of the first readers of *Tractatus* when it appeared in 1922.[4] Since, like most philosophically interested people of our generation I was, like Wittgenstein, much influenced by Ernst Mach, it made a great impression on me.

The next time I met Ludwig Wittgenstein was in the spring of 1928 when the economist Dennis Robertson, who was taking me for a walk through the Fellows' Gardens of Trinity College, Cambridge, suddenly decided to change course because on the top of a little rise he perceived the form of the philosopher draped over a deck-chair. He evidently stood rather in awe of him, and he did not wish to disturb him. Naturally, I walked up to him, was greeted with surprising friendliness, and we engaged in a pleasant but uninterest-ing conversation (in German) about home and family to which Robertson soon left us. Before long Wittgenstein's interest flagged, and evident signs of his not knowing what to do with me made me leave him after a while.

It must have been almost twelve years later that the first of the only real series of meetings I had with him took place. When I went to Cambridge in 1939 with the London School of Economics I soon learned that he was away working at some war hospital. But a year or two later I encountered him most unexpectedly. John

---

[3][Paul Wittgenstein lost his right arm in the First World War. He nonetheless continued performing, commissioning works such as the Concerto for the Left Hand by Maurice Ravel. -Ed.]

[4][Actually 1923, although the book was probably written around 1918. Ludwig Wittgenstein, *Tractatus Logico-Philosophicus* (London: Routledge, 1923; new English translation, by D. F. Pears and Brian F. McGuinness, London: Routledge & Kegan Paul, 1961). -Ed.]

Maynard Keynes had arranged for me to have rooms in the Gibbs building of King's College, and after a while I was asked by Richard Braithwaite to take part in the meetings of the Moral Sciences Club (I think that was the name) which took place in his rooms just below those I occupied.

It was at the end of one of these meetings that Wittgenstein quite suddenly and rather dramatically emerged. It concerned a paper which had not particularly interested me and of the subject of which I have no recollection. Suddenly Wittgenstein leapt to his feet, poker in hand, indignant in the highest degree, and he proceeded to demonstrate with the implement how simple and obvious Matter really was. Seeing this rampant man in the middle of the room swinging a poker was certainly rather alarming, and one felt inclined to escape into a safe corner. Frankly, my impression at that time was that he had gone mad![5]

It was some time later, probably a year or two, that I took courage to go and see him, after having learnt that he was again in Cambridge. He then lived (as always, I think) in rooms several flights up in a building outside the College. The bare room with the

---

[5][Hayek's account was challenged in *Encounter*, November 1977, pp. 93–94, in a Letter to the Editor, "Hayek's Wittgenstein & Popper", by Percy B. Lehning, of Amsterdam, who concluded that Hayek must have been present at the famous 'poker encounter' on October 26, 1946, between Wittgenstein and Karl Popper, described in the latter's autobiography, *Unended Quest* (London: Fontana, 1976), pp. 122–123, in which case either Hayek's dating of the incident was wrong, or "there are at least two incidents at the Moral Sciences Club in which Wittgenstein handled a poker in an aggressive way". To this letter Hayek replied (same issue, p. 94): "I can only conclude that it was a habit of Wittgenstein to drive his point home with a poker. I have, on one occasion, heard a similar story told which, however, must have referred to another occasion, since it did not suggest the violence I recollect from some date certainly before 1946. I am sure I never heard Karl Popper lecture at Cambridge, and I have read his Autobiography only some time after I wrote the note you published." See W. W. Bartley's discussion of the many versions of the Popper-Wittgenstein encounter, "Facts and Fictions", *Encounter*, January 1986, pp. 77–78. Professor Bartley had been preparing a biography of Popper, and in connexion with this incident he related the following: "In my biographical research on Popper, I have been able to determine that Popper's account of his meeting is accurate in all details—with the possible exception of one point of interpretation. In *Unended Quest*, Popper concluded his account by writing: 'Whereon Wittgenstein, in a rage, threw the poker down and stormed out of the room, banging the door behind him.' Professor Peter Munz, of the Victoria University of Wellington, New Zealand, a student of Wittgenstein's who was present at the meeting, assures me that the fact that Wittgenstein may have been in a rage had nothing to do with his banging the door, 'for Wittgenstein *always* banged the door, whatever his mood'. See also Peter Munz, *Our Knowledge of the Growth of Knowledge: Popper or Wittgenstein?* (London: Routledge & Kegan Paul, 1985)." -Ed.]

iron stove, to which he had to bring a chair for me from his bedroom, has often been described. We talked pleasantly on a variety of topics outside philosophy and politics (we knew that we disagreed politically), and he seemed to like the very fact that I strictly avoided 'talking shop', not unlike one or two other curious figures I have met in Cambridge. But, though these visits were quite pleasant and he seemed to encourage their repetition, they were also rather uninteresting and I went along only two or three times more.

After the end of the War, when I had already returned to London, a new kind of contact by letter began when the possibility arose, first to send food parcels, and later to visit our relatives in Vienna. This involved all kinds of complicated contacts with bureaucratic organisations about which, he rightly assumed, I had found out details before he did. In this he showed a curious combination of impracticability and meticulous attention to detail which must have made all contacts with the ordinary business of life highly unsettling for him. However, he did manage to get to Vienna fairly soon after me (I had succeeded for the first time in 1946), and I believe he went there once or twice again.

I think it was in the course of his return from his last visit to Vienna that we met for the last time. He had gone to see his dying sister Minning once more, and he was (though I did not know it) himself already mortally ill.[6] I had interrupted the usual railway journey from Vienna via Switzerland and France at Basel and had boarded there the sleeping car at midnight the next day. Since my fellow occupant of the compartment seemed to be already asleep I undressed in semi-darkness. As I prepared to mount to the upper berth a tousled head shot out from the lower one and almost shouted at me, "You are Professor Hayek!" Before I had recovered sufficiently to realise that it was Wittgenstein and to register my assent, he had turned to the wall again.

When I woke up next morning he had disappeared, presumably to the restaurant car. When I returned I found him deeply engrossed in a detective story and apparently unwilling to talk. This lasted only until he had finished his paperback. He then engaged me in the most lively conversation, beginning with his impressions of the Russians at Vienna, an experience which evidently had shaken him to his depth and destroyed certain long-cherished illu-

---

[6][This must have been in 1949. See W. W. Bartley III, *Wittgenstein*, second edition, revised and enlarged (La Salle: Open Court, 1985), p. 155. -Ed.]

sions. Gradually we were led to more general questions of moral philosophy, but just as it was getting really exciting we arrived at the port (in Boulogne, I believe). Wittgenstein seemed very anxious to continue our discussion, and indeed he said that we must do so on board ship.

But I simply could not find him. Whether he regretted having become so deeply engaged, or had discovered that, after all, I was just another philistine, I do not know. At any rate, I never saw him again.

PART II

THE FORTUNES OF LIBERALISM

THE REDISCOVERY OF FREEDOM: PERSONAL RECOLLECTIONS[1]

It was with great pleasure that I received your invitation to discuss my recollections about the rediscovery of freedom in Germany. I am not generally inclined to indulge in reminiscences, feeling too young as yet and too busy otherwise for such an occupation. So I was somewhat at a loss to think of a way to keep you entertained for half an hour. I had one starting point, however, my having spent some time working together with an earlier generation of participants in the *Verein Deutscher Maschinenbau-Anstalten* (Association of German Machine Construction Companies).

In my talk today I will limit myself by and large to German developments, though it seems curious, in a way, to have a foreigner like myself discussing the development of freedom in Germany. Admittedly, the sad course of events has given my memories a certain scarcity value. An evil fate befell German efforts to defend the ideal of liberty in general and in the field of economics in particular, with the result that today I am almost the only survivor of a generation that set out in the wake of the First World War to devote all its energies to the preservation of a civilised society, a generation that set itself the task to build a better society in a systematic fashion and to learn to understand, and to some extent defend, a tradition that had civilised the world. Primarily under the impetus of Ludwig von Mises, a very small group of us dedicated ourselves to this task in the post-war years. The milieu of the social sciences at that time was anything but sympathetic towards our perspective, being completely under the sway of interventionist ideals that had taken root especially in Germany since the 1870s.

---

[1][Published as "Die Wiederentdeckung der Freiheit—Persönliche Erinnerungen" in Verein Deutscher Maschinenbau-Anstalten (VDMA) und Institut der deutschen Wirtschaft (IW), eds, *Produktivität, Eigenverantwortung, Beschäftigung: Für eine wirtschafts-politische Vorwärtsstrategie* (Cologne: Deutscher Instituts-Verlag, 1983). The essay was delivered as a lecture on the occasion of the Symposium sponsored jointly by the VDMA and the IW on February 1 and 2, 1983, in Bonn-Bad Godesberg, Germany. The translation for this volume is by Dr. Grete Heinz. -Ed.]

The upshot of it was that after the end of the First World War, there were practically no economic theorists left in Germany.[2]

I am hardly overstating the case and will just mention one point as an illustration. When I came back from military service, I met the lucky girls at the University of Vienna who were privileged to attend the lectures of Max Weber in the summer of 1918, while we were still fighting at the front. Weber was Professor of Economics for one semester in Vienna and had mentioned in one of his lectures that he did not feel very qualified, because the first lecture he had heard about economic theory had been his own. It was almost impossible in Germany at that time to become a theorist in the social sciences. Anyone who, like me, had his first scholarly experience with inflation in Austria and then in Germany—and was simultaneously exposed to the caustic comments of his mentor Ludwig von Mises, who kept pointing out what nonsense was being spouted on inflation by German economists, such as Mr. Havenstein's assertion that it was not inflation but a shortage of money that had to be alleviated,[3] or the very prominent author of a widely used textbook on monetary institutions, Helfferich,[4] making the most ridiculous pronouncements about monetary policy—could not help but conclude that economics as a science was defunct in Germany.

Mises, who was anything but kind in this respect, always singled out three or four exceptions. Adolf Weber, he said, was quite a sensible person and so was Passow, who at least defended capitalism. Dietzel showed some insight and Pohle was also a person worthy of respect, if only he would finally get around to publishing something and do more than just propagating Gustav Cassel's work in Germany. But with these exceptions, Mises thought that there were no economists in Germany. And he was not altogether mistaken.

During the 1920s, there finally emerged a theoretical approach, but one that disregarded freedom. The relevance of economic theory was discovered, notably by Bernhard Harms, then the ambi-

---

[2][On the state of German economics at that time see also this volume, chapter 4. -Ed.]

[3][Rudolf Havenstein (1857–1923) was president of the Reichsbank, the German central bank, from 1908 to 1923. For his remarks on this occasion see Fritz K. Ringer, ed., *The German Inflation of 1923* (New York: Oxford University Press, 1969), p. 96. -Ed.]

[4][Karl Helfferich (1872–1924) was director of the Deutsche Bank in Berlin and author of *Das Geld* (Leipzig: Hirschfeld, 1903; sixth edition, 1923). -Ed.]

tious director of the Kiel Institute.[5] He himself was not well versed in economic theory, but on the advice of others he surrounded himself with a group of socialist theoreticians who were presumably the best available theorists. Unfortunately for German theory, Becker,[6] the very influential advisor of the Prussian Ministry of Education, opted for Emil Lederer[7] instead of Joseph Schumpeter for the chair in economics at the University of Berlin which was then vacant. In his disappointment, Schumpeter went to the United States and Lederer—who had also participated in Böhm-Bawerk's seminar but had been by far its weakest member—was appointed to the chair in Berlin.[8]

Aside from this group—who were all not only socialists but also, I think, all without exception Jewish and were of course forced to leave Germany in 1933—there were in fact only two groups of theorists, one of them active as academics, the other in non-academic positions.

The latter consisted of a group of gentlemen that strangely enough had come together within the framework of the Association of German Machine Builders—the VDMA—and which called itself 'Ricardians' to distinguish themselves from the dominant school of economic theorists. Among them were Alexander Rüstow,[9] Hans Gestrich,[10] and Otto Veit.[11] Another member of this circle was Lautenbach,[12] a very gifted theorist who died at a very young age and who was not employed by the VDMA but was in government

---

[5][Bernhard Harms (1876–1939) ran the Institut für Weltwirtschaft at the University of Kiel. Schumpeter calls him "one of the most efficient organisers of research who ever lived". *History of Economic Analysis* (New York: Oxford University Press, 1954), p. 1155. -Ed.]

[6][Carl Heinrich Becker (1876–1933). -Ed.]

[7][Emil Lederer (1882–1939) wrote on a variety of topics in labour and industrial economics. In 1933 he emigrated to New York and became the first Dean of the Faculty of Political and Social Sciences at the New School for Social Research. -Ed.]

[8][This was in 1931. Schumpeter proceeded to accept an appointment at Harvard University the next year. -Ed.]

[9][Alexander Rüstow (1885–1963) was Professor of Economic Geography and Economic History at the University of Istanbul and the author of *Ortsbestimmung der Gegenwart*, 3 vols (Erlenbach-Zurich and Stuttgart: Eugen Rentsch, 1950–57), condensed and translated as *Freedom and Domination* (Princeton, N.J.: Princeton University Press, 1980). -Ed.]

[10][Hans Gestrich (1893–1945) taught at the University of Berlin. -Ed.]

[11][Otto Veit (1898–) was a banker and Professor at the University of Frankfurt. -Ed.]

[12][Wilhelm Lautenbach (1891–1948). -Ed.]

service. Other members of the circle were Dr. Ilau,[13] Friedrich Lutz,[14] and Theodor Eschenburg,[15] with whom I became acquainted only later.

This group of men at the VDMA was in fact the only influential and active circle of theorists in Germany striving earnestly but fruitlessly to achieve a free economy. This circle continued to exist even during the Nazi period, but for the most part its members died young.

I vividly remember the one time I came to Berlin during that period. I generally avoided visiting Germany and crossed only the southwest corner of Germany on my frequent trips between London and Vienna, where I regularly paid visits to Walter Eucken,[16] about which I will report later. I happened to give a lecture in Warsaw at the time and my return trip from Warsaw to London brought me to Berlin, where I made a stopover. That is where I came into contact with this circle of 'Ricardians' and had an extended afternoon discussion at the house of one of its members, I believe that it was Gestrich. I recall vividly that on this occasion, when we moved from purely theoretical topics to more critical subjects, someone—probably the host—jumped up and placed a tea cozy over the telephone to make sure that for heaven's sake no one was listening in on our conversation aside from the members of the circle. This group, which was closely connected with the VDMA, was one of the few that survived the Nazi period without abandoning the liberal tradition.

But to come to my main connexion with today's topic. At a very early date, I am not exactly sure when, perhaps at the meeting of the Association for Social Policy (*Verein für Sozialpolitik*[17]) which was held in Vienna in 1926, I became acquainted with Wilhelm Röpke.[18] For some years I was on very close terms with him, and it was

---

[13][Hans Ilau (1901–?) was later an economist with the Darmstädter und National-bank and the Dresdner Bank and an editor of the *Frankfurter Zeitung*. -Ed.]

[14][Friedrich August Lutz (1901–1975) taught at the University of Freiburg, Princeton University, and the University of Zurich, specialising in capital and interest theory. His wife, Vera Smith Lutz, was Hayek's research student at the London School of Economics. -Ed.]

[15][Theodor Eschenburg (1904–) was later Professor of Political Science at the University of Tübingen. -Ed.]

[16][Walter Eucken (1891–1950) was then Professor of Economics at the University of Freiburg. -Ed.]

[17][The *Verein für Sozialpolitik* (Association for Social Policy) is discussed more fully in this volume, chapter 4. -Ed.]

[18][On Röpke as an economist see the first two Addenda to this chapter. -Ed.]

through Röpke that I came to know the 'Ricardian' group. During the sessions of the *Verein für Sozialpolitik* that took place in subsequent years (Zurich in 1928 and Königsberg in 1930), he was the only bright spot for me, since these sessions were dominated by civil servants such as Sombart and his disciples. They were all very honourable gentlemen, but they were as out of touch with economic theory as they were out of sympathy with personal freedom.

It was through Röpke that I came in contact with Walter Eucken in Freiburg. At that time he was not at all well known, but already had great influence among his closer associates. He was probably the most serious thinker in the realm of social philosophy produced by Germany in the last hundred years. Eucken had published only short studies at that time. Oddly enough, his major work[19] reached me in London during the war. I have always wondered whether this volume, which had been mailed from Zurich by Röpke, was delivered to me because of the negligence of British officials or because they felt that they were keeping an eye on me anyway and leaving me time to compromise myself more seriously. In any case, this book, which had been published in 1940, reached me during the war. It made me realise for the first time what a towering figure Eucken was and to how great an extent Eucken and his circle embodied the great German liberal tradition, which had unfortunately become defunct.

When I mentioned earlier that death had taken its toll prematurely among the German representatives of the ideal of freedom in the last fifty years, I was thinking especially of the Eucken circle, the other of the two groups of theorists I mentioned before. I cannot enumerate them all, but let me at least mention Miksch[20] and Lampe,[21] Eucken's two most promising collaborators, and his closest friend and collaborator in the field of legal philosophy, Franz Böhm,[22] to make you realise what great losses Germany has incurred.

Conceivably an indigenous liberal development might have emerged in Germany. It did manifest itself on a small scale in the

---

[19][Walter Eucken, *Die Grundlagen der Nationalökonomie* (Jena: Gustav Fischer, 1940), translated by T. W. Hutchinson as *The Foundations of Economics: History and Theory in the Analysis of Economic Reality* (London: W. Hodge, 1950). -Ed.]
[20][Leonhard Miksch (1901–1950). -Ed.]
[21][Adolf Lampe (1897–1948). -Ed.]
[22][Franz Böhm (1895–1977). -Ed.]

guise of the *Ordo* Yearbook[23] and the *Ordo* circle, though this was, shall we say, a restrained liberalism. But the *Ordo* circle never matured into a major movement. It lacked the inspired leader that Eucken would have been.

Walter Eucken was a valuable friend for me. In the late 1930s, before the outbreak of the war, when I first acquired a car and made the trip from London to Austria by automobile, I regularly made a stopover in Freiburg just to visit Eucken and to keep in touch with him. Although Eucken had little time left in which to take part in our efforts to defend liberalism, our contacts later had an important consequence. My *Road to Serfdom* was translated into German by Mrs. Röpke shortly after its publication.[24] The German edition was published in Switzerland, but, as I did not realise immediately, for three years the import of the book into Germany was prohibited, so that it was obtainable there only in typescript. An agreement was in effect which obliged the occupying powers to exclude books that took a hostile stand against any one of them. Although this book, which was written at the time that the Russians were our allies, was directed less against communism than against fascism, the Russians instinctively felt that the book was directed against them. They therefore insisted that the occupation authorities ban the import of the book into Germany. Since we are on this subject, let me tell you the end of the story. When I finally visited Germany in 1946, at a time when the import of the book was still prohibited, I had a most moving experience. Although the book was not allowed into the country and only one or two copies had been smuggled in from Switzerland, the book had become well known not only in the abbreviated version published by the *Reader's Digest*[25] but also in a full-length copy.

I happened to come across a typed copy at the time, which I began to read on a railroad trip. I suddenly noticed that it contained passages that were unfamiliar to me. All at once I realised that my book had suffered the same vicissitudes as many of the medieval texts, when copies were made of copies from copies, copies that had come into being because on the original copy someone had made a marginal comment that had been reproduced on the second

---

[23][*Ordo: Jahrbuch für die Ordnung von Wirtschaft und Gesellschaft*, an annual that began publication in 1948; the editors were then Eucken and Böhm. -Ed.]

[24][F. A. Hayek, *Der Weg zur Knechtschaft*, trans. Eva Röpke (Erlenbach-Zurich: Eugen Rentsch, 1945). -Ed.]

[25][F. A. Hayek, "The Road to Serfdom", in *The Reader's Digest*, April 1945, pp. 1–20. -Ed.]

copy, so that contributions by an unknown hand had already been incorporated in the text that had finally reached me. But this leads me far afield from my actual topic.

What I had in mind was to tell about Walter Eucken's role at the very beginning of an international movement, a movement that it would be pretentious to call in the service of freedom, but a movement in the service of understanding the preconditions of freedom. For it is a real problem that many people hold the illusion that freedom can be imposed from above, instead of by creating the preconditions with which people are given the possibility to shape their own fate.

After the publication of *The Road to Serfdom*, I was invited to give many lectures. During my travels in Europe as well as in the United States, nearly everywhere I went I met someone who told me that he fully agreed with me, but that at the same time he felt totally isolated in his views and had nobody with whom he could even talk about them. This gave me the idea of bringing these people, each of whom was living in great solitude, together in one place. And by a stroke of good luck I was able to raise the money to accomplish this.

The story is too amusing to pass over. A Swiss gentleman had raised some money for Röpke to enable him to publish a journal.[26] But as anyone who can guess who the person involved was can readily imagine, this man intended to keep control over the journal. As Röpke refused to go along with this, the two men parted company. My first task consisted in bringing about a reconciliation between this very competent fundraiser and Röpke and to get Röpke's agreement to use the money collected originally for his journal to organise a founding meeting for liberals in Switzerland. His agreement was obtained and as a result it was possible to have the first meeting of the Mont Pèlerin Society on Mont Pèlerin near Vevey in 1947. This session was attended by thirty-seven persons, out of the sixty or so people that I had invited. These were all isolated human beings that I had met on my travels and who had complained that they had found nobody with whom they could discuss their problems.[27]

I had proposed two Germans as participants. One of them was Walter Eucken, of course. The second one that I had in mind was

---

[26][The Swiss gentleman was Albert Hunold (1899–1981). -Ed.]

[27][Hayek's opening address to this conference is reprinted in this volume, chapter 12. For a list of participants see the first footnote to that chapter. -Ed.]

the historian Franz Schnabel.[28] The intention was—and remains my goal even today, although it has not been entirely fulfiled—to have a group consisting not only of pure economists but also social philosophers, jurists, and especially historians. Unfortunately I was unable to get Franz Schnabel to come to Switzerland, but Eucken came. Like most Germans of his generation, he suffered from the language barrier, but his English was at least good enough to participate in discussions. He spoke only German, and it was one of my great pleasures to serve as Eucken's interpreter during this session and to be praised by him for expressing his ideas much more beautifully in English than in the original German.

The reason that I mention all this is because Eucken was greatly acclaimed at this conference. And I believe that Eucken's success in 1947—as the only German attending a scholarly international conference—contributed a little, if I may use this term, to the rehabilitation of German scholars on the international scene. Up to that time, my American friends in particular had been asking, "Do you really dare to invite Germans too?" Such a question is hard to imagine today. I had dared to do so and had had the good luck to find the very person who was the star of the conference.

In some way, the founding and the first conference of the Mont Pèlerin Society, which, I feel entitled to say, was my own idea, although I received a great deal of support in its organisation especially from Röpke as well as from Mises, constituted the rebirth of a liberal movement in Europe.[29] Americans have done me the honour of considering the publication of The Road to Serfdom [1944] as the decisive date, but it is my conviction that the really serious endeavour among intellectuals to bring about the rehabilitation of the idea of personal freedom especially in the economic realm dates from the founding of the Mont Pèlerin Society in 1947.

Almost at the same time as the founding of the Mont Pèlerin Society—one or two years later perhaps—a second development along the same lines took place. A young English pilot who had returned from the war and had made a great deal of money in a few years as an entrepreneur came to me and asked me what he could do to thwart the ominous growth of socialism. I had consider-

---

[28][Franz Schnabel (1887–1966) was Professor of History at the University of Munich and author of the Deutsche Geschichte im neunzehnten Jahrhundert, 4 vols (Freiburg: Herder, 1929–37). -Ed.]

[29][Hayek is alluding here to a dispute in the early 1960s with Röpke and Hunold over the origins and direction of the Mont Pèlerin Society. Details of this episode have not yet been made publicly available. -Ed.]

able trouble persuading him that mass propaganda was futile and that the task consisted rather of convincing intellectuals. To accomplish this we needed to develop an easily understood economic interpretation of the preconditions of liberty, which would require the establishment of institutions geared to that segment of the middle class that I then called, part maliciously and part facetiously, the "secondhand dealers of ideas", a group of decisive importance because it determines what the masses think. I convinced this man by the name of Anthony Fisher of the need to establish such an institution, which led to the founding of the Institute of Economic Affairs in London. Its progress was very slow at first, but today it is not only enormously influential but also serves as the model for a whole set of comparable institutions scattered around the entire western half of the globe, from which sound ideas emanate.[30]

A good deal of detailed information could be reported about recent developments, but I will not dwell on them here. I would like to come back to one point, however, which is especially important for Germany in particular. There was a highly gratifying initial reaction in Germany right after the currency stabilisation in 1949. Germany had the immense luck to possess—I am tempted to say—a man of native talent at the decisive spot. I have known many economists with much greater theoretical sophistication and insight, but I have never met another person with as sound an instinct for the right thing to do as Ludwig Erhard.[31] Ludwig Erhard, who also became a member of the Mont Pèlerin Society at an early stage, deserves far greater credit for the restoration of a free society in Germany than he is given credit for either inside or outside Germany. I have recently learned a great deal of detail about it, because two of my Freiburg friends at the Eucken Institute have compiled an extensive history of the events around 1949. And the intuitive evaluation that I made at the time will be confirmed by this publication. It must be admitted, however, that Erhard could never have accomplished what he did under bureaucratic or democratic constraints. It was a lucky moment when the right person in the right

---

[30][The Institute of Economic Affairs was founded in 1955 and continues to publish books, occasional papers, and the journal *Economic Affairs*. Two of its former directors, Arthur Seldon and Lord Harris of High Cross, are longtime associates of Hayek. For a list of some of these other "comparable institutions" see this volume, Introduction. -Ed.]

[31][Ludwig Erhard (1897–1977) was the West German Minister of Economic Affairs from 1949 until 1963, when he succeeded Konrad Adenauer as Chancellor of the Federal Republic. Among his key advisors were Eucken and Röpke. -Ed.]

spot was free to do what he thought right, although he could never have convinced anybody else that it was the right thing. He himself has gleefully told me how the very Sunday on which the famous decree about the freeing of all prices accompanying the introduction of the new German mark was to be published, the top American military commander, General Clay, called him and told him on the telephone: "Professor Erhard, my advisers tell me you are making a great mistake," whereupon, according to his own report, Erhard replied: "So my advisers also tell me." The freeing of prices was unbelievably successful. In the time that followed, there was in fact a more determined and conscious effort to maintain a free-market economy in Germany than in any other country.

Let me repeat something here that I stated four years ago to the surprise of most listeners and the great satisfaction of the persons concerned, when I had the pleasure of presenting the Erhard prize to Professor Schiller.[32] To the best of my knowledge, Karl Schiller is the man who, next to Ludwig Erhard, deserves the greatest credit for the maintenance and consolidation of a German market economy. Admittedly, even the Social Democratic Party for a while contributed to the maintenance of the market economy.

Although I am much more confident in a way about the prospects of a worldwide restoration of a market economy, I am no longer as confident about the development in Germany. I had been under the impression for some time that Germany might, almost grotesquely, become the world's prime model of classical liberalism. I am afraid that this prospect is now much dimmer. While young people all over the world are in a very large measure rediscovering liberalism—you must forgive me if I use this word that has become so discredited in the United States in its nineteenth-century meaning: I mean liberalism as Jefferson understood this term—and I am delighted about the development of young people in England, France, and Italy, my confidence in Germany's contribution to this movement has retrogressed. As far as I can judge, people in Germany are no longer so convinced that they owe everything to the return to a free-market economy. Old feelings about anti-free trade, anti-competition, and anti-internationalism are again coming to the fore. I am no longer quite sure whether German liberalism is sufficiently deep seated, as I had believed for a while. It is enormously

[32][Karl Schiller (1911–) taught economics at the Universities of Keil and Hamburg before serving in the *Bundesrat* (the upper house of the West German legislature) from 1949 to 1953. He was later an economic adviser to the Social Democratic Party. -Ed.]

important, for the world as well, that Germany maintain its liberal course. I hope that you will keep this in mind. Everyone should share in this concern. In particular you should not assume that in times of crisis exceptions should be made to principles. The current depression will answer the question whether the world keeps on a liberal course or not. You can all contribute decisively to a positive answer.

Addendum: Tribute to Röpke[33]

Having pursued parallel paths for over thirty and in fact almost forty years, having fought for the same ideals and struggled with the same tasks and problems each according to his personal capacity and disposition, I do not find it easy to delineate in its full, rich distinctiveness the figure of a fellow combatant and age mate. One absorbs unconsciously whatever fits into one's own thinking at a given stage when a friend and fellow combatant discovers the answer and the right response to problems which one has tried to solve oneself! How often has it happened that Wilhelm Röpke expressed vividly what was still grey theory for the rest of us or when we had at the very least not yet discovered how to convert a general principle into a relevant response to the problem of the moment!

Those younger than he will record one day how much they learned from Röpke, how great was his impact on the thinking of a new generation, and to what gifts he owed his intellectual leadership. For a contemporary he represents above all a common fate and a common task—an evolution in the course of which our commonly held outlook on the world gradually took shape, without being really able to say in retrospect what each of us contributed to it.

The generation that began to study the economy and society at the end of the First World War was on the lookout, first of all, for genuine economic knowledge. As might be expected of persons looking for a solid foundation, we viewed technical problems of economic theory as our prime concern and the advancing of this discipline as our main task. This was in truth a time when it was essential to gain recognition for theoretical thinking and particularly to participate in the construction of a better technical scaffolding. In Germany economic theory at that time was practically a new discovery, and the enthusiasm for a newly discovered discipline may explain

---

[33][Published along with congratulatory addresses from other friends and colleagues, on the occasion of Röpke's seventy-fifth birthday, in Röpke's *Gegen die Brandung: Zeugnisse eines Gelehrtenlebens unserer Zeit*, collected and edited by Albert Hunold (Erlenbach-Zurich: Eugen Rentsch, 1959), pp. 25–28. An English translation of *Gegen die Brandung*, namely Wilhelm Röpke, *Against the Tide* (Chicago: Henry Regnery, 1969), was published without the tributes. The translation of the present essay is by Dr. Grete Heinz. -Ed.]

the belief of young scholars that nothing could contribute more to the cure of humanity's ills than to give people a better understanding of economics. This knowledge is indispensable for any responsible discussion of the far-reaching problems of social organisation.

Röpke's name first came to my attention in Vienna as that of one of the few young German economists seriously interested in theoretical questions. When we became acquainted shortly thereafter, the basis for a closer contact was primarily his grasp of abstract questions of monetary theory, with which we were concerned in Vienna. But Röpke realised at an early stage, perhaps earlier than most of his contemporaries, that an economist who is nothing but an economist cannot be a good economist. This is a fitting place to mention the influence on all of us of a man of the immediately preceding generation who was a young professor when we were students and whose decisive work had just appeared when we concluded our studies. In his *Gemeinwirtschaft*,[34] which appeared in 1922, Ludwig von Mises had demonstrated how economic thought can serve as the basis for a comprehensive social philosophy and can provide answers to the pressing problems of the time. Irrespective of his success in convincing us immediately, the decisive influence of this work largely determined the common development of our generation, even for those of us who turned to general problems only at a later stage.

What a small handful of people were ready in the 1920s to put their faith in freedom as a matter of principle; how small the number of those who understood that scientific objectivity could be reconciled with an outspoken devotion to an ideal and that all knowledge in social matters could be fruitful, moreover, only linked with the courage of one's convictions! Röpke's passionate involvement in what was happening around him made him a shining example in times of danger and, not much later, one of the first who assumed the burden of exile out of conviction.[35] Whatever losses those of our generation destined to be tossed around in the world incurred by this fate, they did not necessarily feel uprooted. If there now once more exists something like a common ideal of freedom in the Western world—or if such an ideal is in the process of developing—these enforced wanderings constituted one of the most important preconditions for its rebirth.

[34][Ludwig von Mises, *Die Gemeinwirtschaft: Untersuchungen über den Sozialismus* (Jena: Gustav Fischer, 1922), translated by J. Kahane as *Socialism: An Economic and Sociological Analysis* (London: Jonathan Cape, 1936; reprinted, Indianapolis, Ind.: LibertyClassics, 1981). -Ed.]

[35][Röpke was Professor of Economics at the University of Marburg when he was removed from his post for his opposition to National Socialism in 1933, the same year Hayek left Vienna for the London School of Economics. Röpke went on to the University of Istanbul (1933–37) and the Graduate Institute of International Studies in Geneva (1937–66). Mises and Hayek's contemporaries Fritz Machlup, Gottfried Haberler, and Paul Rosenstein-Rodan would all leave Austria by 1935. -Ed.]

It would be presumptuous to discuss the qualities of a contemporary at the height of his creative vigour, when his capacities receive full recognition by the world around him. Röpke's role in the intellectual development of our time must be judged by posterity. But let me at least emphasise a special gift for which we, his colleagues, admire him particularly—perhaps because it is so rare among scholars: his courage, his moral courage. What I have in mind here is not so much his consciously exposing himself to danger, though Röpke did not shirk from that either. But I mean particularly the courage to oppose popular prejudices that are shared by well-intentioned, progressive, patriotic, or idealistic persons at a given time. There are few more disagreeable tasks than taking a stand against movements that are carried along by a wave of enthusiasm and appearing as an alarmist by pointing out dangers when enthusiasts see nothing but good prospects. For an independent-minded social philosopher there is probably no more valuable quality than the moral courage to stand alone in his convictions and to expose himself not only to attacks but to suspicions and denigrations. This is a courage Röpke demonstrated as a young man, at a time when he had not yet consolidated his reputation and his position. It is a courage he continues to demonstrate when he does not hesitate to disappoint his followers and admirers and is as frank in uncovering the illusions of the sixth decade of our century as he was in contending with the illusions of the 1920s. For this he deserves perhaps even greater respect.

Few scholars are lucky enough to exert an influence far beyond their professional circle to the extent that Röpke has done. Since such an influence is only too often acquired at the expense of undue simplification, it must be emphasised that he has never avoided intellectual difficulties. His writings, though intended for a wider audience,[36] offer as much stimulation to his professional colleagues as to the layman. The fact that he does not always and in every respect go along with what is considered particularly 'scientific' at any given time, like many of our generation, is another matter. One is often more realistic and in closer touch with reality in the social sciences when one does not limit oneself to those facts that are measurable and quantifiable. There is also an intermediate realm between 'pure' theory and questions of practical politics where systematic treatment is at least as useful as in pure theory. We will not try to settle the question whether 'political economy', as it used to be called, requires even greater gifts perhaps than pure theory. One thing is certain: that Wilhelm Röpke has been unusually endowed with these special gifts and that, thanks to these gifts, he has had unusual success in holding up to us an ideal for which to strive.

---

[36][For example, Röpke's *Jenseits von Angebot und Nachfrage* (Erlenbach-Zurich: Eugen Rentsch, 1958), translated as *A Humane Economy: The Social Framework of the Free Market* (Chicago: Henry Regnery, 1960). -Ed.]

Addendum: Röpke's Theory of Capital Formation[37]

The present little volume from the well-known series contains a lecture that was received with great interest when its author, Wilhelm Röpke, delivered it at the *Nationalökonomischen Gesellschaft* (Economic Society) in Vienna. With his customary clarity and ease of expression he provides an excellent survey of the most important questions of this area (i.e., capital formation), an area which is, as he emphasises, quite neglected despite its importance. His Introduction argues for a division—one that is quite appropriate in terms both of grouping and of terminology—of the forms of capital formation according to their sources in real or in monetary economics, the latter of which again may be divided into savings, venture-capital formation ('self financing'), and the two sorts of 'forced capital accumulation', that is, through fiscal management and monetary policy.

The investigation of these different types leads Röpke to the conclusion, one which is well worth taking to heart today, that savings in the narrower sense still represents not only the chief but also the only unobjectionable source of capital accumulation. Röpke seems to me to be a bit too leniently disposed, however, with regard to forced capital accumulation through monetary policy, which he also incorrectly, so it seems to me, considers as effective only when the creation of credit brings about a rise in prices, although obviously every allocation of newly created credit to productive ends temporarily increases the demand for productive goods in relationship to the demand for consumer goods, and hence effects an increase in capital.

After this, Röpke investigates very instructively the individual reasons for the scale of saving, distinguishing between the willingness and the capacity to save, and thereby avoiding certain confusions that frequently occur. (The diagram [he gives] illustrating the relationship of these two factors could perhaps have been made clearer by the practical introduction of a third dimension.) Particularly successful here are his concise explanations of the respective relationships between public prosperity, income and division of property, and savings activity, matters which can only be mentioned here without attempting to reproduce the content.

In the last chapter, Röpke takes up again briefly the much-disputed question of whether too much can be saved. So far as he is referring here to the dangerous consequences of capital formation through monetary policy, what he says is obviously to be agreed to without reservation. It is more doubtful, however, whether—as the author implies—even voluntary capital formation can lead to an overcapitalisation that eventually brings about a crisis. However, quite apart from theoretical considerations, the further possibility certainly has to be borne in mind, as Röpke also admits,

---

[37][Review of Röpke's pamphlet, *Die Theorie der Kapitalbildung*, published in the series *Recht und Staat in Geschichte und Gegenwart: Eine Sammlung von Vorträge und Schriften aus dem Gebiet der gesamten Staatswissenschaften*, number 63 (Tübingen: J. C. B. Mohr (Paul Siebeck), 1929). The review was published in the *Zeitschrift für Nationalökonomie*, vol. 1, no. 3, 1929, pp. 474–475. Translated by W. W. Bartley III. -Ed.]

that there could be excessive savings in the sense that the economy as a whole "exchanges a higher present marginal utility for a lower future one". Since interpersonal comparisons of utilities are in principle impossible, such a judgement could, however, be preferred only on the basis of a specified target of economic policy, and never—with objective validity— independently of such a target.

The study is rich in ideas about important current problems such as, especially, that of foreign loans and of the connexions between capital formation and taxation, and also on this account deserves to be disseminated beyond narrow professional circles.

Addendum: Hallowell on the Decline of Liberalism as an Ideology[38]

Few studies in the history of ideas could be more interesting and instructive than a really good account of the decline of liberalism in Germany—a decline which started before it had taken roots outside the realm of theory and closely connected with the fact that to Germany liberalism came not before but simultaneously with nationalism and socialism. To produce such a study would be a task of very considerable magnitude which no one without a very intimate knowledge of German history and German ideas ought to undertake. It is not evident that the author of the brief study before us possesses many of the required qualifications—hardly to be expected in a doctoral dissertation. He confines himself largely to the legal aspects of his problem, the elaboration and transformation of the concept of the *Rechtsstaat*, and there is no reason to quarrel with him on that account; it is a subject quite big enough for a valuable monograph by an author thoroughly familiar with it and with a knowledge not limited to this particular field. But though our present author sees some of the real problems, there is more evidence of dependence on a few secondary authorities, such as E. Troeltsch, H. Heller, and a few articles in the *Encyclopaedia of the Social Sciences* than of a comprehensive study of the original authorities. Even such writers as Fichte or Mazzini are frequently quoted at second hand and it is thus not surprising that e.g., Fichte, because of his early liberal views, is defended against the 'unjust' description as an ideological forerunner of the National Socialists (one wonders whether the author has ever read the *Geschlossene Handelsstaat*[39]). The result is, on the whole, not much more than

---

[38][Review of John H. Hallowell, *The Decline of Liberalism as an Ideology, With Particular Reference to German Politico-Legal Thought* (Berkeley and Los Angeles: University of California Press, 1943). Published in *Economica*, *N.S.*, vol. 11, August 1944, p. 159. -Ed.]

[39][Johann Gottlieb Fichte, *Der geschlossene Handelsstaat (The Closed Commercial State): ein philosophischer Entwurf als Anhang zur Rechtslehre, und Probe einer künftig zu liefernden Politik* (Tübingen: J. G. Cotta, 1800). -Ed.]

a summary of textbook views which, though they illustrate important tendencies, makes them little more intelligible than they were before.

As on the historical so on the conceptual side there are many signs that the author has tackled important problems and with a sound instinct, yet with quite inadequate means and before he has gained sufficient clarity on what precisely he means by the terms he employs. This is well illustrated by two of the central problems of the study, the influence of positivism and the effect of the formalisation of the law. That "the decline of liberalism parallels the degree to which liberal thinkers have accepted positivism" is a just and significant if not original observation. But the elaboration of the argument is vitiated by the ambiguity of the term 'positivism' as it is used, which appears to cover a variety of different and not necessarily connected intellectual attitudes. With regard to the concept of 'formal' law the ambiguity is even more serious; the term appears to be used to describe two aspects of law which are certainly different and perhaps sometimes even contradictory; on the one hand the fact that a rule has been imposed by the proper constitutional machinery, and on the other that it is a true general rule, meant to apply to yet unknown people in circumstances which cannot be foreseen in detail and in this respect different from any legislative measure designed to achieve a specific end.

The ambitious purpose outlined in the Preface, "to ascertain *when* and *how* liberalism as an ideology became decadent" can scarcely be said to have been achieved by this study. It may, however, serve to direct attention to certain limited aspects of a big problem which certainly deserve examination, but on which a great deal of detailed work unknown to the author has already been done, and a great deal more will yet have to be done, before a comprehensive study like the present can be attempted with better prospect of success.[40]

[40][Hayek was later a bit more charitable towards Hallowell's study, which has since become a classic of modern German intellectual history. "Hallowell clearly shows how the leading liberal legal theorists in the Germany of the late nineteenth century by their acceptance of a legal positivism which regarded all law as the deliberate creation of a legislator and who were interested only in the constitutionality of an act of legislation and not in the character of the rules laid down, deprived themselves of any possibility of a resistance to the supersession of the 'material' by the merely 'formal' *Rechtsstaat* and at the same time discredited liberalism by this connexion with a legal positivism with which it is fundamentally incompatible". *Law, Legislation and Liberty*, vol. 2: *The Mirage of Social Justice* (Chicago and London: University of Chicago Press, 1976), p. 167, n 27. -Ed.]

EIGHT

HISTORIANS AND THE FUTURE
OF EUROPE[1]

Whether we shall be able to rebuild something like a common European civilisation after this war will be decided mainly by what happens in the years immediately following it. It is possible that the events that will accompany the collapse of Germany will cause such destruction as to remove the whole of Central Europe for generations or perhaps permanently from the orbit of European civilisation. It seems unlikely that, if this happens, the developments can be confined to Central Europe; and if the fate of Europe should be to relapse into barbarism, though ultimately a new civilisation may emerge from it, it is not likely that this country would escape the consequences. The future of England is tied up with the future of Europe, and, whether we like it or not, the future of Europe will be largely decided by what will happen in Germany. Our efforts at least must be directed towards regaining Germany for those values on which European civilisation was built and which alone can form the basis from which we can move towards the realisation of the ideals which guide us.

Before we consider what we can do to that end, we must try to form a realistic picture of the kind of intellectual and moral situation we must expect to find in a defeated Germany. If anything is certain it is that even after victory we shall not have it in our power to make the defeated think just as we would wish them to; that we shall not be able to do more than assist any promising development; and that any clumsy efforts to proselytise may well produce results opposite to those at which we aim. Two extreme views can still be heard which are equally naive and misleading: on the one hand, that all the Germans are equally corrupted and that therefore only

[1][A paper read to the Political Society at King's College, Cambridge University, on February 28, 1944. The chair was taken by Sir John Clapham. First published in *Studies in Philosophy, Politics and Economics* (London: Routledge & Kegan Paul; Chicago, University of Chicago Press; Toronto: University of Toronto Press, 1967), pp. 135–147. -Ed.]

the complete education of a new generation imposed from outside can change them, or, on the other hand, that the masses of the Germans, once they are freed from their present masters, will quickly and readily embrace political and moral views similar to our own. The position will certainly be more complicated than either of these views suggests. We shall almost certainly find a moral and intellectual desert, but one with many oases, some very fine, but almost completely isolated from each other. The outstanding feature will be the absence of any common tradition—beyond that of opposition to the Nazis and, probably, also to communism—of any common beliefs, a great disillusionment about what can be positively achieved by political action. There will, at first at any rate, be any amount of good will; but nothing will probably be more conspicuous than the powerlessness of good intentions without the uniting element of those common moral and political traditions which we take for granted, but which in Germany a complete break of a dozen years has destroyed, with a thoroughness which few people in this country can imagine.

On the other hand, we must be prepared not only to find an extraordinarily high intellectual level in some of the oases that have been preserved, but even to find that many of the Germans have learnt lessons which we have not yet understood, and that some of our conceptions will appear to their experience-hardened minds very naive and *simpliste*. Hampered as discussion is under the Nazi regime, it has by no means stopped; and from the few samples of German wartime works I have seen (and from the complete list of books published in Germany which I have recently been able to peruse) I have the impression that the intellectual level of the academic discussion of social and political problems in wartime is at least not lower than in this country—probably because many of the best Germans either are precluded, or have voluntarily excluded themselves, from immediate participation in the war effort.

It will be on the Germans who have carried on in this manner—not in proportion to the population of Germany, but numerous enough compared with the number of people who think independently in any country—that our hopes must rest, and to them that we must give any assistance we can. The task of finding them and assisting them without at the same time discrediting them with their own people will be a most difficult and delicate one. If these men are to succeed in making their views prevail, they will need some measure of moral and material support from outside. But they will need almost as much protection against well-intentioned but injudicious attempts to use them by the governmental machinery set up by the victorious powers. While they will probably be anxious to re-establish connexions with, and to obtain the good will of, persons in other countries with whom they share common ideals, they will be rightly reluctant to become in any form instruments of the governmental apparatus of the victors. Unless opportunities are deliberately created for the meeting as equal individuals of persons from both sides who share certain basic ideals, it is not likely that such contacts will soon be re-established. But for a long time such opportunities can be created only by initiative from this side. And it seems to me certain that it must come through the efforts of private individuals and not through governmental agencies if such efforts are to have beneficial effects.

There will be many directions in which international contacts between individuals and groups might be deliberately re-established with beneficial effects. It will probably be easiest, and take place quickest, between the political groups of the Left. But such contacts should clearly not be limited to party groups, and if they were to be confined for some time to the political groups of the Left, this would be very unfortunate from every point of view. If in Germany a more cosmopolitan outlook should once more become, as has largely been true in the past, a prerogative of the Left, this might well contribute to drive the large groups of the Centre again into a nationalist attitude. It will be a more difficult, but in some ways even more important, task to assist the resumption of contacts between those groups where existing alignments in internal politics will not at once provide the channels. And there are tasks for which any grouping on the lines of party politics would be a definite obstacle, though a certain minimum of agreement on political ideals will be essential for any collaboration.

What I want to talk about tonight is more specifically the role which the historians can play in this connexion—where by historians I mean really all students of society, past or present. There can be no doubt that in what is called the 're-education of the German people' the historians will in the long run play a decisive part, just as they did in creating the ideas that rule Germany today. I know that it is difficult for English people to appreciate how great and immediate the influence of academic work of this kind is in Germany, and how seriously the Germans take their professors—almost as seriously as the German professors take themselves. The role which the German political historians of the nineteenth century have played in creating the veneration for the power state and the expansionist ideas which created modern Germany can scarcely be overrated. It was indeed "that garrison of distinguished historians", of which Lord Acton[2] wrote in 1886, "that prepared the Prussian supremacy together with their own, and now hold Berlin like a fortress", who created the ideas "by which the rude strength centred in a region more ungenial than Latium was employed to absorb and to stiffen the diffused, sentimental, and strangely impolitical talent of the studious Germans".[3] There was indeed, to quote Lord Acton again, "probably . . . no considerable group less in harmony with our sentiments in approaching the study of history than that which is mainly represented by Sybel,[4] Droysen,[5] and Treitschke,[6] with Mommsen[7] and Gneist,[8] Bernhardi,[9] and Duncker[10] on the flank", and so much given "to maxims which it has cost the world so much effort to reverse".[11] And it was no accident that it was also Acton the historian who, in spite of all his admiration for much in Germany, foresaw fifty years ago that the tremendous power built up by very able minds, chiefly in Berlin, was "the greatest danger that remains to be encountered by the Anglo-Saxon race".

Though I cannot attempt here to trace in any detail the ways in which the teaching of the historians has helped to produce the doctrines which rule Germany today, you will probably agree with me this influence was very great. Even some of the most repulsive features of the Nazi ideology trace back to German historians whom Hitler has probably never read but whose ideas have dominated the atmosphere in which he grew up. This is true especially of all the race doctrines, which, though I believe the German historians took them first from the French, were mainly developed in Germany. If I had time I could show how in other respects as well scholars of

[2][John Emerich Edward Dalberg-Acton, First Baron Acton (1834–1902). On Acton see also this volume, chapter 9. -Ed.]

[3]["German Schools of History" [1886], in *Essays in the Study and Writing of History*, vol. 2 of *Selected Writings of Lord Acton*, ed. J. Rufus Fears (Indianapolis, Ind.: LibertyClassics, 1985–88), pp. 325–364, esp. p. 352. -Ed.]

[4][Heinrich von Sybel (1817–1895) was Professor at the Universities of Marburg and Bonn and later director of the Prussian archives. -Ed.]

[5][Johann Gustav Droysen (1808–1884) was Professor at the Universities of Kiel, Berlin, and Jena and author of *Geschichte der preussischen Politik* (Berlin: Veit, 1855-86). -Ed.]

[6][Heinrich von Treitschke (1834–1896) was Professor at the Universities of Freiburg, Heidelberg, and Berlin. -Ed.]

[7][Theodor Mommsen (1817–1903) was Professor at the University of Berlin from 1858 to 1903 and specialist on the history of Rome. -Ed.]

[8][Heinrich Rudolf von Gneist (1816–1895). -Ed.]

[9][Theodor von Bernhardi (1803–1887). -Ed.]

[10][Theodor Julius Duncker (1811–1886). -Ed.]

[11]["German Schools of History", op. cit., pp. 355–356. -Ed.]

international fame like Werner Sombart taught a generation ago what to all intents and purposes is the same as the later Nazi doctrines. And I could add, in order not to leave all the blame on the historians, how in a related field my own professional colleagues, the economists, became willingly the instruments of extreme nationalist aspirations so that, e.g., Admiral Tirpitz, when forty or fifty years ago he found the big industrialists rather lukewarm in their reception of his naval policy, could enlist the support of the economists in order to persuade the capitalists of the advantages of his imperialistic ambitions.[12]

There can be little doubt, however, that the influence of the historians proper was the most important; and there is more than one reason why it seems likely that in the future the influence of history for good or bad will be even greater than it was in the past. The complete break in the continuity of most traditions will probably itself produce a turning back to history in search of traditions which provide a foundation for future developments. There will be a great deal of history to be written on the way in which all the misfortunes came about, questions in which the public will take a passionate interest and which are almost bound to become the subject of political disputes.

From our point of view, there is an additional reason why it is urgently to be desired that the Germans should be led to re-examine recent history and to take account of certain facts of which the majority of them are still unaware. The picture of recent history which not only the masses of the German people, but almost everybody in that country still start from, will indeed be the effect of Nazi propaganda which it will be most difficult to remove. It is of great importance that we should remember that many of the facts which have been decisive in forming our opinion of German responsibility and German character will be either unknown to most Germans, or so lightly fixed in their recollections as to carry little weight. Though many Germans will at first be ready to admit that the Allies have reason to distrust them and to insist on far-reaching precautions against another German aggression, even the most reasonable among them will soon be alienated by what to them will

---

[12]In his *Memoirs* Tirpitz records how one of the officers of the information department of the Admiralty was sent "the round of the universities, where all the political economists, including Brentano, were ready to give splendid support. Schmoller, Wagner, Sering, Schumacher, and many others showed that the expenditure on the fleet would be a productive outlay," etc., etc. [Alfred von Tirpitz, *My Memoirs* (New York: Dodd, Mead, 1919), p. 143. -Ed.]

appear excessive restrictions imposed upon them, unless they come to see the full extent of the harm they have inflicted on Europe. After the last war, the gulf which separated the respective views of the two belligerent groups about the facts with which they most reproached each other was never really closed. The admirable willingness to forget, shown at least by the English, brought it about that soon after the last war almost everything which did not fit into the German picture was dismissed as 'atrocity stories'. We may quite possibly find again that not all the reports about the Germans which reached us during the war were true. But this is merely another reason for a careful re-examination of all the facts, a sorting out of what is definitely established from the mere rumours. To follow the natural tendency of letting bygones be bygones and not raking up the mud of the Nazi period would be fatal to the prospect of any real understanding with the Germans. The point at which the more unpleasant facts of recent Germany history are forgotten must not be allowed to come before the Germans have acknowledged their truth to themselves. The air of injured innocence, with which most Germans reacted to the settlement after the last war, was very largely due to real ignorance of the charges of which at that time they were regarded as guilty by nearly everybody in the victorious countries.

These things will have to be discussed—and they certainly will be discussed by ill-informed politicians and by way of recrimination. But if, instead of new causes of future conflict, something like a common view is to emerge, this will depend on these matters not being left entirely to party discussion and nationalist passions, but on their being considered in a more dispassionate spirit by men who wish above all to find the truth. Whether, in Germany in particular, the result of these discussions shall be new political myths or something like the truth will to a great extent depend on the school of historians which will gain the ear of the people. Personally, I can have no doubt that the work which will determine future German opinion will come from inside Germany and not from outside. The suggestion one can now often hear that the victors should produce the textbooks on which future generations of Germans should be brought up appears to me pitifully silly. Such an attempt would be certain to produce the opposite of what is desired. No officially imposed creed, no history written to please another authority in the place of that in the interest of which so much Germany history was written in the past, least of all one inspired by foreign governments (or by emigrants) can hope to gain credence or lasting influence with the German people. The best we can hope, and all we from the outside can usefully work for, is that the history which is to influence the course of German opinions will be written in a sincere effort to find out the truth, subservient to no authority, no nation, race, or class. History must above all cease to be an instrument of national policy.

The most difficult thing to re-create in Germany will be the belief in the existence of an objective truth, of the possibility of a history which is not written in the service of a particular interest. This is where, I believe, international collaboration, if it is collaboration between free individuals, may be of immense value. It would demonstrate the possibility of agreement independent of national allegiance. It would be particularly effective if the historians of the more fortunate countries set the example of not boggling at criticism of their own governments whenever called for. The desire for recognition by and encouragement from his own peers in other countries is perhaps the strongest safeguard against the corruption of the historian by nationalist sentiments, and the closer the international contacts the less will be the danger—just as isolation is almost certain to have the opposite effect. I remember only too well how after the last war the expulsion of all Germans from certain learned societies and their exclusion from certain international scientific congresses was among the strongest of the forces which drove many German scholars into the nationalist camp.

Thus, even insofar as the mere supremacy of truth in the historical teaching of future generations of Germans is concerned, the restoration of contacts with other historians would be of value, and any facilities we can create for this purpose will have a useful role to play. But, supremely important as strict adherence to truth is, I do not believe that it is enough to prevent history from being perverted in its teaching. We must distinguish here between historical research proper and historiography, the exposition of history for the people at large.[13] I am now coming to a very delicate and much disputed subject, and I shall probably be accused of contradicting much of what I have just said. I am convinced, however, that no historical teaching can be effective without passing implicit or explicit judgements, and that its effects will depend very largely on the moral standards which it applies. Even if the academic historian tried to keep his history 'pure' and strictly 'scientific', there will be

---

[13][Hayek is apparently not using the term 'historiography' in its conventional meaning, as the study of the methods and practice of the writing of history. He distinguishes here between original historical research and popular history. -Ed.]

written for the general public histories which will judge and for that reason will have a greater influence. I believe, indeed, that if those German historians who did value truth above everything had so much less influence than their more political colleagues, and if even what influence the former had was in a direction not so very different from that of the latter, it was largely because of their extreme ethical neutrality, which tended to 'explain'—and thereby seemed to justify—everything by the 'circumstances of the time', and which was afraid ever to call black black or white white. It was these scientific historians as much as their political colleagues who inculcated the Germans with the belief that political acts cannot be measured by moral standards, and even that the ends justify the means. I cannot see that the most perfect respect for truth is in any way incompatible with the application of very rigorous moral standards in our judgement of historical events; and it seems to me that what the Germans need, and what in the past would have done them all the good in the world, is a strong dose of what it is now the fashion to call 'Whig history', history of the kind of which Lord Acton is one of the last great representatives. The future historian must have the courage to say that Hitler was a bad man, or else the time he spends on 'explaining' him will only serve to the glorification of his misdeeds.

It is probable that in the cultivation of certain common standards of moral judgement collaboration across frontiers could contribute a great deal—particularly where we have to deal with a country where traditions have been so disrupted and standards so lowered as in Germany of recent years. Even more important, however, is that collaboration will be possible only with those—or at least, that we ought to be willing to collaborate only with those—who are ready to subscribe to certain moral standards, and who in their work have adhered to them. There must be certain common values beyond the sacredness of truth: an agreement, at least, that the ordinary rules of moral decency must apply to political action, and beyond that also a certain minimum agreement on the most general political ideals. The latter need probably be no more than a common belief in the value of individual freedom, an affirmative attitude towards democracy without any superstitious deference to all its dogmatic applications, particularly without condoning the oppression of minorities any more than that of majorities, and, finally, an equal opposition to all forms of totalitarianism, whether it be from the Right or from the Left.

But while it seems that no collaboration would be possible unless it was based on agreement on a common set of values, a kind of agreed programme, it may be doubted whether any programme drawn up for the purpose would be likely to serve this end. No brief statement, however skilfully drawn up, is likely to give satisfactory expression to the set of ideals I have in mind, or would have much chance of uniting a considerable body of scholars. It seems that much more effective than any such programme designed ad hoc would be some great figure who embodies in an especially high degree the virtues and ideals which such an association would have to serve, and whose name could serve as a flag under which men who agree could unite.

I believe that there is one great name available who fits the bill as perfectly as if he had been created for the purpose: I am thinking of Lord Acton. The suggestion I want to put before you is indeed that an 'Acton Society' might form the most suitable agency to assist in the tasks of the historians of this country and of Germany, and perhaps of other countries, which I have attempted to sketch. There are many features united in the figure of Lord Acton that make him almost uniquely suitable as such a symbol. He was, of course, half German by education and more than half German in his training as a historian, and the Germans, for that reason, regard him almost as one of themselves. At the same time he unites, as perhaps no other recent figure, the great English liberal tradition with the best there is in the liberal tradition of the Continent—always using 'liberal' in its true and comprehensive sense, not, as Lord Acton expressed it, for the 'defenders of secondary liberties', but for one to whom individual liberty is of supreme value and "not a means to a higher political end".[14]

If to us Lord Acton perhaps sometimes appears to err by the extreme rigour with which he applies universal moral standards to all times and conditions, this is all to the good, when sympathy with his general outlook is to be a test of selection. I do not know of another figure with regard to whom we can say with equal confidence that, if after the war we find that a German scholar sincerely agrees with his ideals, he is the type of German with whom no Englishman need feel reluctant to shake hands. In spite of all he took from Germany, I think it can be said that he was not only more free of all we hate in the Germans than many a pure Englishman, but also that he had discerned the dangerous aspects of

---

[14][Compare "The History of Freedom in Antiquity" [1877], in *Essays in the History of Liberty*, vol. 1 of *Selected Writings of Lord Acton*, op. cit., pp. 5–28, esp. p. 22. -Ed.]

German developments earlier and more clearly than most other people.

Before I say more about Acton's political philosophy, let me mention one or two other advantages his name seems to combine for our purpose. One is that Acton was a Catholic, even a devout Catholic, yet one who in political matters always preserved complete independence of Rome and never shrank from using the whole austerity of his moral standards in judging the history of the institution he most revered, the Roman Catholic Church. This seems to me very important: not only because, if a more liberal outlook is to be fostered among the great masses who are neither definitely 'Right' or 'Left', any such effort must carefully avoid that hostile attitude towards religion characteristic of much of Continental liberalism, which has done a great deal to drive hosts of decent people into opposition to any kind of liberalism. More important even is that among the real opposition to Hitler in Germany the Catholics have played such an important part that no organisation which, without being itself Roman Catholic, is not at least of such a character as to make it possible for a devout Catholic to collaborate, can hope to gain influence among the great middle groups on which the success of its efforts will so much depend. From what little one can see of German war literature it almost seems as if what spirit of liberalism can still be found in Germany is mainly to be found among the Catholic groups. So far as the historians more especially are concerned, it is almost certainly true that at least some of the Roman Catholic historians (I am thinking particularly of Franz Schnabel and his *Deutsche Geschichte im neunzehnten Jahrhundert*) have kept more free from the poison of nationalism and the veneration of the power state than most other German historians.

Another reason which makes it seem probable that the political philosophy of Lord Acton would have a great appeal to many Germans in the state of mind in which they will be after this war is the extraordinary vogue which, according to all signs, the writings of Jakob Burckhardt[15] are enjoying in Germany today. Burckhardt, though he differs from Acton by his deep pessimism, has much in common with him, above all the ever-reiterated emphasis on power as the arch-evil, the opposition to centralism, and the sympathy for the small and multi-national state. It might indeed be desirable to couple with the name of Acton, though not in the name, yet in the programme of the society, not only the name of Burckhardt, but

---

[15][Jakob Christoph Burkhardt (1818–1897), Swiss historian. -Ed.]

also that of the great French historian who has so much in common with both of them, de Tocqueville.[16] Jointly, these three names indicate probably even better than the single name of Acton the kind of basic political ideals under whose inspiration history might give the future Europe the political re-education which it needs—perhaps because, more than anybody else, these three men continued the tradition of the great political philosopher who, as Acton said, "at his best was England at its best"—Edmund Burke.

If I were to attempt fully to justify my choice of Lord Acton as the main name under which such an effort might be attempted, I should have to give you an outline of his historical maxims and of his political philosophy. But though this would be a task worth attempting (and, significantly, recently attempted by a German scholar[17]), it can hardly be done in a few minutes. All I can do is to read to you from my private Acton anthology some passages which express briefly a few characteristic convictions—though any such selection will give a somewhat one-sided and, in the undesirable sense, too 'political' impression.

I can be very brief about Acton's notion of history. "My notion of history", he wrote, "is of a thing the same for all men, not open to treatment from special and exclusive standpoints". This implies, of course, not only the singleness of truth, but also Acton's belief in the universal validity of moral standards. I will remind you in this connexion of the famous passage from the Inaugural Lecture in which he says that

> the weight of opinion is against me when I exhort you never to debase the moral currency or to lower the standard of rectitude, but to try others by the final maxim that governs your own lives, and to suffer no man and no cause to escape the undying penalty which history has power to inflict on wrong. The plea in extenuation of guilt and mitigation of punishment is perpetual.[18]

an argument which Acton develops more fully in a well-known letter to a fellow historian, which I should like to quote at length, but from which I can read only a sentence or two. He argues there against the thesis that great historical figures must be judged

---

[16][Alexis de Tocqueville (1805–1859), author of *Democracy in America* (London: Saunders & Otley, 1835). -Ed.]

[17][Probably a reference to Ulrich Noack, who wrote several studies of Acton in the late 1930s and 1940s. -Ed.]

[18]["The Study of History" [1895], in *Essays in the Study and Writing of History*, op. cit., pp. 504–552, esp. p. 546. -Ed.]

unlike other men, with a favourable presumption that they did no wrong. If there is any presumption it is the other way against holders of power, increasing as the power increases. Historic responsibility has to make up for the want of legal responsibility. Power tends to corrupt and absolute power corrupts absolutely. Great men are almost always bad men, even when they exercise influence and not authority: still more when you superadd the tendency or certainty of corruption by authority. There is no worse heresy than that the office sanctifies the holder of it. That is the point at which the negation of Catholicism and the negation of Liberalism meet and keep high festival.[19]

And he concludes: "The inflexible integrity of the moral code is, to me, the secret of the authority, the dignity, the utility of history."[20]

My illustrations of Acton's political philosophy must be even more unsystematic and incomplete, selected mainly for their relevance to the present situation and to what I have already said. I shall give the few quotations without comment, and only hope that they will have more freshness than the somewhat hackneyed passages I have just quoted. But perhaps recent events make it easier to appreciate the significance of some of these statements, such as the following discussion of what we now call 'totalitarianism':

Whenever a single definite object is made the supreme end of the State, be it the advantage of a class, the safety or the power of the country, the greatest happiness of the greatest number, or the support of any speculative idea, the State becomes for a time inevitably absolute. Liberty alone demands for its realisation the limitation of the public authority, for liberty is the only object which benefits all alike, and provokes no sincere opposition.[21]

Or take the following:

The true democratic principle, that none shall have power over the people, is taken to mean that none shall be able to restrain or elude its power. The true democratic principle, that the people shall not be made to do what it does not like, is taken to mean that it shall never be required to tolerate what it does not like. The

[19][Letter to Bishop Mandell Creighton, April 5, 1887, in *ibid.*, pp. 378–388, esp. p. 383. -Ed.]

[20][*Ibid.*, p. 384. -Ed.]

[21]["Nationality" [1862], in *Essays in the History of Liberty*, op. cit., pp. 409–433, esp. p. 424. -Ed.]

true democratic principle, that every man's free will shall be as unfettered as possible, is taken to mean that the free will of the collective people shall be fettered in nothing.[22]

Or:

A theory that identified liberty with a single right, the right of doing all that you have the actual power to do, and a theory which secures liberty by certain unalterable rights, and founds it on truth which men did not invent and cannot abjure, cannot both be formative principles in the same Constitution. Absolute power and restrictions on its exercise cannot exist together. It is but a new form of the old contest between the spirit of true freedom and despotism in its most dexterous disguise.

And finally:

Liberty depends on the division of power. Democracy tends to unity of power. To keep asunder the agents, one must divide the sources; that is, one must maintain, or create, separate administrative bodies. In the view of increasing democracy, a restricted federalism is the one possible check on concentration and centralism.[23]

Perhaps the most important argument, too long to quote, is that of the essay on nationality where Acton courageously opposed to the dominant doctrine that (as expressed by J. S. Mill) "it is in general a necessary condition of free institutions, that the boundaries of governments should coincide in the main with those of nationalities"[24] the opposite view that the "co-existence of several nations under the same State is a test, as well as the best security of its freedom. It is also one of the chief instruments of civilisation; and, as such, it is in the natural and providential order, and indicates a state of greater advancement than the national unity which is the ideal of modern liberalism."[25] Nobody who knows central Europe will deny that we cannot hope there for lasting peace and advance

---

[22]["Sir Erskine May's 'Democracy in Europe'", in *ibid.*, pp. 54–85, esp. p. 80.-Ed.]

[23][Letter to Mary Gladstone, February 20, 1882, in the *Letters of Lord Acton to Mary, Daughter of the Right Hon. W. E. Gladstone*, ed. Herbert Paul (London: Macmillan, 1913), p. 98. -Ed.]

[24][John Stuart Mill, *Considerations on Representative Government* [1861], in *Essays on Politics and Society*, vol. 19 of the *Collected Works of John Stuart Mill* (Toronto: University of Toronto Press; London: Routledge & Kegan Paul, 1965), pp. 371–577, esp. p. 548. -Ed.]

[25][Acton, "Nationality", op. cit., pp. 425. -Ed.]

of civilisation unless these ideas become at last victorious, nor that the most practical solution of the problems of that part of the world is a federalism of the kind Acton advocated.

Do not say that these ideals are utopian and therefore not worth working for. It is *because* they are ideals which can only be realised in the more or less distant future that they are the kind of ideals by which the historian can allow himself to be guided without the risk of becoming involved in party passions. As a teacher, and the historian cannot help being the political teacher of the future generations, he must not allow himself to be influenced by considerations of what is now possible, but ought to be concerned with making what decent people agree to be desirable, but what seems impracticable in view of the existing state of opinion. It is because, whether he wills it or not, the historian shapes the political ideals of the future, that he himself must be guided by the highest ideals and keep free from the political disputes of the day. The higher the ideals which guide him, and the more he can keep independent from political movements aiming at immediate goals, the more he may hope in the long run to make possible many things for which the world may not yet be ready. I am not even sure that we may not, by keeping distant ends in view, exercise a greater influence than the 'hard-boiled realist' of the kind that is now fashionable.

I have little doubt that a considerable group of historians, or, I should rather say, students of society, pledged to the ideals embodied in the work of Lord Acton, could become a great force for good. But what, you will ask, can any formal organisation, such as the Acton Society I have suggested, contribute towards this end? To this my answer is, first, that I should not expect so much from its action as a body, but a great deal from it as an instrument for making possible in the near future the resumption of numerous individual contacts across the boundaries. I need not again emphasise why it is so important that what help or encouragement we can give should not come mainly through official or governmental channels. But for the individual it will for a long time be very difficult to do anything in isolation. The purely technical difficulties of seeking out individually the persons on the other side with whom one would wish to collaborate will be even greater. In all this such a society (or it would rather have to be a kind of club with selected membership) would be of great help.

But though I regard this facilitating of contacts between individuals as the more important purpose, and though it is scarcely possible now to sketch in any detail what the collective activities of the society might be, I believe that there will be not inconsiderable scope for such activities, mainly of an editorial kind. A good deal could be done to revive and popularise the works of those German political writers who in the past have represented a political philosophy more in accord with the ideals we wish to foster than those who had the greatest influence during the past seventy years. Even a journal largely devoted to the common discussion of problems of recent history might well prove beneficial, and might canalise discussion into a direction more profitable than the 'war-guilt' bickerings after the last war. It is possible that both in this country and in Germany a journal devoted not to the results of historical research proper but to the exposition of history to the general public might prove both successful and have a real role to play if conducted by responsible historians. The society as such would, of course, never presume to decide any of the controversial questions, but in providing a forum for discussion and opportunity for collaboration between historians from different countries it would probably perform a very useful service.

But I must not let myself be led into any discussion of detail. My purpose has been not to solicit support for a definite project, but rather to submit a tentative suggestion to your criticism. While the more I think about the potential good such a society might do, the more I am attracted by the idea, it does not seem worth pursuing it further without first trying it out on other people. So if you will tell me whether you think that some attempt in the direction indicated seems to you worthwhile, and whether the name of Lord Acton appears to you a suitable symbol under which such an association might be formed, this will be of great help to me in deciding whether to pursue the idea further or to drop it.[26]

---

[26][Hayek did of course pursue it, by arranging the conference in Switzerland that became the Mont Pèlerin Society. See his opening address to the conference, reprinted in this volume, chapter 12. -Ed.]

NINE

THE ACTONIAN REVIVAL:
ON LORD ACTON (1834-1902)[1]

With a sure instinct where the strength of his opponents rested, the late Professor Harold Laski once wrote that "a case of unanswerable power could . . . be made out for the view that [de Tocqueville] and Lord Acton were the essential liberals of the nineteenth century".[2] That this is at least partially true is now increasingly recognised. The Whig tradition which they represented, the British element in the incongruous mixture which European liberalism then constituted, is gradually being separated from the elements of French intellectualist democracy which had overlaid many of its most valuable features. As the totalitarian propensities of that French tradition come to be more and more clearly seen,[3] it becomes increasingly important to recover the sources of the great tradition which Lord Acton had in mind when he wrote that "Burke at his best is England at its best". It seems that after more than a hundred years the basic truth is at last recognised which that great American, Francis Lieber, so brilliantly expressed in his essays on "Anglican and Gallican Liberty".[4]

It is as the last great representative of the English Whig tradition and its most important development in the American Revolution that Lord Acton is of such importance today. He himself was perfectly aware of this intellectual ancestry, and most of his charac-

[1][Published as "The Actonian Revival", a review of Gertrude Himmelfarb, *Lord Acton: A Study in Conscience and Politics* (Chicago: University of Chicago Press, 1952), and of G. E. Fasnacht, *Acton's Political Philosophy: An Analysis* (New York: Viking, 1953), in *The Freeman*, March 23, 1953, pp. 461–462. -Ed.]

[2][Harold J. Laski, "Alexis de Tocqueville and Democracy", in F. J. C. Hearnshaw, ed., *The Social and Political Ideas of Some Representative Thinkers of the Victorian Age* (London: George C. Harap, 1933), p. 100. Harold Laski (1893–1950) was Professor of Political Science at the London School of Economics from 1920 until 1950 and Chairman of the British Labour Party. -Ed.]

[3]See particularly J. L. Talmon's important study on *The Origins of Totalitarian Democracy* (London: Secker and Warburg, 1952).

[4][Francis Lieber, *Civil Liberty and Self-Government* [1849], third edition, ed. Theodore D. Woolsey (London: J. B. Lippincott, 1881), pp. 51–55 and 279–296. -Ed.]

216

teristic maxims could easily be traced to seventeenth- and eighteenth-century sources (compare, e.g., Milton's fear that "long continuance of power may corrupt sincerest men"[5]). Although Acton himself never achieved a systematic exposition of his views, the corpus of his historical essays and lectures is probably still the most complete summation of that true liberalism which sharply differed from the radicalism that led to socialism, and which to me still appears as the finest set of values which Western civilisation has produced. It is incalculable how much misery at least the European continent would have been spared if that tradition had prevailed instead of the intellectualist version of liberalism which by its fierce and intolerant attitude to religion divided Europe hopelessly into two camps.

The widespread revival of interest in the writings of Lord Acton—and de Toqueville—is thus a welcome and promising sign. Within the last few years we have had, apart from numerous articles on him in learned journals, Bishop Mathew's study on Acton's youth, a valuable essay on him by Professor Herbert Butterfield, and Miss Himmelfarb's earlier collection of some of Acton's essays published in 1948 under the title *Freedom and Power*.[6] An edition of Acton's complete works has been announced,[7] and simultaneously with the two volumes under review,[8] a most welcome edition of his *Essays on Church and State* has been brought out by Mr. Douglas Woodruff.[9]

The two books under review—Miss Himmelfarb's *Lord Acton: A Study in Conscience and Politics*, and G. E. Fasnacht's *Acton's Political Philosophy: An Analysis*—are nevertheless the first satisfactory accounts of Acton's ideas as a whole. Moreover, they are complementary rather than competing with each other. Miss Himmelfarb's is a very skilful account of the evolution of Acton's ideas, while Mr. Fasnacht surveys them systematically topic by topic. Both authors have drawn

---

[5][*The Readie and Easie Way to Establish a Free Commonwealth* [1660], in *The Complete Prose Works of John Milton*, ed. Harold Kollmeir (New Haven, Conn.: Yale University Press, 1980), vol. 7, p. 434, line 20. -Ed.]

[6][David Mathew, *Acton, the Formative Years* (London: Eyre & Spottiswoode, 1946); Herbert Butterfield, *Lord Acton*, Pamphlets of the English Historical Association, no. 69 (London: G. Philip, 1948); Acton, *Essays on Freedom and Power*, selected and with an Introduction by Gertrude Himmelfarb (Boston: Beacon Press, 1948). -Ed.]

[7][But at this date is not yet published. Meanwhile see J. Rufus Fears, ed., *Selected Writings of Lord Acton*, op. cit. -Ed.]

[8][See this chapter, note 1. -Ed.]

[9][Douglas Woodruff, ed., *Essays on Church and State* (London: Hollis & Carter, 1952). -Ed.]

heavily on the great volume of Acton manuscripts preserved in the library of Cambridge University, and as a result a great deal of new light is thrown on many of Acton's ideas which he had expressed only aphoristically in his occasional publications. Although I have myself for a long time been a student and admirer of Acton, I have gratefully to admit that many of the apparent contradictions in his writings have resolved themselves for me only as a result of Miss Himmelfarb's sympathetic description of the slow growth and gradual change of his views. She also reconstructs from the accessible documents an intelligible account of the most crucial episode in Acton's life, his reaction to the declaration of papal infallibility by the Vatican Council in 1870, which the suppression of his relevant letters of that period had so far concealed.[10] The book is certainly the best introduction to Acton's thought, even though the author probably exaggerates the extent to which Acton in later life had abandoned the Whig position of the early Burke; it is perhaps also for this reason that she is unduly puzzled by the fact that Acton, who had nothing but praise for the American Revolution, remained highly critical of the French Revolution.

Prepared by Miss Himmelfarb's introduction the reader will turn with advantage to Mr. Fasnacht's less readable but no less careful and scholarly presentation of Acton's mature thought. It is a straightforward exposition, largely in Acton's own words. Though Mr. Fasnacht is fully aware of the development of Acton's ideas, his aim is mainly to show that they form a coherent system and to provide as much material as possible from which the gaps in the fragmentary statements left by Acton himself can be filled. It makes a fascinating book to study. We get many of the more suggestive notes from the hundreds of card boxes in which Acton had accumulated the material for his "History of Liberty", the "greatest book that has never been written". There is material there, not only for many Ph.D. theses, but also for some good books which I hope will some day appear. And the thoughtful reader will find ample stimulus to exercise his own intelligence on some of the toughest problems of political philosophy.

[10][See *Lord Acton on Papal Power*, compiled by H. A. MacDougal (London: Sheed & Ward, 1973). -Ed.]

TEN

IS THERE A GERMAN NATION?[1]

Difficult as it is for the ordinary man to believe that all he has heard of the Germans can be true, it becomes almost impossible for those who have direct acquaintance with a particular side of German life. Those who are really aware of the crimes committed by tens of thousands of Germans during [the Second World] War find it hard to believe that this does not show the common character of all Germans, and they often strive to forget whatever else they may have known about them. Those, on the other hand, who ever knew intimately one of the better sides of German life find themselves, against all evidence, clinging to the belief that what we hear now must be greatly exaggerated and the work of comparatively few. Yet all such attempts to arrive at a consistent picture by suppressing part of the facts are fatal to an understanding of the German problem. Any true picture of that people must begin by the realisation that extreme opposites form part of it.

It is the great merit of Professor Vermeil's new survey of German history[2] that he has not distorted it by any attempt at false consistency. His book, the latest and ripest product of the great school of French *Germanistes* at the Sorbonne, is a remarkable work in many ways. It is admirable in spirit, catholic in interest, almost incredibly learned in the remotest corners of German history and literature, and astonishing in its capacity for sympathy with what are often strange phenomena. He covers an enormous field in great compression, and the frequent brief allusions to less-known figures and events are a high tribute to the education of the French readers to

---

[1][Review of Edmond Vermeil, *Germany's Three Reichs* (London: A. Dakers, 1944), published in *Time and Tide*, March 24, 1945, pp. 249–250. Hayek notes there that "[i]n the quotations from the book I omit all the italics, the lavish use of which throughout the work is the one serious blemish of an otherwise remarkably good production". -Ed.]

[2][See preceding note. -Ed.]

whom it was originally addressed. Such a guide through a forest, who makes us stop here and there in a rapid journey to notice characteristic details, cannot always be easy reading. At times what one sees is like the parts of an intricate mosaic, too big ever to be seen in its entirety. Yet unsatisfactory as this may seem at first, it may yet be the truest picture that can be given where perhaps there is no true whole.

Of the strictly historical part of the book no more can be said here than that all the essential ingredients which went to the making of modern Germany are there, from "the splendid but brief career of the towns" in the fourteenth and fifteenth centuries to the forced development of the economy under Bismarck, which substituted for the lacking bourgeoisie a class of *nouveaux riches* "desperately in search of a tradition they did not possess", the intellectual development from the great ages of Leibnitz and Bach, or Goethe and Beethoven, to Nietzsche's later work and to H. S. Chamberlain,[3] and the religious development from Lutheranism to a religious indifferentism which the religious instinct "disappointed and deceived, turned to science, or to art and literature, or finally, to the nation conceived as an imperial community". Even where a statement at first surprises, such as the remark about the docile majority on which Bismarck counted but which he never had, or about Hitler as "the man of compromise, perhaps in that respect the successor of Bismarck", it proves on reflection both true and illuminating.

The history of Germany provides, however, only a framework within which Professor Vermeil pursues his main purpose, the "explanation of that aggressiveness in principle" characteristic of the Third Reich. He does not make his task easy and he is certainly not blind to what is great and admirable in German history. He even emphasises that "there always has been, and is to this day behind the Hitler façade, a humanist Germany" and that while "[a] minority in Germany extol war[,] the majority hate it but accept and wage it". Yet all this is part of an argument which tries to explain why "as an organised nation, Germany becomes intolerable". To some people the strict justice with which Professor Vermeil concedes and even stresses all the good points in the Germans will condemn the book. I find the true story how a mixture containing so many good

---

[3][Houston Stewart Chamberlain (1855–1927), author of *Die Grundlagen des neunzehnten Jahrhunderts* (Munich: F. Bruckmann, 1899), translated as *Foundations of the Nineteenth Century* (London and New York: John Lane, 1910). -Ed.]

elements has produced the Nazi horror both more illuminating and more horrifying than one drawn in uniform black.

The conclusion of the book, called "Psychological Sketch and Future Perspectives", with its description of the different character of the German tribes and with its profound comparison of Germany and Russia, is a little masterpiece which even those should read who have no time for a long book. But it is during the gradual approach to this culmination that some of the most penetrating observations occur. One of the most pregnant is the brief passage in which Professor Vermeil corrects the familiar German contrast between "civilisation" and "culture" by substituting for it the true opposition between civilisation and policy. I should like to quote many other such brief but significant remarks from the book, but I must content myself with one more. I don't think I misunderstand Professor Vermeil when I feel that his main conclusion occurs early in the book when he states that "Germany has never been, has never been able to be, and, owing to her circumstances, no doubt never will be, a true national state".

Perhaps I can best illustrate the meaning of this by a point which I owe indirectly to Professor Vermeil, who has made clear to me the significance of a fact of which I had been vaguely aware. It shows a fundamental difference between the national feeling of the German and that of most other, or at least all the older, nations. If an Englishman, or a Frenchman, or an American, wants for any reason to be particularly English, French, or American, he looks at his fellows and tries to be like them. Not so the German: He invents a theory of what the German ought to be like and tries to live up (or down) to it—however different this may make him from his fellows. This sounds absurd; but the question is: What else can he do? There would be no difficulty if he tried to be particularly Bavarian, or Prussian, or Swabian. But what are, or were, the characteristics which the majority of Germans have in common? It is true that during the past seventy years many qualities which used to be regarded as specifically Prussian have become fairly widespread in Germany. But that did not make them generally popular or desirable even in Germany, and what hold they gained was largely due to that desperate striving for a common national character which later made even Germans who approved of nothing in Hitler's programme see 'something good' in the Nazi movement.

It is this lack of common features which explains why there is scarcely a virtue which some German has not claimed as a national characteristic, and hardly a vice which they could not be made to embrace if it seemed to give them at last something in common.

This craving to become a nation seems indeed the only common trait of the modern Germans. It is dreadful to think that Hitler may indeed for the first time in history have created one German nation. But this result need not be beyond remedy, and the fascination of a new unifier not a permanent danger. It is true that to impose upon the Germans a permanent partition would almost certainly merely rekindle that craving for unity. But there may be better methods of preventing Germany from re-emerging as the kind of organised nation as which she is intolerable. If any central government she retains after the defeat remains for a long period under Allied control, and development of far-reaching autonomy of the parts becomes the only road to independence, and if these parts have the prospect of being received into the Western community of nations, one by one as they succeed in creating stable representative institutions, it is not too much to hope that, without any formal prohibition of re-union, they may in the end remain satisfied with a loose federal tie. But that will largely depend on the framework that Western Europe has to offer, that is, on how far in the interval the other European nations will succeed in putting the common house in order.

ELEVEN

A PLAN FOR THE FUTURE OF GERMANY[1]

Neither legal scruples nor a false humanitarianism should prevent the meting out of full justice to the guilty individuals in Germany. There are thousands, probably tens of thousands, who fully deserve death; and never in history was it easier to find the guilty men. Rank in the Nazi party is almost certain indication of the degree of guilt. All the Allies need to do is to decide how many they are prepared to put to death. If they begin at the top of the Nazi hierarchy, it is certain that the number they will be shooting in cold blood will be smaller than the number who deserve it. The danger, not less from the point of view of the future Germany than from that of the world, is that we may falter at this task and later, because the demand for retribution is not satisfied, let our plans for long-term policy be affected by a desire for future punishment when nothing but the effectiveness of our policy should count. The Germans will still be numerous and seated in the heart of Europe; and unless we can regain them for Western civilisation, the war will have been lost in the long run. If Germany becomes permanently totalitarian, the European continent will follow.

The long-term policy of guiding the Germans back into Western civilisation has three main aspects: political, economic, and educational or psychological. Of these the last is probably the most important. If I still begin with a discussion of the desirable political and economic structure, it is because I believe we will have to approach the problem of re-education largely indirectly. Yet before we can turn to this it is necessary explicitly to discard certain current misconceptions which make much of the popular discussion run in terms of extremes which are equally misleading. It is neither true that the corruption of the German mind is confined to a Nazi minority or that it is merely the result of developments since the last war, nor that the Germans have always been like that. Their

[1][Published with the subtitle "Decentralisation Offers Some Basis for Independence" in *The Saturday Review of Literature*, June 23, 1945, pp. 7–9, 39–40. -Ed.]

present state of mind has been created by a long and gradual process which for most of Germany began with the creation of the Reich by Bismarck seventy-five years ago. It would be difficult to deny that a hundred years ago most of Germany was still an integral part of Western civilisation, essentially indistinguishable from the rest. But we must also face the fact that by now the majority of Germans will be affected to a greater or lesser extent by Nazi ideals, including most of those who themselves think that they made every effort to escape the influence of Nazi propaganda.

There can be little doubt that what we shall find in Germany will be little better than a moral and intellectual desert. There will be isolated oases in it, small groups of upright and courageous men who in most respects share our opinions and who moreover have been tested in their convictions as none of us ever have. But these few men and women will be almost completely isolated from each other. With the rest of the people it will very likely not be the definite beliefs they hold, but rather the absence of any beliefs, a deep scepticism and cynicism toward all political ideals, and an appalling ignorance of what has really happened, which will present the main problem. There will be, at first at any rate, much good will and readiness to make a new start. But nothing will probably be more conspicuous than the powerlessness of good intentions without that uniting element of common moral and political traditions which we take for granted, but which during the last twelve years have been destroyed in Germany to an extent which it is difficult to realise.

This is a difficult but not a hopeless position. It would be hopeless if there were in Germany no men or women at all who still adhere to the beliefs that we wish to see again victorious. But unless during the last two years they have all been killed, there is good reason to believe that we shall find in Germany such men and women, a small number it is true, but not so few in comparison with the number of people who think independently in any nation. It is on them that we must base our hopes, for whom we must create the opportunities and provide chances of bringing their people back into what was once a common European civilisation.

The political problem is mainly one of directing German ambitions away from the ideal of a highly centralised German Reich, a nation unified for common action, as even before 1914 the Germans were unified like no other civilised nation. There seems no doubt possible that we must prevent the reappearance of such a highly centralised German Reich because a centralised and highly integrated Germany will always be a danger to peace.

Here we face, however, a serious dilemma. The direct method of breaking Germany into parts and prohibiting their reunion would almost certainly fail in the long run. It would be the surest way to reawaken the most violent nationalism and to make the creation of a reunified and centralised Germany the main ambition of all Germans. We should be able to prevent this for some time. But in the long run no measure will succeed which does not rest on the acquiescence of the Germans; and it surely must be our fundamental maxim that any successful settlement must have a chance of continuing when we are no longer ready to maintain it by the continuous exercise of force.

There seems to be only one solution of this difficulty: to tell the Germans that whatever common central government they will have will remain under Allied control for an indefinite period; but that they can progressively escape this control by developing representative and democratic institutions on a smaller scale in the individual states of which the Reich is composed; that this is their only road to independence in the near future; and that it depends only on them when they will reach it.

These individual German states include, of course, those which have long been absorbed into Prussia as well as those which had retained some degree of autonomy till 1933. Indeed, there is not only no objection to the breaking up of Prussia and the reconstituting of such states as Hanover, Westphalia, or the Rhineland, but this is an essential condition for the success of any plan. There need be no fear that this will produce a nationalistic reaction such as a similar direct dismemberment of the Reich would produce. Most of the people in the state would welcome it, and the tradition of their separate existence is far from dead.

The time when the individual German states would be likely to earn their emancipation from direct Allied control would probably greatly differ from state to state. Those of the West and of the Southwest, like Baden and Württemberg, and the old Hanse towns, like Hamburg and Bremen, still have considerable remnants of a democratic tradition and would probably succeed in a few years. Others will take much longer, and some, like old Prussia, which has practically no such tradition, may take very long indeed. This gradual character of the process, the intervals between the dates at which the various states would achieve some independence, would, however, be very important.

This process of emancipation would have to move towards a state of affairs in which the Allied control would increasingly become confined to the role of the government of federation or even of a

225

confederation. The importance of this gradual process of devolution of powers to the individual states lies in that otherwise the Allied control might merely help to prepare another highly centralised system of government ultimately to be handed over to the Germans. An Allied-controlled central government of this kind would not long have to rely on a large army of occupation. All it would need, but would need so long as it existed, would be a comparatively small, but highly efficient, striking force to ensure obedience of recalcitrant states.

Nothing need or should be announced about any permanent prohibition of the German states reuniting later. The fact that they become ripe for release from Allied control at very different dates, and that most of them would have to build up a new order of their own while much of the rest of Germany was still under Allied control, would in itself operate in the right direction. One may hope that by the time the first of the separate states is ripe for emancipation, this will not have to mean that it must become an entirely independent state. A fully satisfactory solution could only be achieved if by that time some other federation of European states were ready to receive such states into their organisation. Release from Allied control would then mean transfer from a quasi-federation, in which the 'federal' power was exercised under Allied control, to a federation with non-German states, in which the German states would become equal members. The western German states might thus gradually be transferred to a federation, consisting of, say, Holland, Belgium, and Scandinavia. Some other German states might at first be allowed to enter into similar arrangements with Czechoslovakia, Austria, and perhaps Switzerland. In the course of time, as more of the German states achieved this status, the balance could of course be preserved only in a much more comprehensive European federation which included France and Italy.

But even if these hopes should prove utopian, there is good reason for expecting that after a period of separate existence the individual German states would be far from anxious once again to merge their individuality in a highly centralised Reich. This at least may be expected if Allied policy, particularly economic policy, during the transition period succeeds in entangling the individual states as closely as possible with their non-German neighbors.

This raises the extremely important problem of economic policy and economic control. There is again probably only one kind of such control which will be effective and practicable in the long run: to impose free trade on the whole of Germany. This is an essential part of this plan without which it would not work; and it solves many problems which are otherwise probably insoluble.

When I described the powers of the Allied-controlled central government as similar to those of a federal government, this meant, of course, that they included control of trade policy. To leave the power of the foreign trade in the hands of the individual states would give them far too much power over their economic system. To retain a common tariff system for the whole of Germany, on the other hand, would have the effect that the German economic system would be built up again as a highly centralised and self-sufficient system, which is precisely what we must prevent. What we want to achieve is that Germany should become specialised in the fields where she can make the greatest contribution to the world's prosperity but at the same time should become so mixed up with the economy of other countries that she can only prosper by the continuous exchange of her goods with the outside world.

This is precisely what free trade will bring about—and bring about by means of only one control, and that a control which cannot be evaded. Germany would thereby be given a chance of becoming prosperous again without becoming dangerous. She would become largely dependent on imports of food grains, and would have to buy them by the export of manufactures. Even if in particular branches of manufacture it might be possible for a German government to counteract the effects of free trade by secret subsidies, it would not be possible to do that for all the essential foods and raw materials which under free trade she could not produce within the country. And controls of imports, whether by tariffs or other restrictions, are almost the only measure which cannot be imposed secretly, since the countries whose exports are excluded must of necessity be the first to notice them.

While it will be essential to create conditions which provide an inducement for the Germans to develop in the direction which we wish they should, this would of course solve only part of the problem. There is also a real task of re-education which is an exceedingly difficult and delicate one and where in particular the proposals which are most frequently heard are still of a kind which are likely to produce the opposite from what they aim at. The idea that the Germans can be made to think as the Allied powers would wish them to by supplying suitable textbooks on which the future generation of Germans are to be brought up, and by imposing on them a new official creed instead of the old one, is not only to fall into the totalitarian error; it is childishly silly and would be certain to discredit the very ideas which we will want to spread. No, if there is

to be any lasting change in the moral and political doctrines dominating Germany, it must come by a gradual process from within, in
which those Germans who have understood the corruption must
take the lead. Even if their number should prove still smaller than I
believe it will be, this is still our only hope. What we have to aim at
is not a new indoctrination but a revival of the belief in truth and
objective moral standards, not only in private life but in politics,
and a readiness to receive and to examine new ideals, which is not
encouraged by forcing down a people's throat a ready-made set of
principles. The process, like all spreading of ideals, will have to be a
gradual one, going down the intellectual ladder from the people
who have learned to think critically to those who merely accept
what reaches them through the ear or the printed word. The
problem will be to find and to assist the men and women in Germany who can get this process started, without, at the same time,
discrediting them with their own people, as would undoubtedly
happen if they were to become the instruments of the Allied governments. But before considering the practical measures which can
be taken for this end, it is necessary to say a little of the main aims
towards which these efforts must be directed.

There is much to be learned for this from the process by which
German moral and political standards became gradually detached
from the common Western tradition and by which the peculiar
conceptions and ideals of present-day Germany were shaped. If in
the sphere of politics and public morals the Germans during the
last seventy years moved progressively away from what we regard as
civilised standards, the beginning of this development must be
traced to the events and struggles which accompanied the unification of Germany. Bismarck's achievement has so thoroughly blinded
even Western historians to his great responsibility for starting a
growth which ended with the Nazis that it is worthwhile recalling
some characteristic events of that period—particularly as our main
problem will be how far we must accept Bismarck's work as unalterable, or how far it will have to be undone.

How profoundly the means of Bismarck's complete lack of scruple
has affected German standards is clearly brought out by his latest
and best biography.[2] Especially the story of the years 1865 to 1871,

---

[2]Erich Eyck, *Bismarck*, 3 vols (Erlenbach-Zurich: Eugen Rentsch, 1941–44). [Con-
densed English version, *Bismarck and the German Empire* (London: Allen & Unwin,
1950). Hayek reviewed the German edition in an article called "The Historian's
Responsibility" in *Time and Tide*, January 13, 1945, pp. 27–28, from which the
following discussion of Bismarck is taken. Some parts of the review not reproduced

when Bismarck achieved his greatest success and turned his severest critics into his most enthusiastic admirers, is highly instructive. Till 1865 most enlightened people, in Germany as much as outside, had regarded him as little better than an unscrupulous adventurer. His achievement of the unification of Germany led to a complete change of opinion. And during the later years, when he came to be regarded as the main guarantee of European peace, the infamy of his earlier policy was forgotten, by his most outspoken German critics as much as by most foreign observers—so much so, indeed, that even now such a description of his policy will probably sound exaggerated.

Yet, till success seemed to justify his methods, many of the Germans who later became his most ardent admirers used language quite as strong as this. That was during the years in which the Prussian Diet fought against Bismarck one of the great fights for the law in German history—and Bismarck won by creating against the law the army with which he defeated Austria and France. If the full duplicity of his policy was then only suspected, there can be now no doubt about it. The man who, when reading the intercepted report of one of his dupes among foreign ambassadors in which the latter passed on a solemn assurance he had just received from Bismarck, was capable of scribbling on the margin, "He really believed it!" and the master of corruption from the influence of whose secret funds the German press never fully recovered, deserves all that has been said about him. It is now practically forgotten that Bismarck came near rivalling the Nazis in his brutal treatment of democratic Frankfurt, when he sanctioned the extortion of an exorbitant war contribution by the threat of bombarding, starving out, and sacking a German town which had never taken up arms, or by his threat to shoot innocent hostages in Bohemia. And the story of how he engineered the conflict with France as the only means of making an unwilling South Germany forget its dislike of Prussian military dictatorship has only recently been fully understood.

At first Bismarck's proceedings caused in Germany widespread and genuine indignation freely expressed and even among some of the Prussian conservatives. The historian Sybel, later one of his main eulogists, described him as "frivolously unprincipled", Gustav Freytag[3] as "miserable and shamelessly dishonest", and the jurist

---

in the text of the present essay have been added as footnotes to this chapter. -Ed.]

[3][Gustav Freytag (1816–1895), novelist and historian. -Ed.]

Ihering[4] spoke of his "revolting shamelessness" and "horrible frivolity". Yet only a few years later most of the same men joined the chorus of unqualified praise and one of these publicly admitted that for such a man of action he was willing to give a hundred men of powerless honesty.[5]

But while foreign observers showed themselves in fact little more impervious to the corrupting influence of success, theirs were temporary lapses and the effect in other countries not great enough to cause such change in moral standards as it did in Germany. There the question at issue was that of her being united as a single nation; it was the achievement of the ambition of generations which had become inextricably mixed up with the methods by which it had been brought about. These methods could not be defended without either grave distortion of facts, or a defence of deception and lying, bribery and brutal terror. A dilemma was created between truth or moral rectitude on the one hand, and what was regarded as patriotic duty, and patriotism proved to be stronger. The principles became firmly established that the end justified the means and that public actions could not be measured by moral standards but only by their fitness for ends.[6]

[4][Rudolf von Ihering (1818–1892) was Professor of Law at the University of Göttingen. -Ed.]

[5][Ihering, quoted in Eyck, op. cit., vol. 2, p. 318. In his review of Eyck's book (see this chapter, footnote 2) Hayek adds at this point: "That all this is unfortunately merely human and by no means peculiarly German baseness is shown by the similar reactions in other countries. I do not know whether a history of Bismarck's reputation has ever been written; it would be a most instructive lesson in the ways in which the standards are formed by which we judge public action. But the samples of British reactions which I know are scarcely less striking than the German ones. *The Spectator*, for example, which had been very frank in its comments, had already early in 1866 come to grant that 'it is hard even for Englishmen not to admit that they have been unjust to Count Bismarck. The man's policy is detestable, but his objects are great, his plans adequate, and his ability marvelous'. And Sir William Russell, the great correspondent of *The Times*, on whom Bismarck had played one of his dirtiest tricks, was nevertheless able to say of him: 'If I were a Prussian, I could fall down and worship him for his work'". -Ed.]

[6][In the Eyck review Hayek continues: "It takes a long time, nevertheless, till a whole people learn to look with changed eyes on public affairs, and in view of the process of re-education the Germans will need, it is well worth while to give some attention to the way in which the principles of Bismarckian *Realpolitik* were disseminated. Bismarck himself, of course, acted not only by his example but also through his *Memoirs* (*Gedanken und Erinnerungen* (New York and Stuttgart: Cotta, 1898)), the first political *Volksbuch* in Germany and (with the possible exception of H. S. Chamberlain's *Foundations of the Nineteenth Century*, which appeared a year later) the only book which in circulation and influence can be compared with *Mein Kampf*. But the main responsiblity must be sought elsewhere. The masses take their opinions ready

I cannot go here into the other main part of the Bismarck story, the way in which, after he had unified the Reich, he skilfully used the promise of economic benefit to harness both capital and labour into an all-German economic organisation on the Prussian model, how with him the deliberate efforts began to unify the Germans not only politically but to unite them in common beliefs. But it is necessary to say a little more about the process by which the views on political and moral questions of which he was the great representative gradually gained mastery over the minds of the Germans.

The point which I want particularly to stress, and which seems to emerge so clearly from the history of this period, is the predominant role which the German historians played by their efforts to justify and defend Bismarck and how in this way they spread the veneration of the power state and the expansionist ideas characteristic of modern Germany. Nobody says that more clearly than the great English historian Lord Acton, who knew Germany as well as his own country and who as early as 1886 could speak of "that garrison of distinguished historians that prepared the Prussian supremacy together with their own, and now hold Berlin like a fortress", a group "almost entirely given to maxims which it has cost the world so much effort to reverse".[7] And it was the same Lord Acton who in spite of his admiration for much in Germany was able to foresee fifty years ago that the tremendous power built up by very able minds, chiefly in Berlin, was "the greatest danger that remains to be encountered by the Anglo-Saxon race".[8]

These glances at history are necessary if we are to appreciate the specially important task that will fall to the historians and teachers of history in the re-education of the Germans. They are, of course,

---

made, and for the great events of the past, and particularly among a people so well schooled as the Germans, it is mainly the historian who sets the standards by which they are judged. The role which the historians have played in this connexion points indeed to a very important task they will have in the future." -Ed.]

[7][Acton, "German Schools of History", op. cit., pp. 352 and 355–356. -Ed.]

[8][Here Hayek adds: "The influence of the historian, moreover, extends far beyond the interpretation of the events most intimately connected with the fate of his country. No better illustration of this can be given than the curious change which occurred in the attitude of German historians towards the famous struggle between Philip of Macedon and the Greeks. Philip became in their eyes a sort of classical Bismarck whose craft was employed to unify the Greek nation while Demosthenes' defence of Athenian independence was represented as a shortsighted and reprehensible particularism, accountable only by dishonourable motives. Thus even classical education was made an instrument of inculcating the youth with the new standards of political morals." -Ed.]

not the only ones who will have to work for this end, but their position is so important that it will be justified if, turning now to the practical problem, we use the term 'historian' for all those students and writers in the humanities who formulate the ideas which in the long run govern society.

Our problem is how we can effectively assist those among these men in Germany on whose influence we must mainly base our hopes for a better future Germany. That they will need assistance, material, and even more moral assistance is certain. These isolated men will, in the first instance, need the assurance that they are not moral outcasts but that they are striving for the same ends as many men all over the world. While there are many German scholars with whom we neither wish nor ought ever again to have any commerce, it would be fatal to extend such ostracism to all, including those whom we should wish to help. But in a situation where one must feel doubts about everybody except the few of whom one has personal knowledge, the difficulty of distinguishing the records of the various persons might produce the same result unless deliberate efforts are made to facilitate contacts. If these men are to be again made active members of the community of Western civilisation, they will soon have to be given an opportunity for exchanging opinions, for obtaining books and periodicals, and even for travel, which will for long be impossible for most Germans.

There is not only the difficulty how to find these individuals. There is the even greater difficulty of how the help can be administered without discrediting them with their own people. On the first point, what is needed is clearly some pooling of the knowledge of individual German scholars possessed by their fellows in the Allied countries. On the second, the main consideration must be that these men ought to be neither expected nor induced to become the tools of the Allied authorities. If these efforts are to have any chance of success, there must not be the slightest ground for the suspicion that these men serve merely another power instead of that which their opponents served, and not the slightest doubt that they are committed to anything but the truth. Indeed they will probably need, just as much as positive help, protection against well-meant but ill-directed attempts to use them in the service of the Allied government machinery.

The only practical solution of this problem would seem the creation by independent scholars of an international academy, or society of elected members, in which those scholars of the Western countries who take an active interest in these problems join with the individual Germans whom they regard as worthy of such support.[9] Such a society could bring together all those on both sides who are willing to serve the two great ideals of truth in history and moral standards in politics, and whose past record justifies the confidence that they will do so.

These general ideas would, of course, have to be more clearly defined, since the aim of the society presupposes agreement of its members on the general principles of the basic liberalism of Western civilisation which it wishes to preserve. To express these principles in a manifesto drawn up for the purpose is scarcely practicable. After much consideration of the various possibilities I feel that the best way of defining that philosophy would be to express it by the names of one or two great men who were its outstanding representatives. And no two men seem to me more clearly to express these ideals, and better to express the particular task of such a society, than the English historian Lord Acton and his French counterpart, Alexis de Tocqueville. Both men represented the same liberal philosophy at its best and combined a passion for truth with a profound respect for the moral forces in history. And while Lord Acton, the Englishman, knew the Germans in their bad and their good sides as well as he knew his fellow countrymen, the Frenchman de Tocqueville was of course one of the greatest students and admirers of American democracy. I do not see how the political ideals of such an international academy could be better expressed than by calling it the Acton-Tocqueville Society. It is to the men and women who know what these names stand for and who are willing to subscribe to the ideals of these two men that such an organisation must first appeal.

There is no need at this stage to describe the functions of such a society in detail. I do not claim that this kind of organisation is necessarily the best. But I am convinced that there is a great problem which needs careful thought and preparation and on which, at present, not enough thinking is done, because it is not a problem which can be solved by governmental activities. It is the independent scholars and thinkers who must take the initiative; and the time is now short if a great opportunity is not to be missed.

[9][On this proposal, see this volume, chapter 12. -Ed.]

Addendum: The Future of Austria[10]

With Russian armies at the gates of Vienna the future of Austria becomes an urgent issue. So little is known about many of the factors which will determine the country's destiny that it is not surprising that authoritative statements have been few and not very definite. But this uncertainty does not affect the question which seemed foremost not so long ago. That Austria will be permanently separated from Germany is not only settled Allied policy; it can confidently be assumed to be the wish of the Austrian people and—unless serious mistakes are made—to remain so. The important point to realise is that the pro-Anschluß movement was based much less on senti-mental-nationalist grounds than on purely rational calculation: It was the hope of a poor and weak country to gain by inclusion in the prosperity of its wealthy neighbour. It is not likely that from an economic point of view inclusion in Germany will be a particularly attractive proposition for some time to come. That the emotional grounds for such a desire will by now have been thoroughly changed into the opposite, no one in the least degree familiar with Austria since the occupation can doubt.

But this is only the beginning of the problem. Although it has never been quite true to say that Austria is incapable of maintaining her population, it is true that under conditions like those between the two wars she could do so only at a very low standard. The insoluble dilemma of that period was that, just at the time when Austria had become very poor, her working classes had for the first time gained great strength, and inevitably used it to press for a considerable improvement of their standard of living. For a time they succeeded, by forcing the employers to draw on the accumulated capital, a process whose outcome became visible in the successive collapse of Austria's financial institutions and the progressive sale of her industrial assets to Germany. But even if, for some time after this war, the Austrians know that they must be content with very modest standards, it is not to be expected that the mass of a highly intelligent industrial population, which till 1934 had been among the best organised (and its leaders among the most radical) in Europe, will long be satisfied with the prospects in a self-contained Austria. This problem, before the war largely one of Vienna and her immediate surroundings, is likely to have become even more acute as a result of recent developments. It seems that the Nazis have created large new industrial districts all along Austria's eastern border (including some around newly opened oilfields) and manned largely with imported workers, not all of whom may wish to return to the countries from which they have been recruited. It is on the economic prospects of these industrial districts (the largest in Central Europe) that the stability of Austria will ultimately depend. Many difficult problems are involved, not least that of the future ownership and management of these industries in a country where the old

---

[10][Published in *The Spectator*, London, April 6, 1945, p. 306–307. -Ed.]

bourgeoisie, always small, has been largely expelled or discredited. Only the wider political problems can be considered here.

The one rational solution of this and many other problems of Central Europe, the formation of a comprehensive federation, including not only the territory of former Austria-Hungary, but all of Yugoslavia, Romania, and probably Bulgaria (and preferably with such bones of contention as Transylvania, Croatia, or Slovakia as separate member states) seems still to be barred by Russian opposition. And to the next-best solution, a close combination of Austria and Czechoslovakia, which might form a nucleus for a later larger federation, the impression that Czechoslovakia has committed herself rather far with Russia is likely to form an obstacle with both the Austrian Social Democrats and Catholics. Thus we may well find Austria again not only independent but thrown back on her meagre resources, with little scope for her comparatively large industrial population.

There is not much that can be done to remedy this by altering frontiers. The only important change that certainly ought to be made is the re-incorporation in Austria of the South Tyrol (i.e., the German-speaking district of Bozen, not, of course, the Italian-speaking Trentino). It would be important for economic reasons, and even more so because the attachment of the people of Austria generally centres mainly round their particular *Land*, and the partition of the heart of the old Tyrol has deprived the Tyrolese of their centre of gravitation and thereby inevitably set up centrifugal tendencies. (For the same reasons it would also be a fatal mistake to concede certain new Yugoslav claims for those parts of Carinthia which in the plebiscite of twenty-six years ago opted with an overwhelming majority for Austria.) Perhaps the suggestion recently made to hand over to Austria the salient of Berchtesgaden, formerly part of the *Land* Salzburg, should also be seriously considered, since it would not only substantially shorten one of Austria's main lines of interior communication, but also prevent Berchtesgaden from becoming a German national shrine. Quite a different problem is that of access to a seaport. An actual incorporation of Trieste into Austria, though in the interests of both, is probably neither practicable nor desirable. But it may well be advisable to make Trieste a free city under international control on the model of Danzig, with guaranteed free-port facilities for both Austria and Czechoslovakia.

None of these possible changes would, however, fundamentally alter Austria's economic problems. But there might be another possibility if Vienna were, as has often been suggested, to become the seat of the new League of Nations or whatever the corresponding organisation may be called. With the future shape of Europe as it seems to emerge, Vienna might well prove to be the most suitable neutral spot on the common boundary of what, in some sense, will probably be the Western and the Russian spheres of influence. This would in itself solve many of the peculiar problems of Vienna. But one might go one step further and make Vienna, together with the adjoining industrial areas, a really neutral district, with full internal autonomy but international control of all its foreign relations. This would make it possible to turn it into a completely free-trade area, from which industrial Vienna would derive nothing but gain, and which would give her a position as a commercial centre in accord with her equipment, but which as part of a small and largely agricultural country she would not be likely to achieve. There would still be enough manufacturing industry left in the rest of Austria not to reduce her to a purely agricultural country; but that excessive urban and manufacturing aggregation which could find no place within the small country would be given appropriate scope without anyone having to fear that its revival as an economic centre might be followed by a restoration of its political influence.

At this point many readers will probably ask whether Austria deserves so much consideration as these reflections suggest. There has recently been a tendency, to which Mr. Eden[11] has given countenance, to argue that the Austrians have yet to earn their right to be treated differently from the Germans. The suggestion that the Austrians have it in their power to rise betrays some misapprehension of the position in a country which the Germans were allowed to overrun eighteen months before the outbreak of war. The Austrians are not more, but considerably less, able to organise any effective opposition than, say, the Czechs or the Norwegians are. Not only is a considerably higher proportion of their youth away from home, conscripted at a time when there was no prospect of foreign help and largely dispersed among German units; there is also another factor which makes the position specially difficult. No one can doubt that in any occupied country the number of quislings would have been many times higher if they had been able to appear in the nationalist cloak under which they can appear in Austria. But a rise in the proportion of potential traitors from, say, one in 500 to one in 50 creates a difference not merely of degree but of kind. It turns secret organisation for resistance from a risk worth taking to suicidal folly. The younger men who might be ready thus to sacrifice themselves are not there; and the older men are probably right in feeling that it is more important for them to survive to help build up a new Austria than die in a senseless demonstration. The number who do is still considerable.

Whatever the merits of that question, the decisive consideration must be that to treat Austria as Germany's partner is probably the one way to drive her, however unwillingly, to behave as Germany's partner. This applies particularly to the question of reparations. There will be some German assets in Austria to which the Allies may rightly lay claim; but to exact reparations beyond that would be fatally to weaken a country whose political instability has always been due to its economic weakness. To put it bluntly, Austria's independence, as is probably true of any country not held together by either linguistic or historical unity, must be economically worth while to be lasting.

---

[11][Anthony Eden (1897–1977), later Lord Avon, was British Foreign Secretary from 1931 to 1938 and succeeded Winston Churchill as Prime Minister in 1955. He resigned in 1957 following the Suez Canal crisis. -Ed.]

TWELVE

OPENING ADDRESS TO A CONFERENCE AT MONT PÈLERIN[1]

I must confess that now, when the moment has arrived to which I have looked forward so long, my feeling of intense gratitude to all of you is much tempered by an acute sense of astonishment at my temerity in setting all this in motion, and of alarm about the responsibility I have assumed in asking you to give up so much of your time and energy to what you might well have regarded as a wild experiment. I will, however, confine myself at this stage to a simple but profoundly sincere "thank you".

It is my duty, before I step down from the position I have so immodestly assumed, and gladly hand over to you the task of carrying on what fortunate circumstances have enabled me to initiate, to give you a somewhat fuller account of the aims which have guided me in proposing this meeting and suggesting its programme. I shall endeavour not to tax your patience too much, but even the minimum of explanation which I owe you will take some little time. The basic conviction which has guided me in my efforts is that, if the ideals which I believe unite us, and for which, in spite of so much abuse of the term, there is still no better name than liberal, are to have any chance of revival, a great intellectual

---

[1][Address delivered April 1, 1947, at Mont Pèlerin near Vevey, Switzerland, and previously published in *Studies in Philosophy, Politics and Economics*, op. cit., pp. 148–159. -Ed.] The members of the conference were the following: Maurice Allais, Paris; Carlo Antoni, Rome; Hans Barth, Zurich; Karl Brandt, Stanford, Calif.; John Davenport, New York; Stanley R. Dennison, Cambridge; Aaron Director, Chicago; Walter Eucken, Freiburg; Erich Eyck, Oxford; Milton Friedman, Chicago; Harry D. Gideonse, Brooklyn, N.Y.; Frank D. Graham, Princeton, N.J.; F. A. Harper, Irvington-on-Hudson, N.Y.; Henry Hazlitt, New York; T. J. B. Hoff, Oslo; Albert Hunold, Zurich; Carl Iversen, Copenhagen; John Jewkes, Manchester; Bertrand de Jouvenel, Chexbres, Vaud; Frank H. Knight, Chicago; [H. de Lovinfosse, Waasmunster, Belgium]; Fritz Machlup, Buffalo, N.Y.; L. B. Miller, Detroit, Mich.; Ludwig von Mises, New York; Felix Morley, Washington, D.C.; Michael Polanyi, Manchester; Karl R. Popper, London; William E. Rappard, Geneva; Leonard E. Read, Irvington-on-Hudson, N.Y.; Lionel Robbins, London; Wilhelm Röpke, Geneva; George J. Stigler, Providence, R.I.; Herbert Tingsten, Stockholm; François Trevoux, Lyon; V. O. Watts, Irvington-on-Hudson, N.Y.; C. V. Wedgwood, London.

task must be performed. This task involves both purging traditional liberal theory of certain accidental accretions which have become attached to it in the course of time, and also facing up to some real problems which an over-simplified liberalism has shirked or which have become apparent only since it has turned into a somewhat stationary and rigid creed.

The belief that this is the prevailing condition has been strongly confirmed to me by the observation that in many different fields and in many different parts of the world, individuals who have been brought up in different beliefs and to whom party liberalism had little attraction have been rediscovering for themselves the basic principles of liberalism and have been trying to reconstruct a liberal philosophy which can meet the objections which in the eyes of most of our contemporaries have defeated the promise the earlier liberalism offered.

During the last two years I have had the good fortune to visit several parts of Europe and America and I have been surprised by the number of isolated men whom I found in different places, working on essentially the same problems and on very similar lines. Working in isolation or in very small groups they are, however, constantly forced to defend the basic elements of their beliefs and rarely have opportunity for an interchange of opinion on the more technical problems which arise only if a certain common basis of conviction and ideals is present.

It seems to me that effective endeavours to elaborate the general principles of a liberal order are practicable only among a group of people who are in agreement on fundamentals, and among whom certain basic conceptions are not questioned at every step. But not only is, at this time, the number of those who in any one country agree on what seems to me the basic liberal principles small, but the task is a very big one, and there is much need for drawing on as wide an experience under varying conditions as possible.

One of the most instructive observations to me was that the farther one moves to the West, to countries where liberal institutions are still comparatively firm, and people professing liberal convictions still comparatively numerous, the less are these people prepared really to re-examine their own convictions and the more are they inclined to compromise, and to take the accidental historical form of a liberal society which they have known as the ultimate standard. I found on the other hand that in those countries which either had directly experienced a totalitarian regime, or had closely approached it, a few men had from this experience gained a clearer conception of the conditions and value of a free society. The more I discussed these problems with people in different countries, the more I was driven to the conviction that the wisdom is not all on one side, and that the observation of the actual decay of a civilisation taught some independent thinkers on the European Continent lessons which I believe have yet to be learnt in England and America if these countries are to avoid a similar fate.

Yet it is not only the students of economics and politics in various countries who have much to profit from each other and who, by joining their forces across the national frontiers, could do much to advance their common cause. I was no less impressed by the fact of how much more fruitful the discussion of the great problems of our time could be between, say, an economist and a historian, or a lawyer and a political philosopher, if they shared certain common premises, than the discussion is between students of the same subjects who differed on these basic values. Of course, a political philosophy can never be based exclusively on economics or ex-pressed mainly in economic terms. It seems that the dangers which we are facing are the result of an intellectual movement which has expressed itself in, and affected the attitude towards, all aspects of human affairs. Yet while in his own subject every one of us may have learnt to recognise the beliefs which are part and parcel of the movement that leads to totalitarianism, we cannot be sure that as economists, for example, we do not, under the influence of the atmosphere of our time, accept as uncritically as anyone else ideas in the field of history or philosophy, morals or law, which are part and parcel of the very system of ideas which we have learnt to oppose in our own field.

The need for an international meeting of representatives of these different subjects seemed to me especially great as a result of the war which not only has for so long disrupted many of the normal contacts but also inevitably, and in the best of us, created a self-centredness and nationalist outlook which ill accords with a truly liberal approach to our problems. Worst of all, the war and its effects have created new obstacles to the resumption of international contacts which to those in the less fortunate countries are still practically unsurmountable without outside help, and are serious enough for the rest of us. There seemed clearly to exist a case for some sort of organisation which would help to reopen communica-tions between people with a common outlook. Unless some sort of private organisation were created, there would be serious danger that contacts beyond national frontiers would become increasingly the monopoly of those who were in one way or another tied up in the existing governmental or political machinery and were bound to serve the dominating ideologies.

It was evident from the beginning that no permanent organisation of this kind could be created without some experimental meeting at which the usefulness of the idea could be tried out. But as this, in the present circumstances, seemed hardly possible to arrange without considerable funds, I did little but talk about this plan to as many people as would listen, until, to my own surprise, a fortunate accident suddenly placed this within the range of possibility. One of our Swiss friends here, Dr. Hunold, had raised funds for a cognate but different project which for accidental reasons had to be abandoned, and he succeeded in persuading the donors to turn the amount over for this new purpose.

It was only when thus a unique opportunity offered itself that I fully realised what a responsibility I had taken on, and that, if the chance was not to be missed, I must undertake to propose this conference and, worst of all, to decide who was to be invited. You will perhaps sympathise enough with the difficulty and the embarrassing nature of such a task to make it unnecessary for me to apologise at length for the manner in which I have discharged it.

There is only one point in this connexion which I ought to explain: As I see our task, it is not sufficient that our members should have what used to be called 'sound' views. The old liberal who adheres to a traditional creed *merely* out of tradition, however admirable his views, is not of much use for our purpose. What we need are people who have faced the arguments from the other side, who have struggled with them and fought themselves through to a position from which they can both critically meet the objection against it and justify their views. Such people are even less numerous than good liberals in the old sense, and there are now few enough even of them. But when it came to drawing up a list I discovered to my pleasant surprise that the number of people whom I thought had a title to be included in such a list was a good deal larger than I had expected or than could be asked to the conference. And the final selection had inevitably to a large extent to be arbitrary.

It is a matter of great regret to me that, largely as a result of my personal shortcomings, the membership of the present conference is somewhat unevenly balanced and that the historians and political philosophers, instead of being as strongly represented as the economists, are a comparatively small minority. This is partly due to the fact that my personal contacts among this group are more limited, and to the fact that even among those who were on the original list a particularly high proportion of the non-economists was unable to attend, but partly also to the fact that at this particular juncture economists seem perhaps to be more generally aware of the immediate dangers and of the urgency of the intellectual problems which we must solve if we are to have a chance to guide developments in a more desirable direction. There are similar disproportions in the national distribution of the membership of this conference and I particularly regret that both Belgium and Holland are entirely unrepresented. I have no doubt that, apart from these faults of which I am conscious, there are other and perhaps more serious blunders which I have unwittingly committed, and all I can do is to ask for your indulgence, and to beg your help so that in future we shall possess a more complete list of all those from whom we may expect sympathetic and active support in our efforts.

It has given me much encouragement that not a single one of all those to whom I sent invitations did not express his sympathies with the aim of the conference and the wish to be able to take part. If nevertheless many of them are not here, this is due to physical difficulties of one kind or another. You will probably like to hear the names of those who have expressed their wish that they could be with us and their sympathy with the aims of this conference.[2]

In mentioning those who cannot be with us for temporary reasons I must also mention others on whose support I had particularly counted but who will never again be with us. Indeed the two men with whom I had most fully discussed the plan for this meeting both have not lived to see its realisation. I had first sketched the plan three years ago to a small group in Cambridge[3] presided over by Sir John Clapham who took a great interest in it but who died suddenly a year ago. And it is now less than a year since I discussed the plan in all its detail with another man whose whole life had been devoted to the ideals and problems with which we shall

---

[2]I then read out the following list of names: Costantino Bresciani-Turroni, Rome; William H. Chamberlin, New York; René Courtin, Paris; Max Eastman, New York; Luigi Einaudi, Rome; Howard Ellis, Berkeley, Calif.; A. G. B. Fisher, London; Eli Heckscher, Stockholm; Hans Kohn, Northampton, Mass.; Walter Lippmann, New York; Friedrich Lutz, Princeton; Salvador de Madariaga, Oxford; Charles Morgan, London; W. A. Orton, Northampton, Mass.; Arnold Plant, London; Charles Rist, Paris; Michael Roberts, London; Jacques Rueff, Paris; Alexander Rüstow, Istanbul; Franz Schnabel, Heidelberg; W. J. H. Sprott, Nottingham; Roger Truptil, Paris; D. Villey, Poitiers; E. L. Woodward, Oxford; H. M. Wriston, Providence, R. I.; G. M. Young, London. Though not present at the meeting at Mont Pèlerin, all those named later agreed to join the society there formed as original members.

[3][See this volume, chapter 8. -Ed.]

be concerned: Henry Simons of Chicago.[4] A few weeks later he was no more. If with their names I mention that of a much younger man who had also taken a great interest in my plans and whom, if he had lived, I should have hoped to see as our Permanent Secretary, a post for which Etienne Mantoux would have been ideally suited, you will understand how heavy are the losses which our group has suffered even before it first had an opportunity to meet.

If it had not been for these tragic deaths I should not have had to act alone in summoning this conference. I confess that at one time these blows had completely shaken my resolution to pursue the plan further. But when the opportunity came I felt it a duty to make of it what I could.

There is another point connected with the membership of our meeting which I should briefly mention. We have among us a fair number of regular writers for the periodical press, not in order that the meeting should be reported, but because they have the best opportunity to spread the ideas to which we are devoted. But to reassure other members it may be useful to mention that unless and until you should decide otherwise, I think this should be regarded as a private meeting and all that is said here in the discussion as 'off the record'.

Of the subjects which I have suggested for systematic examination by this conference, and of which most members seem to have approved, the first is the relation between what is called 'free enterprise' and a really competitive order. It seems to me to be much the biggest and in some ways the most important problem and I hope that a considerable part of our discussion will be devoted to its exploration. It is the field where it is most important that we should become clear in our own minds, and arrive at an agreement about the kind of programme of economic policy which we should wish to see generally accepted. It is probably the set of problems in which the largest proportion among us are actively interested and where it is most urgent that the work which has been conducted independently in parallel directions in many parts of the world should be brought together. Its ramifications are practically endless, since an adequate treatment involves a complete programme of a liberal economic policy. It is likely that after a survey of the general problem you may prefer to split it up into more

---

[4][For a recent appraisal of Simons in this connexion see J. Bradford De Long, "In Defense of Henry Simons's Standing as a Classical Liberal", *Cato Journal*, vol. 9, no. 3, Winter 1990, pp. 601–618. -Ed.]

special questions to be discussed in separate sessions. We could probably in this manner find room for one or more of the additional topics which I mentioned in one of my circulars, or for such further problems as that of the inflationary high-pressure economy which, as has been justly observed by more than one member, is at the moment the main tool by which a collectivist development is forced on the majority of countries. Perhaps the best plan will be that, after devoting one or two sessions to the general issue, we set aside half an hour or so at the end of one of these discussions to decide on the further course of our deliberations. I propose that we devote the whole of this afternoon and evening to a general survey of this topic and perhaps you will allow me to say a few words more about it this afternoon. I have taken the liberty to ask Professor Aaron Director of Chicago, Professor Walter Eucken of Freiburg and Professor Maurice Allais of Paris to introduce the debate on this subject and I have no doubt that we shall then have more than enough food for discussion.

Profoundly important as the problems of the principles of economic order are, there are several reasons why I hope that we will, still during the first part of the conference, have time also for some of the other topics. We are probably all agreed that the roots of the political and social dangers which we face are not purely economic and that, if we are to preserve a free society, a revision not only of the strictly economic concepts which rule our generation is required. I believe it will also help to make us more rapidly acquainted if during the early part of the conference we range over a rather wider field and look at our problems from several angles before we attempt to proceed to more technical aspects or problems of detail.

You will probably agree that the interpretation and teaching of history has during the past two generations been one of the main instruments through which essentially anti-liberal conceptions of human affairs have spread; the widespread fatalism which regards all developments that have in fact taken place as inevitable consequences of great laws of necessary historical development, the historical relativism which denies any moral standards except those of success and non-success, the emphasis on mass movements as distinguished from individual achievements, and not least the general emphasis on material necessity as against the power of ideas to shape our future, are all different facets of a problem as important and almost as wide as the economic problem. I have suggested as a separate subject for discussion merely one aspect of this wide field, the relation between historiography and political education, but it is an aspect which should soon lead us to the wider problem. I am very glad that Miss Wedgwood and Professor Antoni have consented to open the discussion on this question.

It is, I think, important that we fully realise that the popular liberal creed, on the Continent and in America more than in England, contained many elements which on the one hand often led its adherents directly into the folds of socialism or nationalism, and on the other hand antagonised many who shared the basic values of individual freedom but were repelled by the aggressive rationalism which would recognise no values except those whose utility (for an ultimate purpose never disclosed) could be demonstrated by individual reason, and which presumed that science was competent to tell us not only what is but also what ought to be. Personally I believe that this false rationalism, which gained influence in the French Revolution and which during the past hundred years has exercised its influence mainly through the twin movements of positivism and Hegelianism, is an expression of an intellectual hubris which is the opposite of that intellectual humility which is the essence of the true liberalism that regards with reverence those spontaneous social forces through which the individual creates things greater than he knows. It is this intolerant and fierce rationalism which is mainly responsible for the gulf which, particularly on the Continent, has often driven religious people from the liberal movement into reactionary camps in which they felt little at home. I am convinced that unless this breach between true liberal and religious convictions can be healed there is no hope for a revival of liberal forces. There are many signs in Europe that such a reconciliation is today nearer than it has been for a long time, and that many people see in it the one hope of preserving the ideals of Western civilisation. It was for this reason that I was specially anxious that the subject of the relation between liberalism and Christianity should be made one of the separate topics of our discussion; and although we cannot hope to get far in exploring this topic in a single meeting, it seems to me essential that we should explicitly face the problem.

The two further topics which I have suggested for discussion are questions of the practical application of our principles to the problems of our time rather than questions of principles themselves. But both the problem of the future of Germany, and that of the possibilities and prospects of a European federation, seemed to me problems of such immediate urgency that no international group of students of politics should meet without considering them, even if we cannot hope to do more than clear our own minds a little by an exchange of views. They are both questions on which the present state of public opinion more than anything else is the great obstacle to any reasonable discussion and I feel that it is a special duty not to shirk their consideration. It is a symptom of their complexity that I have had the greatest difficulty in persuading any members of this conference to open the discussion on these two subjects.

There is one other topic which I should have liked to see discussed because it seems to me central to our problem, namely the meaning and conditions of the rule of law. If I did not actually suggest it, it was because, in order to discuss this problem adequately, it would have been necessary to extend our membership even further and to include lawyers. It was again largely lack of knowledge on my part which prevented this, and I mention it largely in order to make it clear how wide we shall have to cast our net if in any permanent organisation we are to be competent adequately to deal with all the different aspects of our task. But the programme I have suggested is probably ambitious enough for this one conference and I will now leave this point and turn to one or two other matters on which I ought to comment briefly.

So far as the first of these, the formal organisation of this conference, is concerned, I don't think we need to burden ourselves with any elaborate machinery. We could not have wished for a person better qualified to preside over us at this first meeting than Professor Rappard and I am sure you will allow me to thank him on your behalf for having consented. But we should not expect him or anyone else to carry this burden throughout the conference. The most appropriate arrangement will probably be to have this task rotate and, if you agree, one of the acts of this first meeting will be to elect chairmen for the next few meetings. If the meeting will agree on a programme at least for the first part of the conference, little formal business should arise until we have to consider the agenda for the second part, which I have suggested we might do at a special meeting on Monday evening. It would probably be wise if in addition we set up, at this meeting, a small standing committee of five or six members to fill in any details of the programme on which we agree now or to make any changes which circumstances may show to be desirable. You may also feel it desirable to appoint a secretary to the conference, or perhaps still better, two secretaries, one to look after the programme and another to be in charge of general arrangements. I believe this would be amply sufficient at this stage to regularise our proceedings.

There is another point of organisation which I should probably mention at this stage. I shall of course see that proper minutes will be kept of the business part of our discussions. But no arrangements have been made or seemed practicable for obtaining a shorthand record of our discussions. Apart from the technical difficulties, this would also have impaired the private and informal character of our discussions. But I hope that the members will themselves keep some notes of their major contributions so that, if the conference should decide to embody its main results in some kind of written record, it will be easy for them to put on paper the essence of their remarks.

There is also the question of language. In my preliminary correspondence I have tacitly assumed that all the members are familiar with English, and as this is certainly true of the majority of us, it would greatly facilitate our deliberations if English were mainly used. We are not in the fortunate position of official international bodies which command a staff of interpreters. It seems to me that the rule should be that every member should use the language in which he can hope to make himself most widely understood.

The immediate purpose of this conference is, of course, to provide an opportunity for a comparatively small group of those who in different parts of the world are striving for the same ideals, to get personally acquainted, to profit from one another's experience, and perhaps also to give mutual encouragement. I am confident that at the end of these ten days you will agree that this meeting will have been well worth while if it has achieved no more than this. But I rather hope that this experiment in collaboration will prove so successful that we shall want to continue it in one form or another.

However small the total number of people of our general outlook may be, there are of course among them many more competent scholars actively interested in the problems I have outlined than the small number present. I could myself have drawn up a list two or three times as long, and from the suggestions I have already received I have no doubt that together we could without difficulty compile a list of several hundred men and women in the various countries who share our general beliefs and would be willing to work for them. I hope we will compile such a list, selecting the names rather carefully, and design some means of continued contacts between these people. A beginning of such a list I am placing on the table and I hope you will add to it as many names as you think desirable, indicate by your signatures which of the other proposals you wish to support, and also perhaps let me know privately if any of the other persons appearing on the list seem to you to be unsuitable for inclusion among the members of a permanent organisation. We should probably not include any name unless it receives the support of two or three members of our present group and it may be desirable, later during the conference, to set up a small scrutiny committee to edit a final list. I assume that all those who were invited to this conference but were unable to attend will as a matter of course be included in this list.

There are of course many forms in which such regular contacts might be provided. When in one of my circulars I employed the somewhat highflown expression of an "International Academy for Political Philosophy" I meant to emphasise by the term "Academy" one aspect which seems to me essential if such a permanent organisation is to fulfil its purpose: It must remain a closed society, not open to all and sundry, but only to people who share with us certain common convictions. This character can only be preserved if membership can be acquired only by election, and if we treat admission into our circle as seriously as the great learned academies. I did not mean to suggest that we call ourselves an Academy. It will be for you, if you decide to form a Society, to choose a name for it. I have been rather attracted by the idea of calling it the Acton-Tocqueville Society, and somebody has suggested that it might be appropriate to add Jakob Burckhardt as a third patron saint. But this is a question we need not yet consider at this stage.

Beyond the important point that, as it seems to me, whatever permanent body we form must be a closed society, I have no strong view about its organisation. Much is to be said for giving it, at first at least, the loosest possible form and making it, perhaps, no more than a kind of correspondence society in which the list of members serves no other purpose than to enable them to keep in direct contact with each other. If it were practicable, as I fear it is not, to arrange that all the members provided one another with reprints or mimeographed copies of their relevant writings, this would in many ways be one of the most useful things we could do. It would, on the one hand, avoid the danger, which a specialised journal would create, that we would talk only to those already converted, but it would, on the other, keep us informed of the parallel or complementary activities of others. But the two desiderata, that the efforts of the members of our group should reach a great variety of audiences and not be confined to those who are already converted, and that at the same time the members of our group should be kept fully informed of one another's contributions, should somehow be reconciled, and we shall at least have to consider the possibility of sooner or later issuing a journal.

But it may well be that for some time to come such a loose and informal arrangement as I have suggested is all that we can achieve, since more would require greater financial means than we shall be able to raise from our midst. If there were larger funds available, all sorts of possibilities might open up. But, desirable as this might be, I shall be content with such a modest beginning if that is all we can do without in any manner compromising our complete independence.

This conference itself of course illustrates how the pursuit of our aims is dependent on the availability of some financial means, and we cannot expect to be often so fortunate as we have been this time in securing the necessary funds for it mainly from Swiss and, so far as the travelling expenses of the American members are concerned, from American sources, without any strings or conditions being attached to the offer. I wanted to take the earliest opportunity explicitly to reassure you on this point and at the same time to say how grateful we must be to Dr. Hunold who has raised the Swiss funds, and to Mr. W. H. Luhnow of the William Volker Charities Trust in Kansas City, who has made possible the participation of our American friends, for their help in this respect. To Dr. Hunold we are further indebted for undertaking all the local arrangements; and all the pleasures and comforts we are now enjoying we owe to his efforts and foresight.

I feel that it will be best if we do not turn to any discussion of the practical task I have mentioned until we are much better acquainted with one another and have more experience of the possibilities of collaboration than we have now. I hope there will be a good deal of private conversation on these questions during the next few days and that in the course of these our ideas will gradually crystallise. When after three days of work and another three days of more informal companionship we resume our regular business meetings, one of those meetings should probably be set aside for a systematic examination of the possibilities. I will defer till then any attempt to justify the name which I have tentatively suggested for the permanent society or any discussion of the principles and aims which would have to govern its activity.

For the time being we are just the Mont Pèlerin Conference to which you will have to give your own laws and whose procedure and destiny is now entirely in your hands.

THIRTEEN

THE TRAGEDY OF ORGANISED HUMANITY: DE JOUVENEL ON POWER[1]

Though few people seem yet to be aware of it, we are beginning to pay the price for one of the most fateful delusions which have ever guided political evolution. About a hundred years ago political wisdom had learnt to comprehend, as a result of centuries of bitter experience, the essential importance of manifold checks and barriers to the expansion of power. But after power seemed to have fallen into the hands of the great mass of the people, it was suddenly thought that no more restrictions on power were necessary. The delusion arose, described by Lord Acton in a phrase less hackneyed but not less profound than that which is now constantly quoted, "that absolute power may, by the hypothesis of its popular origin, be as legitimate as constitutional freedom".[2] But power has an inherent tendency to expand and where there are no effective limitations it will grow without bounds, whether it is exercised in the name of the people or in the name of a few. Indeed, there is reason to fear that unlimited power in the hands of the people will grow farther and be even more pernicious in its effects than power exercised by few.

This is the tragic theme on which M. de Jouvenel has written a great book. It is a theme which has always occupied the profoundest political thinkers and which during the last decades has challenged several of the most eminent of them to devote the mature wisdom of their old age to its study. Little more than twenty years ago the economist Friedrich von Wieser concluded a distinguished career with a treatise on *Das Gesetz der Macht*[3] which did not yet find the public ready for a discussion of the problem. Some ten years

---

[1] [Review of Bertrand de Jouvenel, *Power: The Natural History of its Growth* (London and New York: Hutchinson, 1948), published as "The Tragedy of Organised Humanity" in *Time and Tide*, November 6, 1948, p. 119. -Ed.]

[2] [The other phrase alluded to is the famous "power tends to corrupt and absolute power corrupts absolutely". On Acton see this volume, chapters 8 and 9.-Ed.]

[3] [Friedrich von Wieser, *Das Gesetz der Macht* (Vienna: J. Springer, 1926). On Wieser, Hayek's teacher at the University of Vienna, see this volume, chapter 3. -Ed.]

later the historian Guglielmo Ferrero similarly devoted one of his last works to a short and pregnant study of *Pouvoir*.[4] And more recently Bertrand Russell has given us a thoughtful book on *Power*.[5] It is probably as much a sign of the increasing urgency of the problem as a testimony to the exceptional gifts of the author that now a much younger man has given us a monumental study of the same subject which by its restrained passion and obvious relevance to the events of the moment surpasses in impressiveness those expressions of mature wisdom. It is probably a result of the circumstances of the time that apparently in all instances the later authors were unacquainted with the earlier works. But that the books are so wholly dissimilar is probably less due to this than to the infinite diversity of the subject which no work can treat in all its aspects.

M. de Jouvenel, however, comes surprisingly near this. He achieves it by not attempting a theoretical system but by building up a picture from an extraordinary amount of detail. It is the cumulative effect of his illustrations of all the various facets of power rather than a clear-cut theoretical structure by which he tries to make us understand the phenomenon. This is quite deliberate. With some justification he feels that in such an attempt "abstract ideas must be kept imprecise so as not to exclude the transmission of further particulars". As it should be, his picture of one of the great historical forces is a work of art at least as much, if not more, than a scientific treatise. Perhaps he has not altogether escaped the danger of obscuring the great outline by over-elaboration of particular points. There is certainly danger that the many brilliant phrases and aperçus may detract attention from the main aim of the work. The temptation of the reviewer to strengthen this impression by culling a collection of the more striking *obiter dicta* is almost irresistible. But this would give an unjust impression of the book.

M. de Jouvenel's method is not only deliberate, it is also the expression of a more fundamental attitude, his distrust of that facile rationalism which would rather force complex facts into a simple scheme that our limited reason can fully comprehend than ever admit that reason itself may teach us the limits of its power. Indeed, he rightly puts much of the blame for the threatening doom on this intellectualist bias:

---

[4][Ferrero's *Pouvoir* was not published until it appeared in English translation as *The Principles of Power* (New York: G. Putnam's Sons, 1942), though it was written some years earlier. -Ed.]

[5][Bertrand Russell, *Power: A New Social Analysis* (London: Allen & Unwin, 1938). -Ed.]

So soon as the intellectual imagines a simple order of things he is serving the growth of Power. For the existing order, here as elsewhere, is complex and rests on a whole mass of supports, authorities, sentiments, and adjustments of the most varied kind. If it is thought to make one spring do the work of so many, how strong must be the force of its recoil; or if one pillar must support henceforward what many supported, it must be of the stoutest! Only Power can be that spring or that pillar—and what a Power it must be! Simply because speculative thought tends to neglect the usefulness of a crowd of secondary factors which make for order, it leads inevitably to the reinforcement of the central authority and never more surely than when it is unsettling every kind of authority, the central included; for Authority there must be, and when it rises again it is, inevitably, in the most concentrated forms open to it. . . .
And so the credulous tribe of philosophers works on Power's behalf, vaunting its merits right up to the point at which Power disillusions it; whereupon, it is true, it breaks into cursings, but still it serves the cause of Power in general, by placing its hopes in a radical and systematic application of its principles, being a thing which only a capacious Power can achieve.

It is through a succession of such glances at the links of the process which builds power that M. de Jouvenel achieves his masterly and frightening picture of the impersonal mechanism by which power tends to expand until it engulfs the whole of society. It is a picture which few will forget who have read the work and of which they will only too frequently be reminded by events. He succeeds in this without falling into any of the intellectual traps which threaten such an attempt. Though the language sometimes personifies Power, it is never really represented anthropomorphically but throughout as what it is, an impersonal force resulting from the problems of men's collaboration, from their individual appetites, desires and beliefs, often innocent and almost all common to most men. Indeed, though the language rises sometimes to almost poetical flights, the dominating character of the book is its hard realism, its almost terrifying freedom from illusions and its sober description of social processes in their true nakedness.

It is almost impossible to select any part of such an exposition as more significant or important than any other. But for those who wish to sample the book before embarking on a systematic study, I would particularly recommend the brilliant chapter 13 on "Imperium et Democratie" (the title is one of the few instances where the accomplished translator has not succeeded in quite rendering the meaning of the original French) and especially the highly interesting discussion of Rousseau and the rule of law—a somewhat surprising but illuminating interpretation of Rousseau which the author has since expanded in his Introduction to a splendid edition of *Du contrat social*.[6] It has convinced me that Rousseau understood the meaning of the rule of law better than any other writer known to me.

It is part of M. de Jouvenel's reaction against the over-rationalist views of the last two centuries that his emphasis is almost entirely on the external mechanism of power and that he tends to under-stress the role of opinion. There are few specific statements on this to which one could take exception, apart from such asides as that a particular "distortion of doctrine, incomprehensible though it is to the dealer in ideas, seems natural enough to the observer of the social mechanism". On the abstract level it is perhaps no more than a slight difference in the balance of emphasis, though a difference which is most important in its consequences. If I am not mistaken it is this difference which from closely similar starting points will lead one to a position which is liberal in the old sense and relatively optimistic, and the other to a conservative and profoundly pessimistic attitude. And it seems to me that it is his scepticism with regard to the role of opinion which leads M. de Jouvenel in the end to a more conservative position than is in accord with his ardent love of liberty and which makes him regard even more of the political evils of this world as inevitable than may be necessary. But, it must be confessed, I know not the student of power who has not been driven to similarly pessimistic conclusions.

---

[6][Jean-Jacques Rousseau, *Du contrat social, précédé d'un essai sur la politique de Rousseau, par Bertrand de Jouvenel* (Geneva: Éditions du Chevalailé, 1947). -Ed.]

FOURTEEN

BRUNO LEONI (1913–1967)
AND LEONARD READ (1898–1983)

Bruno Leoni[1]

Even three months after the tragic event it is difficult to believe that Bruno Leoni is no longer among us. Lovable and dynamic, he lived life with such an intensity that more than most men he seemed to embody life itself. By a cruel fate he was taken from us at the height of his powers when great accomplishments justified the expectation of even greater achievements. He had a nature so rich that even after many years of friendship one constantly discovered new and unsuspected facets of a great personality of a kind for which we sometimes envy past ages, but which we scarcely ever encounter in our own time. Perhaps Italy is fortunate in still producing more such figures whom elsewhere we associate with the Renaissance. Among the citizens of the world of whom he had become one and among whom I mainly met him, he was unique.

Though this very lecture hall evokes the poignant memory that less than four years ago I was privileged to speak here under Bruno Leoni's chairmanship—and to enjoy his and Mrs. Leoni's hospitality at their home at Turin—it was mostly in distant parts of the world, in the United States and Japan as well as in various cities of Europe, that I mainly knew him.[2] I can therefore tell nothing of the greater part of his life, at Pavia, Turin, and Sardinia, of which you all know much more than I do. I must confine myself to speaking about Bruno Leoni as a scholar and international figure, the man who gained devotion and respect wherever he went, and of whom I am proud to speak as much in the name of our common friends all over the world as in my own name.

---

[1][Published as "Bruno Leoni, the Scholar" in *Il Politico*, University of Pavia, vol. 33, 1968, pp. 21-25. For a recent evaluation of Leoni's thought see Peter H. Aranson, "Bruno Leoni in Retrospect", *Harvard Journal of Law and Public Policy*, vol. 11, Summer 1988, pp. 661–711; and Leonard P. Liggio and Tom G. Palmer, "Freedom and the Law: A Comment on Professor Aranson's Article", *ibid.*, pp. 713–725. -Ed.]

[2][At the meetings of the Mont Pèlerin Society. -Ed.]

We all soon found that there was much more in the man whom we chiefly knew as a distinguished scholar, a devoted adherent of the cause of freedom, and a tireless and inventive organiser in the service of this cause.

We soon caught glimpses of a deep understanding of the arts and of music, especially of oriental art and also of oriental philosophy—and not least of the arts of life, of the skill and zest in enjoying all the fine and beautiful things which the world has to offer. Of all these many sides of Bruno Leoni which made his companionship so attractive, I do however not know enough to speak about them at any length. In what follows I must confine myself to the three aspects of his work in which for some ten or twelve years our efforts had run parallel courses and where in consequence I had come to know him rather well. The first is his effort to overcome the departmentalisation of the social sciences and especially to bridge the gulf which has come to separate the study of law from that of the theoretical social sciences. The second is the effort to provide a satisfactory intellectual foundation for the defence of individual freedom, in which he so strongly believed. The third point will be certain important suggestions contained in his literary work which to me seem to point the way to the solution of some central intellectual difficulties of political theory, but where, since Bruno Leoni was not given time to work them out fully, it will be the task of those who wish to honour his memory to try to continue where he left off.

But before I turn to my chief task, I must say a few words about the character of my association with Bruno Leoni. The honour that your venerable university has done me in asking me to speak on this sad occasion makes it seem desirable that I explain what limited authority I have for the performance of this task. I first met Bruno Leoni fourteen years ago at the University of Chicago where I was then teaching[3] and where he had gone, I believe, mainly to deepen his acquaintance with Anglo-American law and political institutions. We soon discovered on how many points our interests and ideals coincided and this brought him soon into that international organisation of scholars and publicists for the study of the conditions requisite for the preservation of individual freedom, the Mont Pèlerin Society, which I had started a few years earlier and to

[3][Hayek was with the Committee on Social Thought at the University of Chicago from 1950 to 1962, where he conducted a regular seminar on various problems in the social sciences. -Ed.]

whose affairs he was later to give so much of his time and energy. We again spent some time together almost ten years ago at Claremont College, California, at a seminar devoted to the problems of liberty, where he delivered that course of lectures on *Freedom and the Law* about which I shall have to speak more fully later.[4] It was then that I first came to see Bruno Leoni's capacity of inspiring an audience, his untiring readiness to discuss intellectual problems at every hour of day and night, and his general zest for life which made him grasp all opportunities for instruction and enjoyment which the environment of the moment offered. I may be permitted to mention here a little episode which occurred on that occasion. We lecturers at the seminar were kept pretty busy and valued the three hours after the midday meal during which we had no definite obligations. When Bruno Leoni regularly disappeared during that period, we drew at first the natural conclusion. But how wrong we were! He had discovered an opportunity of taking flying lessons at a nearby aerodrome and spent at the controls of an airplane the hours we others used for rest!

Not long after this I again encountered Bruno Leoni in the United States, not in person but following in his footsteps and noticing the deep impressions he had left behind: In 1961 I succeeded him as Distinguished Visiting Professor at the Thomas Jefferson Center of Studies in Political Economy of the University of Virginia and could feel the great impact he had made.

But even before that we had been drawn more closely together by the invaluable services he rendered in a crisis in the affairs of the international society to which I have referred already and of which he thereby became and remained to the moment of his death the driving spirit. Since Bruno Leoni had nothing to do with the origin of this conflict, I need not enter here into the nature of this crisis which arose, as may happen in any group, out of a certain incompatibility of temperaments, but which at one time threatened to wreck the society.[5]

Elected its secretary in the midst of this conflict and for a time, after the resignation of the president, chiefly responsible for its affairs, he steered it with sure hands through the turbulent waters not only into a calmer sea but into a new period of flourishing

---

[4][This was the Fifth Institute on Freedom and Competitive Enterprise held in June 1958. The lectures were published as Bruno Leoni, *Freedom and the Law* (Princeton, N.J.: D. Van Nostrand, 1961; reprinted, Los Angeles: Nash, 1972). -Ed.]

[5][On this see this volume, p. 192, note 29. -Ed.]

activity. The annual meetings at Turin, at Knokke-sur-mer in Belgium, on the Semmering in Austria, at Stresa, at Tokyo, and at Vichy, which he organised, were among the most successful our society has had. At the last meeting at Vichy, only six months ago, he was with general acclamation elected president following in that office on Friedrich Lutz and, earlier, John Jewkes, Wilhelm Röpke, and myself. How great an asset he was to the society we are becoming only too aware now when we are so tragically soon faced with the task of finding a successor to him.

I must now turn to his scholarly and literary work of which I know well only what he published in English and only a small part of what appeared in Italian.

Bruno Leoni was one of those increasingly rare men who had the courage to transcend the limits of a specialism and to try to see the problems of society as a whole. With his tremendous energy and quickness of perception he succeeded in escaping the dangers of dilettantism which such a broadening out into several fields of study so easily produces. He was, of course, primarily a lawyer and, I understand, highly successful as a practising lawyer. But even within the field of law he was as much a philosopher, sociologist, and historian of law as a master of positive law. That he was also an eminent political scientist is perhaps only natural in a teacher of constitutional law as interested in the history of ideas as he was. He also contributed to the development of political science in Italy and abroad with the review *Il Politico* of which he was a founder and editor for many years. But this exhausts by no means the full extent of the range of his curiosity; I can testify that he was no mean economic theorist and had worked through some of the more difficult parts of mathematical economics and shown a deep insight into some of the methodological difficulties which modern developments in this field raise. This was of course closely connected with another chief concern of his which I have left last: the general philosophy of science. He was, if I am not mistaken, one of the originators and most active members of the Centro di Studi Metodologici and the work he did in this connexion led him to some of the fundamental problems of general philosophy.

A glance at a list of Bruno Leoni's publications shows how varied his interests were. The list I have before me enumerates more than eighty publications of which more than seventy date from the last twenty years. Much of this is difficult of access to a foreigner and unknown to me. I hope somebody will collect his more important occasional writings into a volume to honour his memory.[6] It is particularly to be regretted that he did not find time to prepare for publication the suggestive and original first volume of his *Lezioni di Filosofia del Diritto* which deals with the thought of classical antiquity and which in 1949 he had issued in mimeographed form for his students. Especially his treatment of the relation between *physis* and *nomos* in ancient Greek thought seems to me to contain much that would deserve development. From my incomplete knowledge of his writings it seems to me, however, that the one published systematic book of his, which is available only in English and Spanish,[7] is much the most important of his works, both for what it explicitly says and even more for the hints it contains of further developments, problems it raises without fully answering them and which it now remains for us, his friends and admirers, to take up and to develop. In this chief contention it is so unconventional, and even directly opposed to much that is today almost universally accepted, that there is some danger that it may not be taken as seriously as it deserves or dismissed as a crotchety speculation of a man out of sympathy with his time.

It would perhaps be possible to distort the spirited account of his chief thesis in the assertion that the invention of legislation was a mistake and that the world would do better to renounce legislation altogether and to rely exclusively on the development of the law by judges and jurisconsults as has been true of the development of the ancient Roman law and of the common law of England. But though a few isolated statements in the book might lend themselves to such an interpretation, Bruno Leoni explicitly rejects it. What I believe he was trying to say is the highly important point that the law which emerges from jurisdiction and the work of the jurists of necessity possesses certain properties which the products of legislation may need but not possess, but which are essential if individual freedom is to be preserved. He has explicitly brought out only some of those properties which judge-made law necessarily possesses but which all law ought to possess in a society of free men. He argues persuasively, and has convinced me, that although the codification of the law was intended to increase the certainty of the law, it did at

[6][A compilation of Leoni's works was collected by Pasquale Scaramozzino and published in Italian as *Omaggio a Bruno Leoni* (Milan: A. Giuffrè, 1969). -Ed.]

[7][I.e., *Freedom and the Law*, op. cit. The Spanish edition is *La Libertad y La Ley* (Buenos Aires: Centro de Estudios Sobre la Libertad, 1961). The 1972 English edition includes a Foreword by Arthur Kemp containing some additional biographical information on Leoni. -Ed.]

most enhance the short-run certainty of the law, and I am no longer sure that even this is strictly true, while the habit of altering the law by legislation certainly decreases its long-run certainty. He did show further that one characteristic of the rules of just conduct which emerge from the spontaneous process of law was that these rules were essentially negative, rules aiming at the determination of a protected domain for each individual and as such an effective guarantee of individual liberty. As to many other profound thinkers the task of the law was to him not so much to create justice as to prevent injustice. And in his stress on the Golden Rule, "Do not do to others what you do not wish others to do to yourself"—a rule which, as he was fond of pointing out, Confucianism had in common with Christianity—he suggested an equally negative test of the justice of such rules by the consistent application of which we might hope progressively to approach justice.

Perhaps the richness of suggestions which this book contains will be fully apparent only to those who have already been working on similar lines. Bruno Leoni would have been the last to deny that it merely points a way and that much work still lies ahead before the seeds of new ideas which it so richly contains can blossom forth in all their splendour. It is part of the tragedy of the sudden termination of this rich life that we can see how much more there was that he might still have given us.

If I have regarded it as my chief task today to speak about Bruno Leoni the scholar, it was not only because this was the side of him which I best knew but also because, just because his work is unfinished, there is some danger that it may not be properly appreciated. But to those who stood nearer to him this will seem but a small part of Bruno Leoni the man. Even to those who knew him mainly professionally this world must seem a poorer place without him. I can conceive what his loss must mean to his students to whom he gave so much of his devotion and energy. But our deepest sympathy must go out to those for whom he was the centre of life, to whom he was able not only to offer a harmonious and beautiful home but all the kindness of a generous heart, and where he leaves a gap that nobody can fill. We know that he was much more than only a scholar; but we hope that it will be at least some consolation to those whom he has left behind if we pay this tribute to Bruno Leoni the scholar.

Leonard Read[8]

The institution Leonard Read has built up, and through which he has wielded such great influence, bears the modest and prosaic name of a Foundation for Economic Education.[9] I am sure that with his unfailing flair in such things he has chosen the name under which it was most likely to succeed. Yet, I want to suggest that this name describes the aim of this institution—and of Leonard Read's work—much too narrowly; that he has really set his goal much higher. It seems to me that on an occasion like this we ought to try to spell out more fully what it really is that he and, I think, all of you who are here tonight are chiefly concerned about. I cannot do so adequately in a few words, but I will try to put it in less than the time allocated to me. Indeed, I believe I can put the central idea into eight words. I will first give you the formula and then briefly comment on the various parts of it. I believe that what the Foundation for Economic Education, with Leonard Read at its head, and all his co-fighters and friends are committed to is nothing more nor less than *the defence of our civilisation against intellectual error.*

I do not mean this as the kind of high-flown phrase that one is apt to coin for an occasion such as this. I mean it literally, as the best definition of our common task. I have chosen every one of these eight words advisedly and will now try to explain what I mean by them.

In the first instance I wanted to emphasise that what is threatened by our present political trends is not just economic prosperity, not just our comfort, or the rate of economic growth. It is very much more. It is what I meant to be understood by the phrase "our civilisation". Modern man prides himself that he has built that civilisation as if in doing so he had carried out a plan which he had before formed in his mind. The fact is, of course, that if at any point in the past man had mapped out his future on the basis of the then-existing knowledge and then followed this plan, we would

---

[8][Published in *What's Past Is Prologue: A Commemorative Evening to the Foundation for Economic Education on the Occasion of Leonard Read's Seventieth Birthday* (Irvington-on-Hudson, N.Y.: The Foundation for Economic Education, 1968), pp. 37–43. The speech on which this essay was based was given on October 4, 1968, at the Waldorf Astoria Hotel, New York. The reader may also wish to consult the series of testimonials published by FEE following Read's death in 1983, *In Memoriam, Leonard E. Read, 1898–1983.* -Ed.]

[9][The Foundation for Economic Education, Irvington-on-Hudson, New York. FEE continues to sponsor educational events and to publish the monthly journal *The Freeman*. -Ed.]

not be where we are. We would not only be much poorer, we would not only be less wise, but we would also be less gentle, less moral: In fact we would still have brutally to fight each other for our very lives. We owe the fact that not only our knowledge has grown, but also our morals have improved—and I think they *have* improved, and especially that the concern for our neighbour has increased—not to anybody planning for such a development, but to the fact that in an essentially free society certain trends have prevailed because they made for a peaceful, orderly, and progressive society.

This process of growth to which we owe the emergence of what we now most value, including the growth of the very values we now hold, is today often presented as if it were something not worthy of a reasonable being, because it was not guided by a clear design of what men were aiming at. But our civilisation is indeed largely an unforeseen and unintended outcome of our submitting to moral and legal rules which were never 'invented' with such a result in mind, but which grew because those societies which developed them piecemeal prevailed at every step over other groups which followed different rules, less conducive to the growth of civilisation. It is against this fact to which we owe most of our achievements that the rationalist constructivism so characteristic of our times revolts. Since the so-called Age of Reason it seemed to an ever-increasing number of people not worthy of a rational being that he should be guided in his actions by moral and legal rules which he did not fully understand; and it was demanded that we should not regard any rules obligatory on us except such as clearly and recognisably served the achievement of particular, foreseeable aims.

It is, of course, true that we only slowly and gradually begin to understand the manner in which the rules which we traditionally obey constitute the condition for the social order in which civilisation has arisen. But in the meantime, uncomprehending criticism of what seemed not 'rational' has done so much harm that it sometimes seems to me as if what I am tempted to call *the destruction of values by scientific error* were the great tragedy of our time. They are errors which are almost inevitable if one starts out from the conception that man either has, or at least ought to have, deliberately made his civilisation. But they are nevertheless intellectual errors which bid fair to deprive us of values which, though we have not yet learned to comprehend their role, are nevertheless indispensable foundations of our civilisation.

This has already brought me to the second part of my definition of our task. When I stressed that it is genuine intellectual error that we have to fight, what I meant to bring out is that we ought to remain aware that our opponents are often high-minded idealists whose harmful teachings are inspired by very noble ideals. It seems to me that the worst mistake a fighter for our ideals can make is to ascribe to our opponents dishonest or immoral aims. I know it is sometimes difficult not to be irritated into a feeling that most of them are a bunch of irresponsible demagogues who ought to know better. But though many of the followers of what we regard as the wrong prophets are either just plain silly, or merely mischievous troublemakers, we ought to realise that their conceptions derive from serious thinkers whose ultimate ideals are not so very different from our own and with whom we differ not so much on ultimate values, but on the effective means of achieving them. I am indeed profoundly convinced that there is much less difference between us and our opponents on the ultimate values to be achieved than is commonly believed, and that the differences between us are chiefly intellectual differences. We at least believe that we have attained an understanding of the forces which have shaped civilisation which our opponents lack. Yet if we have not yet convinced them, the reason must be that our arguments are not yet quite good enough, that we have not yet made explicit some of the foundations on which our conclusions rest. Our chief task therefore must still be to improve the argument on which our case for a free society rests.

But I must not allow this to degenerate into a lecture. I referred to these purely intellectual problems in order to say that while there are quite a number of us who devote ourselves exclusively to these intellectual problems—and often express our results in a manner that is intelligible only to our fellow specialists—and quite a number of practical men who clearly and rightly see that there is something wrong in the now dominant beliefs, there is hardly anyone who at the same time sees the great issues of our time as intellectual problems and also is so familiar with the thinking of the practical man that he can put the crucial arguments in a language which is meaningful to the man of the world.

If Leonard Read's position is probably unique today, it is precisely because he possesses both capacities. I will frankly admit that I have only slowly and gradually discovered this. When twenty-one years ago some friends helped me to organise that meeting on Mont Pèlerin in Switzerland, some of them told me that there was in the United States a man extremely good in interpreting libertarian ideas to the public. And as it had from the beginning been the aim of that group not to confine itself to theoreticians, but to include persons who would interpret its conclusions to the general public,

Leonard Read seemed to be an ideal person to invite. He certainly has fulfilled this expectation, but having considered him from the beginning chiefly from that angle, I continued for a while to regard him as an interpreter rather than as an original thinker—after all, somebody who can put ideas in simple words often is. I want to use this occasion, however, publicly to admit that in that view of Leonard Read I was mistaken and that in the course of these twenty-one years my estimate of him progressively changed. I found not only that he knew much more than most of the rest of us about the opinions governing current policies, and was therefore much more effective in meeting the errors in them: I had rather hoped that, though I did not know how well it could be done. But I found also that he was a profound and original thinker who disguised the profundity of his conclusions by putting them into homely everyday language, and that those of us who for a time, and perhaps somewhat condescendingly, had seen in him mainly a populariser found that they had a great deal to learn from him.

Leonard Read has indeed become in our circle, in which the nonacademics are still a small minority, not only one of the best liked but one of the most respected members, one on whom they rely not only to spread the gospel, but as much to contribute to the development of ideas. Nothing, therefore, gives me greater pleasure than to be able to join in this celebration of his achievement. And, if one who is his junior only by a few months may conclude on a personal note, the greatest pleasure in this is that on this occasion one may still expect even more from him in the future than he has already done in the past.

EDITOR'S ACKNOWLEDGEMENTS

The Editor's most profound debt is to the late W. W. Bartley III, to whom the original plan and much of the preliminary research for this volume is due. He is also grateful to Dr. Grete Heinz for her fine translations; to Professor Ralph Raico of the State University of New York, College at Buffalo, and to Mr. Leif Wenar of Harvard University, for their assistance with the text; to Dr. David Gordon and an anonymous reader for suggestions related to the introduction; and to Ms. Leslie Graves for her thorough reading of the manuscript. In addition, he has gained profoundly from participation in scholarly conferences on Austrian economics sponsored by the Ludwig von Mises Institute, Auburn University; the Department of Economics and Special Collections Department, Duke University; the Institute for Humane Studies, George Mason University; the Foundation for Economic Education, Irvington-on-Hudson, New York; and Hillsdale College, Hillsdale, Michigan. He thanks all these institutions for arranging such events, and in particular the Mises Institute for financing much of his travel expense. Finally, he is grateful to Ms. Gene Opton for her work in readying the manuscript for publication, and to Mr. Stephen Kresge for his sound guidance and exceptional patience. None of these people or organisations, of course, is responsible for remaining errors in the text.

Peter G. Klein
Berkeley, California
January 1991

CHRONOLOGICAL LIST OF CONTENTS

Date	Title as Originally Published, Chapter in This Volume
1948	"The Tragedy of Organised Humanity" [Review of de Jouvenel's *Power*], Chapter 13
1953	"The Actonian Revival", Chapter 9
1954	Review, Schumpeter's *History of Economic Analysis*, Chapter 5
1956	"Tribute to Ludwig von Mises", Chapter 4
1959	"On Röpke" [in Röpke's *Gegen die Brandung*], Prologue to Part II, Addendum
1963	"The Economics of the 1920s as Seen from Vienna", Prologue to Part I
1964	Review, Mises's *Epistemological Problems of Economics*, Chapter 4
1967	"Diskussionsbemerkungen über Ernst Mach und das sozialwissenschaftliche Denken in Wien (Ernst Mach and the Social Sciences in Vienna)", Chapter 7
1968	"Economic Thought: The Austrian School", Chapter 1
1968	"Bruno Leoni, the Scholar", Chapter 14
1968	"Leonard Read", Chapter 14
1973	"Tribute to von Mises, Vienna Years", Chapter 4
1973	"The Place of Menger's *Grundsätze* in the History of Economic Thought", Chapter 2, Addendum
1976	Preface to 1976 edition, Mises's *Interventionism*, Chapter 4
1977	Einleitung, Mises's *Erinnerungen (Notes and Recollections)*, Chapter 4

CHRONOLOGICAL LIST OF CONTENTS

INDEX

Acton, Lord, 204, 209–15, chapter 9, 231, 233, 247, 249
Adler, Friedrich, 173
Adler, Karl, 93n
Adler, S., 132n
Adler, Victor, 173n
Agassi, Joseph, 50n
Allais, Maurice, 237n, 243
Allen, R.G.D., 53n
Amonn, Alfred, 51
Antoni, Carlo, 237n, 244
apriorism, 9, 10–11, 13, 55, 148, 152, 158
Aranson, Peter H., 253n
Arendt, Hannah, 5
Aris, R., 162n
Aristotle, 43
Arrow, Kenneth, 44n
Auersperg, Adolf, 76
Auspitz, Rudolf, 25, 47, 66n, 67n
Austrian school of economics, 2, 5, 6, 7, 13, 21n, chapter 1, 130, 166, 168, 170, *passim*; first and second generations, 22, 119n, 166; third generation, 51, 130, 145, 157, 166; fourth generation, 2, 8, 52, 53, 166; and Clark, 39; modern, 6, 9, 12, 54, 107, 157; and University of Vienna, 46n
Avenarius, Richard, 174
Axelrod, Robert, 7n

Bach, J.S., 220
Barth, Hans, 237n
Bartley, W.W. III, ix, 11n, 143n, 176n, 179n, 180n, 198n
Bastiat, Frédéric, 38, 64n
Bauer, Otto, 51n, 138

Bauer, Stefan, 93n
Becker, Carl Heinrich, 187
Beethoven, Ludwig van, 220

Benson, Bruce L., 7n
Bergson, Abram, 10
Bernhardi, Theodor von, 204
Bettelheim, Bruno, 5
Birck, L.V., 112n
Bismarck, Otto von, 13, 220, 224, 228–31
Block, Maurice, 83
Blum, Mark E., 52n, 173n
Boese, Franz, 77n, 146n
Böhm, Franz, 189, 190n
Böhm-Bawerk, Eugen von, 21, 22n, 29n, 48, 51, 70, 72n, 73, 81–2, 86, 90, 104, 111–13, 121, 138, 156, 163, 166; on capital, 85, 111; on cost, 112; Georgescu-Roegen on, 74n; on interest, 150; on liberalism, 28–9, 127; and Marshall, 33; and Menger, 45n, 46 & n, 62, 75 & n, 112, 114; and Mises, 130; on price theory, 112; Schumpeter on, 120n, 163; seminar of, 22, 34, 51, 130, 138, 144, 160, 168, 187; and Wieser, 121n
Boland, Lawrence A., 50n
Bonar, James, 48n, 84
Born, Karl Erich, 138n
Bostaph, Samuel, 50n
Braithwaite, Richard, 179
Brandt, Karl, 237n
Braun, Martha Stefanie, later Browne, 155
Brentano, Franz, 145n
Brentano, Lujo, 77n, 145 & n, 205n
Bresciani-Turroni, Costantino, 241n
Browne, *see* Braun
Buchanan, James M., 54
Bücher, Karl, 77n
Bunge, Mario A., 55n

Hayek, F.A., 19n, 21n, 27n, 28n,
31n, 37n, 40n, 42n, 44n, 45n,
49n, 50n, 51n, 52, 53 & n, 54n,
55n, 56n, 61n, 62n, 63n, 67n,
68, 70n, 84n, 92n, 95n, 96n,
108n, 117n, 126n, 128n, 129n,
132n, 133n, 134n, 142n, 143n,
144n, 145n, 146n, 147n, 154n,
157n, 160n, 163n, 164n, 170n,
174n, 176n, 179n, 188n, 196n,
200n, 207n, 215n, 219n, 228n
Hazlitt, Henry, 237n
Hearn, William Edward, 64n
Hearnshaw, F.J.C., 216n
Hébert, Robert F., 164n
Heckscher, Eli, 241n
Heilbroner, Robert, 1
Heinz, Grete, 108n, 166, 170n,
172n, 185n, 195n
Held, Adolf, 77n
Helfferich, Karl, 186
Heller, H., 199
Heller, Walter, 13, 14n
Helmholz, Hermann von, 175
Henderson, Leon, 13
Hennings, Klaus H., 45n, 51n
Herkner, Heinrich, 145
Hermann, Friedrich B.W., 44n,
64, 71, 76n, 144, 156
Hicks, John R., 8 & n, 28n, 53,
66n, 89n, 96n
Hildebrand, Bruno, 75, 76n
Hilferding, Rudolf, 51n
Himmelfarb, Gertrude, 216n,
217–18
historical school of economics, x,
40, 49, 50, 63, 79, 84, 98, 113,
143, 156; older, 75, 78n;
younger, 77, 78n
historicism, x, 78n
Hitler, 208, 220, 221
Hoff, T.J.B., 237n
Hollander, Jacob Harry, 35
Hoppe, Hans-Hermann, 153n,
169n
Hoppe, Margaret Rudelich, 169n
Howey, Richard S., 99n

Human Action (Ludwig von Mises),
128, 134, 140, 146, 147, 149n
Hume, David, 50, 78n
Huncke, George D., 46n
Hunold, Albert, 191n, 192n, 195n,
237n, 240, 248
Husserl, Edmund, 32, 174n
Hutchinson, T. W., 8n, 11n, 14n,
28n, 79n, 189n

Ihering, Rudolf von, 230
Ilau, Hans, 188
Illy, Leo (Leo Schönfeld), 30, 31n,
51, 155, 166
imputation, 48, 73, 112n, 114;
Wieser on, 116; *see also* orders
of goods
Institute of Economic Affairs, 193
institutionalist school of economics,
36, 40, 78n
interest, Böhm-Bawerk on, 150;
Mises on, 149–50
international trade, 38, 150, 151n
*Investigations into the Method of the
Social Sciences* (Carl Menger), 28
& n, 50n, 77–81, 105; on
money, 88
Iverson, Carl, 237n

Jaffé, William, 43n, 63n, 65n, 66n
Jefferson, Thomas, 198
Jenks, Jeremiah W., 35
Jevons, William Stanley, 8n, 21n,
48, 52, 53, 66, 75, 76, 97, 98;
as anticipator of Menger, 45; as
equilibrium theorist, 71n;
influence of, 104; on marginal
utility, 42 & n, 43, 62, 63n, 65,
74n
Jewkes, John, 237n, 256
John, Andrew, 6n
Jouvenel, Bertrand de, 237n,
chapter 13

Kahane, Jacques, 141, 196n
Kahn, Hans, 172n
Kaldor, Nicholas, 37n
Kant, Immanuel, 174